COMPANION

HALLMARK
KEEPSAKE
ORNAMENTS

Mary Sieber

©2007 Krause Publications

Published by

krause publications
An Imprint of F+W Publications

700 East State Street • Iola, WI 54990-0001
715-445-2214 • 888-457-2873
www.krausebooks.com

Our toll-free number to place an order or obtain
a free catalog is (800) 258-0929.

Library of Congress Catalog Number: 2006935631

ISBN: 978-0-89689-509-6

Designed by Marilyn McGrane
Edited by Mary Sieber

Printed in China

Contents

Introduction

Who among us doesn't have at least one Hallmark Keepsake Ornament hanging on our Christmas tree? Perhaps you have a Baby's First Christmas ornament commemorating the birth of a child, or an Our First Christmas Together ornament you received as a wedding gift. Or maybe you're lucky, and being a "Star Trek" fan has finally paid off because the Starship Enterprise ornament you got back in 1991 is now worth some serious money.

For nearly 35 years, Hallmark Keepsake Ornaments—produced by Hallmark Cards Inc. of Kansas City, Missouri—have transformed Christmas trees everywhere into 3-D scrapbooks of memories that capture and preserve times, events, and special occasions. When the first 18 ornaments were introduced in 1973, Christmas tree decorations went from simple colored glass balls to creative and fun designs. Soon, Americans started a new tradition that changed the way they viewed ornaments. No longer were ornaments just pretty decorations for the tree. Suddenly they became unique, year-dated and available only for a limited time, making them an instant hit with collectors.

Appropriately titled
Dream Book, Hallmark's
annual catalog of ornaments is
eagerly awaited by collectors. Dream Books
from 1995 through 2006 are shown here.

In 1973 Hallmark issued a handful of ornaments, six in ball shape and 12 made of yarn. Today the Keepsake line releases more than 200 new ornaments each year. Collectors eagerly anticipate Hallmark's Keepsake Ornament Premiere every July, where they have their first opportunity to purchase that year's new ornaments. In October Hallmark holds its Keepsake Ornament Debut, offering even more new releases. Each year Hallmark also publishes a full-color catalog, called the Dream Book, showcasing the new ornaments.

A total of more than 6,000 Hallmark ornaments have been produced since the company began issuing them in 1973, and more than 11 million U.S. households collect them.

How It All Began...

Hallmark Cards Inc. was founded by Joyce C. Hall, who began his career selling postcards when he was a teenager in the early 1900s. With money pooled from his brothers Rollie and William, the three opened the Norfolk Postcard Company in 1908.

Two years later, J.C., as he was called, filled two shoeboxes with postcards and traveled to Kansas City, Missouri, to look for new business. Rollie eventually joined his brother in Kansas City, and together they opened Hall Brothers, a specialty store dealing in postcards, gifts, books, and stationery in downtown Kansas City.

Despite a devastating fire in 1915, the business succeeded. The brothers borrowed money to buy an engraving firm, setting the stage for the creation of the first original Hallmark designs. Then in 1921 William Hall joined his brothers in Kansas City.

All three brothers were active in the company during their business lives. Rollie was vice president and director of national sales; William was vice president and treasurer.

J.C. Hall passed away in 1982 at the age of 91.

Beloved Ornaments

Collectors are continually drawn to Hallmark ornaments because they evoke memories and emotions, mark milestones in our lives, celebrate significant relationships, and are just plain fun. They also take us back to our childhoods with ornaments that reflect our American culture.

Hallmark's first collectible ornament series featuring Betsey Clark designs began in 1973 and ended in 1985 after a 13-year run. Her designs returned in 1986 in the Betsey Clark: Home for Christmas series and again in 1998 in celebration of Hallmark's 25th anniversary.

Other significant ornament collections in Hallmark's colorful history include the 27-year-long Frosty Friends series, which debuted in 1980 and is still going strong. Each ornament in the series features a cute snowsuit-clad Inuit child participating in a variety of joyous wintertime activities.

Another longtime favorite is the Nostalgic Houses and Shops series, which was introduced in 1984 and continues today. The Rocking Horse collection, which began in 1981 and ended in 1996, was another successful series. (See "Hallmark Timeline" for more popular series.)

Hallmark's many licensed property lines include Peanuts, Barbie, Mickey Mouse and a host of other Disney characters, Lionel trains, and many more. Famous movies also replay again and again in the Hallmark ornament theater: Star Wars, Gone With the Wind, and The Wizard of Oz are just a few.

Hallmark also produces miniature ornaments, which were introduced in 1988 and are desirable to collectors because of their small size and intricate detail. In addition, Hallmark offers ornaments that celebrate springtime and Halloween.

Hallmark Keepsake Ornament Collector's Club

Founded in 1987, the national Hallmark Keepsake Ornament Collector's Club was created in response to requests from collectors of Hallmark ornaments. It celebrates its 20th anniversary in 2007.

The first club convention was held in Kansas City, Missouri, in 1991. Hallmark ornament aficionados everywhere eagerly anticipate these yearly conventions. To celebrate its anniversary milestone, there are three club events planned for 2007.

Membership offers many perks, including complimentary ornaments as well as the opportunity to purchase ornaments that are not available to the general public.

Hundreds of local chapters of the national club are active in the United States and Canada. Local Hallmark retailers sponsor most of these independent clubs.

How Prices Are Determined

Hallmark ornaments have truly become a treasured collectible not only for their holiday significance, but for their secondary market value also.

The secondary market is the market collectibles enter after they have left the original, primary point of retail sales. This market exists because a buyer is searching for an item no longer available through regular retail distribution channels. Secondary market transactions are represented by sales between individual collectors as well as dealers who may or may not be involved with primary retail selling.

Because secondary market prices can vary from region to region, and even within a given locale, values listed in *Warman's Hallmark Keepsake Ornaments* are simply guides to help collectors, insurance agents, appraisers, and others determine the "going" or "asking" price. These values reflect the most often asked-for or sold-for prices. *Warman's Hallmark Keepsake Ornaments* is not published to determine exact pricing information on ornaments and should not be taken as such.

Inside this book you'll find secondary market values for more than 6,000 Hallmark ornaments from 1973 through 2006. The prices published in this book are average or fair trend values at which mint condition ornaments with their boxes are currently trading hands. Several steps were taken to arrive at these prices. This included researching everything available on Hallmark: acquiring the company's Dream Books; reading other books; studying Internet auctions; working with secondary market dealers and exchange specialists; and talking with readers and collectors.

Please keep in mind this book is simply a guide to be used in conjunction with every other bit of information you can obtain to determine a realistic value for your Hallmark ornaments. In the end, enthusiasts like you determine the true value of ornaments when you actively buy and sell them on the secondary market.

How to Use This Book

Warman's Hallmark Keepsake Ornaments is divided into decades starting with the 1970s, when Hallmark launched its ornament line. Each decade features full-color pictures and secondary market information for ornaments produced during that time.

Each photograph is fully identified with the name of the ornament, the year it was produced, the series in which it appeared (if applicable), and the current secondary market value of the ornament.

The secondary market listings are arranged in alphabetical order by ornament name. These listings include:
- title (name) of the ornament;
- identifying number;
- series in which the ornament appeared (if applicable);
- year the ornament was issued;
- issue price of the ornament (the price it retailed for when new), rounded to the nearest dollar; and
- current secondary market trend price

Hallmark Keepsake Ornament Timeline

1979: Here Comes Santa series begins
1980: Frosty Friends series begins

1973: Ornament line begins with the Betsey Clark series
1975: First figural ornaments appear
1976: First commemorative ornament issued, titled Baby's First Christmas
1977: Peanuts characters debut as Hallmark ornaments

1981: Rocking Horse series begins

1984: Nostalgic Houses and Shops series begins; first Magic Ornaments offered
1985: Chris Mouse series begins
1987: Hallmark Keepsake Ornament Collector's Club is formed
1988: Hallmark introduces miniature ornaments; Mary's Angels series begins
1989: Crayola Crayon series begins

1991: Classic American Cars series begins; Hallmark introduces Easter ornaments; Star Trek series begins with Starship Enterprise ornament

1992: Hallmark offers five pedal car replicas and begins the Kiddie Car Classics line

1993: Barbie and Looney Tunes characters both debut in the Hallmark line

1994: Kiddie Car Classics ornament series begins; The Lion King and The Wizard of Oz movies inspire new ornaments

1995: All-American Trucks series begins

1996: Hallmark introduces first Star Wars ornament and first Lionel trains ornament

1998: Hallmark Keepsake Ornaments' 25th anniversary

2001: Ornaments featuring Hot Wheels cars debut

2003: Hallmark Keepsake Ornaments' 30th anniversary

Special Thanks

This book never would have existed without the generous help of Hallmark ornament maven Merna Dudley of Wisconsin. Her collection of hundreds of Hallmark ornaments—along with the collections of her daughter, Merry, and sons, Roger Jr. and Mike—account for more than 500 pictures in this book. Merna fell in love with Hallmark ornaments in the 1970s. Among her earliest ornaments are the Currier & Ives glass balls from 1974, Chickadees glass ball from 1976, and Peanuts satin ball from 1977. Her collecting really began in earnest in 1978. Today, 30 years later, Merna remains a devoted Hallmark collector. Thank you, Merna!

Our sincere appreciation also goes to collectors Marilyn Mortenson, of Iola, Wisconsin, and her children Steve, Heidi, and Jill; Joan Johnson of Amherst, Wisconsin; and Hester Shingleton of Roanoke, Virginia, for allowing us to photograph their rare, vintage 1970s ornaments.

1970s

The 1970s mark the birth of Hallmark Keepsake Ornaments and the beginning of America's love affair with them.

When Hallmark entered the ornament arena, Christmas tree decorations went from simple colored glass balls to creative and fun designs. Ornaments suddenly became unique, year-dated and available only for a limited time, making them an instant hit with collectors.

The first year of production was 1973, when Hallmark issued 18 ornaments: six in ball shape and 12 made of yarn. Among them was a series of ball ornaments featuring Betsey Clark designs of children. (Clark was an artist for Hallmark Cards for 25 years.)

The first figural-type ornaments appeared in 1975. The first commemorative ornament, Baby's First Christmas, was issued in 1976. The Peanuts characters—Charlie Brown, Snoopy, Linus, and others from that gang—debuted as ornaments in 1977. In 1979 the decade drew to a close with the introduction of the Here Comes Santa series, with an ornament titled Santa's Motorcar.

1970s Pricing

Ornament Title	Series	Year	Issue Price	Current Value
25th Christmas Together 350QX269-3	Commemoratives	1978	$4	$15
Angel 125XHD78-5	Yarn Ornaments	1973	$1	$29
Angel 150QX103-1	Yarn Ornaments	1974	$2	$29
Angel 175QX220-2	Cloth Doll Ornaments	1977	$2	$45
Angel 250QX110-1	General Line	1974	$2	$80
Angel 300QX176-1	Tree Treats	1976	$3	$85
Angel 350QX354-3	Colors Of Christmas	1978	$4	$50
Angel 400QX139-6	Handcrafted Ornaments	1978	$4	$70
Angel 450QX171-1	Twirl-Abouts	1976	$4	$100
Angel 500QX182-2	Nostalgia	1977	$5	$62
Angel 600QX172-2	Yesteryears	1977	$6	$70
Angel Delight 300QX130-7	Little Trimmers	1979	$3	$72
Angel Music 200QX343-9	Sewn Trimmers	1979	$2	$19
Angel Tree Topper 900HD230-2	Tree Topper	1977	$9	$425
Angels 800QX150-3	Handcrafted Ornaments	1978	$8	$200
Animal Home 600QX149-6	Handcrafted Ornaments	1978	$6	$160
Antique Car 500QX180-2	Nostalgia	1977	$5	$40
Antique Toys Carousel 1st Ed. 600QX146-3	Carousel Series	1978	$6	$175
Baby's First Christmas 250QX211-1	General Line	1976	$2	$129
Baby's First Christmas 350QX131-5	General Line	1977	$4	$85
Baby's First Christmas 350QX200-3	Commemoratives	1978	$4	$31
Baby's First Christmas 350QX208-7	Commemoratives	1979	$4	$28
Baby's First Christmas 800QX154-7	Commemoratives	1979	$8	$100
Behold The Star 350QX255-9	Decorative Ball Ornaments	1979	$4	$30
Bell 350QX154-2	Christmas Expressions Collection	1977	$4	$40
Bell 350QX200-2	Colors Of Christmas	1977	$4	$40
Bellringer 600QX192-2	Twirl-Abouts	1977	$6	$62
Bellswinger 1st Ed. QX147-9	Bellringer Series	1979	$10	$170
Betsey Clark (2) 350QX167-1	General Line	1975	$4	$38
Betsey Clark (3) 450QX218-1	General Line	1976	$4	$60
Betsey Clark (4) 450QX168-1	General Line	1975	$4	$35
Betsey Clark 1st Ed. 250XHD110-2	Betsey Clark	1973	$3	$100
Betsey Clark 250QX157-1	Adorable Adornments	1975	$2	$230
Betsey Clark 250QX163-1	General Line	1975	$2	$20
Betsey Clark 250QX210-1	General Line	1976	$2	$45
Betsey Clark 250XHD100-2	General Line	1973	$2	$45
Betsey Clark 2nd Ed. 250QX108-1	Betsey Clark	1974	$3	$45
Betsey Clark 3rd Ed. 300QX133-1	Betsey Clark	1975	$3	$40
Betsey Clark 4th Ed. 300QX195-1	Betsey Clark	1976	$3	$60
Betsey Clark 5th Ed. 350QX264-2	Betsey Clark	1977	$4	$350
Betsey Clark 6th Ed. 350QX201-6	Betsey Clark	1978	$4	$40
Betsey Clark 7th Ed. 350QX201-9	Betsey Clark	1979	$4	$19

Betsey Clark, 1973, **$45**, and Christmas 1973, 1st in the Betsey Clark series, **$100.**

Photo courtesy Hallmark

Christmas is Love, 1973, **$75.**

Elves, 1973, **$40.**

Santa With Elves, 1973, **$80.**

Angel, 1974, **$29.**

Norman Rockwell, 1974, **$45.**

Photo courtesy Hallmark

The original Baby's First Christmas ornament, 1976, **$129.**

Ornament Title	Series	Year	Issue Price	Current Value
Bicentennial '76 Commemorative QX203-1	Bicentennial Commemoratives	1976	$2	$20
Bicentennial Charmers 300QX198-1	Bicentennial Commemoratives	1976	$3	$50
Black Angel 350QX207-9	Decorative Ball Ornaments	1979	$4	$25
Blue Girl 125XHD85-2	Yarn Ornaments	1973	$1	$25
Boy Caroler 125XHD83-2	Yarn Ornaments	1973	$1	$19
Buttons & Bo (2) 350QX113-1	General Line	1974	$4	$50
Buttons & Bo (4) 500QX139-1	General Line	1975	$5	$38
Calico Mouse 450QX137-6	Handcrafted Ornaments	1978	$4	$50
Candle 350QX203-5	Colors Of Christmas	1977	$4	$60
Candle 350QX357-6	Colors Of Christmas	1978	$4	$85
Cardinals 225QX205-1	Decorative Ball Ornaments	1976	$2	$30
Caroler 175QX126-1	Yarn Ornaments	1976	$2	$22
Charmers (2) 350QX215-1	General Line	1976	$4	$25
Charmers 250QX109-1	General Line	1974	$2	$20
Charmers 300QX135-1	General Line	1975	$3	$50
Charmers 350QX153-5	General Line	1977	$4	$60
Chickadees 225QX204-1	Decorative Ball Ornaments	1976	$2	$40
Choir Boy 125XHD80-5	Yarn Ornaments	1973	$1	$27
Christmas Angel 350QX300-7	Holiday Highlights	1979	$4	$100
Christmas Carousel 2nd Ed. 650QX146-7	Carousel Series	1979	$6	$115
Christmas Cheer 350QX303-9	Holiday Highlights	1979	$4	$40
Christmas Chickadees 350QX204-7	Decorative Ball Ornaments	1979	$4	$32
Christmas Collage 350QX257-9	Decorative Ball Ornaments	1979	$4	$40
Christmas Eve Surprise 650QX157-9	Handcrafted Ornaments	1979	$6	$70
Christmas Heart 650QX140-7	Handcrafted Ornaments	1979	$6	$45
Christmas Is For Children 500QX135-9	Handcrafted Ornaments	1979	$5	$45
Christmas Is Love 250XHD106-2	General Line	1973	$2	$75
Christmas Mouse 350QX134-2	Decorative Ball Ornaments	1977	$4	$60
Christmas Star Tree Topper QX702-3	Tree Topper	1978	$8	$40
Christmas Traditions 350QX253-9	Decorative Ball Ornaments	1979	$4	$40
Christmas Treat 500QX134-7	Handcrafted Ornaments	1979	$5	$42
Christmas Tree 350QX302-7	Holiday Highlights	1979	$4	$50
Colonial Children (2) 400QX208-1	Bicentennial Commemoratives	1976	$4	$10
Currier & Ives (2) 250QX164-1	Currier & Ives	1975	$2	$40
Currier & Ives (2) 350QX112-1	Currier & Ives	1974	$4	$38
Currier & Ives (2) 400QX137-1	Currier & Ives	1975	$4	$40
Currier & Ives 250QX209-1	Currier & Ives	1976	$2	$40
Currier & Ives 300QX197-1	Currier & Ives	1976	$3	$50
Currier & Ives 350QX130-2	Currier & Ives	1977	$4	$50
Della Robia Wreath 450QX193-5	Twirl-Abouts	1977	$4	$42
Desert 250QX159-5	Beauty Of America Collection	1977	$2	$42
Disney (2) 400QX137-5	General Line	1977	$4	$55
Disney 350QX133-5	General Line	1977	$4	$70
Disney 350QX207-6	General Line	1978	$4	$42
Dove 350QX310-3	Holiday Highlights	1978	$4	$50
Dove 450QX190-3	Handcrafted Ornaments	1978	$4	$45

Partridge, 1976, from the Yesteryears series, **$62.**

Drummer Boy, 1976, from the Yesteryears series, **$85.**

Bicentennial '76 Commemorative, 1976, **$20.**

Angel, 1976, from the Twirl-Abouts series, **$100.**

Partridge, 1976, from the Twirl-Abouts series, **$100.**

Ornament Title	Series	Year	Issue Price	Current Value
Downhill Run, The 650QX145-9	Handcrafted Ornaments	1979	$6	$120
Drummer Boy 175QX123-1	Yarn Ornaments	1975	$2	$13
Drummer Boy 175QX123-1	Yarn Ornaments	1976	$2	$26
Drummer Boy 250QX136-3	Little Trimmers	1978	$2	$78
Drummer Boy 250QX161-1	Adorable Adornments	1975	$2	$175
Drummer Boy 350QX130-1	Nostalgia	1975	$4	$168
Drummer Boy 350QX252-3	Decorative Ball Ornaments	1978	$4	$42
Drummer Boy 350QX312-2	Holiday Highlights	1977	$4	$62
Drummer Boy 400QX130-1	Nostalgia	1976	$4	$83
Drummer Boy 500QX184-1	Yesteryears	1976	$5	$85
Drummer Boy, The 800QX143-9	Handcrafted Ornaments	1979	$8	$75
Elf 125XHD79-2	Yarn Ornaments	1973	$1	$26
Elf 150QX101-1	Yarn Ornaments	1974	$2	$26
Elves 250XHD103-5	General Line	1973	$2	$40
First Christmas Together 350QX132-2	Commemoratives	1977	$4	$48
First Christmas Together 350QX218-3	Commemoratives	1978	$4	$48
For Your New Home 350QX217-6	Commemoratives	1978	$4	$25
For Your New Home 350QX263-5	Commemoratives	1977	$4	$35
Friendship 350QX203-9	Commemoratives	1979	$4	$25
Granddaughter 350QX208-2	Commemoratives	1977	$4	$19
Granddaughter 350QX211-9	Commemoratives	1979	$4	$38
Granddaughter 350QX216-3	Commemoratives	1978	$4	$38
Grandma Moses 350QX150-2	General Line	1977	$4	$34
Grandmother 350QX252-7	Commemoratives	1979	$4	$18
Grandmother 350QX260-2	Commemoratives	1977	$4	$50
Grandmother 350QX267-6	Commemoratives	1978	$4	$18
Grandson 350QX209-5	Commemoratives	1977	$4	$35
Grandson 350QX210-7	Commemoratives	1979	$4	$40
Grandson 350QX215-6	Commemoratives	1978	$4	$40
Green Boy 200QX123-1	Yarn Ornaments	1978	$2	$28
Green Girl 125XHD84-5	Yarn Ornaments	1973	$1	$25
Green Girl 200QX126-1	Yarn Ornaments	1978	$2	$28
Hallmark's Antique Card Coll. 350QX220-3	Decorative Ball Ornaments	1978	$4	$44
Happy Holidays Kissing Balls QX225-1	General Line	1976	$5	$225
Happy The Snowman (2) QX216-1	General Line	1976	$4	$50
Heavenly Minstrel Tabletop QHD 921-9	Table Decor	1978	$35	$145
Holiday Memories Kissing Ball QHD 900-3	General Line	1978	$5	$120
Holiday Scrimshaw 400QX152-7	Handcrafted Ornaments	1979	$4	$135
Holiday Wreath 350QX353-9	Colors Of Christmas	1979	$4	$42
Holly & Poinsettia Ball 600QX147-6	Handcrafted Ornaments	1978	$6	$60
Holly & Poinsettia Table Decor OHD320-2	Table Decor	1977	$8	$132
House 600QX170-2	Yesteryears	1977	$6	$70
Ice Hockey Holiday 1st Ed. 800QX141-9	Snoopy & Friends	1979	$8	$160
Jack-In-The-Box 600QX171-5	Yesteryears	1977	$6	$67
Joan Walsh Anglund 350QX205-9	General Line	1979	$4	$35
Joan Walsh Anglund 350QX221-6	General Line	1978	$4	$40

Locomotive, 1976, from the Nostalgia series, **$110.**

Nativity, 1977, from the Nostalgia series, **$97.**

Antique Car, 1977, from the Nostalgia series, **$40.**

Weather House, 1977, from the Twirl-Abouts series, **$35.**

Ornament Title	Series	Year	Issue Price	Current Value
Joy 350QX132-1	Nostalgia	1975	$4	$143
Joy 350QX201-5	Colors Of Christmas	1977	$4	$50
Joy 350QX254-3	Decorative Ball Ornaments	1978	$4	$44
Joy 350QX310-2	Holiday Highlights	1977	$4	$50
Joy 450QX138-3	Handcrafted Ornaments	1978	$4	$44
Light Of Christmas, The 350QX256-7	Decorative Ball Ornaments	1979	$4	$30
Little Girl 125XHD82-5	Yarn Ornaments	1973	$1	$25
Little Girl 175QX126-1	Yarn Ornaments	1975	$2	$22
Little Miracles (4) 450QX115-1	General Line	1974	$4	$60
Little Miracles (4) 500QX140-1	General Line	1975	$5	$40
Little Trimmer Collection QX132-3	General Line	1978	$9	$320
Little Trimmer Set QX159-9	General Line	1979	$9	$340
Locomotive (Dated) 350QX127-1	Nostalgia	1975	$4	$113
Locomotive 350QX356-3	Colors Of Christmas	1978	$4	$60
Locomotive 400QX222-1	Nostalgia	1976	$4	$110
Love 350QX258-7	Commemoratives	1979	$4	$38
Love 350QX262-2	Commemoratives	1977	$4	$27
Love 350QX268-3	Commemoratives	1978	$4	$60
Love 350QX304-7	Holiday Highlights	1979	$4	$55
Mandolin 350QX157-5	Christmas Expressions Collection	1977	$4	$40
Manger Scene 250XHD102-2	General Line	1973	$2	$90
Marty Links (2) 400QX207-1	General Line	1976	$4	$55
Marty Links 300QX136-1	General Line	1975	$3	$50
Mary Hamilton 350QX254-7	General Line	1979	$4	$28
Matchless Christmas 400QX132-7	Little Trimmers	1979	$4	$39
Merry Christmas (Santa) 350QX202-3	Decorative Ball Ornaments	1978	$4	$20
Merry Christmas 350QX355-6	Colors Of Christmas	1978	$4	$55
Merry Santa 200QX342-7	Sewn Trimmers	1979	$2	$8
Mother 350QX251-9	Commemoratives	1979	$4	$18
Mother 350QX261-5	Commemoratives	1977	$4	$35
Mother 350QX266-3	Commemoratives	1978	$4	$40
Mountains 250QX158-2	Beauty Of America Collection	1977	$2	$35
Mr. & Mrs. Snowman Kissing Ball QX225-2	General Line	1977	$5	$100
Mr. Claus 200QX340-3	Yarn Ornaments	1978	$2	$23
Mr. Santa 125XHD74-5	Yarn Ornaments	1973	$1	$25
Mr. Snowman 125XHD76-5	Yarn Ornaments	1973	$1	$24
Mrs. Claus 200QX125-1	Yarn Ornaments	1978	$2	$22
Mrs. Santa 125XHD75-2	Yarn Ornaments	1973	$1	$22
Mrs. Santa 150QX100-1	Yarn Ornaments	1974	$2	$22
Mrs. Santa 175QX125-1	Yarn Ornaments	1975	$2	$19
Mrs. Santa 175QX125-1	Yarn Ornaments	1976	$2	$19
Mrs. Santa 250QX156-1	Adorable Adornments	1975	$2	$125
Mrs. Snowman 125XHD77-2	Yarn Ornaments	1973	$1	$24
Nativity 350QX253-6	Decorative Ball Ornaments	1978	$4	$125

Bell, 1977, from the Colors of Christmas series, **$40.**

Joy, 1977, from the Holiday Highlights series, **$50.**

Snowman, 1977, from the Twirl-Abouts series, **$78.**

Peanuts, 1977, **$80.**

Bellringer, 1977, from the Twirl-Abouts series, **$62.**

Ornament Title	Series	Year	Issue Price	Current Value
Nativity 350QX309-6	Holiday Highlights	1978	$4	$95
Nativity 500QX181-5	Nostalgia	1977	$5	$97
New Home 350QX212-7	Commemoratives	1979	$4	$24
Night Before Christmas 350QX214-7	Decorative Ball Ornaments	1979	$4	$40
Norman Rockwell 250QX106-1	General Line	1974	$2	$45
Norman Rockwell 250QX111-1	General Line	1974	$2	$84
Norman Rockwell 250QX166-1	General Line	1975	$2	$62
Norman Rockwell 300QX134-1	General Line	1975	$3	$20
Norman Rockwell 300QX196-1	General Line	1976	$3	$78
Norman Rockwell 350QX151-5	General Line	1977	$4	$65
Old Fashion Customs Kissing Ball QX225-5	General Line	1977	$5	$147
Ornaments 350QX155-5	Christmas Expressions Collection	1977	$4	$45
Our First Christmas Together 350QX209-9	Commemoratives	1979	$4	$68
Our Twenty-Fifth Anniversary 350QX250-7	Commemoratives	1979	$4	$14
Outdoor Fun 800QX150-7	Handcrafted Ornaments	1979	$8	$120
Panorama Ball 600QX145-6	Handcrafted Ornaments	1978	$6	$140
Partridge 450QX174-1	Twirl-Abouts	1976	$4	$100
Partridge 500QX183-1	Yesteryears	1976	$5	$62
Partridge In A Pear Tree 350QX351-9	Colors Of Christmas	1979	$4	$40
Peace On Earth (Dated) 350QX131-1	Nostalgia	1975	$4	$93
Peace On Earth 350QX311-5	Holiday Highlights	1977	$4	$60
Peace On Earth 400QX223-1	Nostalgia	1976	$4	$90
Peanuts (2) 400QX163-5	Peanuts Collection	1977	$4	$90
Peanuts 250QX162-2	Peanuts Collection	1977	$2	$80
Peanuts 250QX203-6	Peanuts Collection	1978	$2	$60
Peanuts 250QX204-3	Peanuts Collection	1978	$2	$70
Peanuts 350QX135-5	Peanuts Collection	1977	$4	$80
Peanuts 350QX205-6	Peanuts Collection	1978	$4	$70
Peanuts 350QX206-3	Peanuts Collection	1978	$4	$60
Peanuts: Time To Trim 350QX202-7	General Line	1979	$4	$45
Praying Angel 250QX134-3	Little Trimmers	1978	$2	$40
Quail, The- 350QX251-6	Decorative Ball Ornaments	1978	$4	$40
Rabbit 250QX139-5	Decorative Ball Ornaments	1977	$2	$90
Raggedy Andy 175QX122-1	Yarn Ornaments	1975	$2	$40
Raggedy Andy 175QX122-1	Yarn Ornaments	1976	$2	$40
Raggedy Andy 250QX160-1	Adorable Adornments	1975	$2	$275
Raggedy Ann & Raggedy Andy 400QX138-1	General Line	1975	$4	$65
Raggedy Ann & Raggedy Andy 450QX114-1	General Line	1974	$4	$90
Raggedy Ann 175QX121-1	Yarn Ornaments	1976	$2	$40
Raggedy Ann 175QX121-1	Yarn Ornaments	1975	$2	$40
Raggedy Ann 250QX159-1	Adorable Adornments	1975	$2	$160
Raggedy Ann 250QX165-1	General Line	1975	$2	$50
Raggedy Ann 250QX212-1	General Line	1976	$2	$40
Ready For Christmas 650QX133-9	Handcrafted Ornaments	1979	$6	$50
Red Cardinal 450QX144-3	Handcrafted Ornaments	1978	$4	$150

Angel, 1978, **$70.**

Candle, 1978, from the Colors of Christmas series, **$85.**

Angel, 1978, from the Colors of Christmas series, **$50.**

Merry Christmas, 1978, from the Colors of Christmas series, **$55.**

Grandmother, 1978, **$18.**

Calico Mouse, 1978, **$50.**

Granddaughter, 1978, **$38.**

Hallmark's Antique Card Collection Design, 1978, **$44.**

Ornament Title	Series	Year	Issue Price	Current Value
Reindeer 300QX178-1	Tree Treats	1976	$3	$55
Reindeer 600QX173-5	Yesteryears	1977	$6	$71
Reindeer Chimes 450QX320-3	Holiday Chimes	1978	$4	$35
Reindeer Chimes 450QX320-3	Holiday Chimes	1979	$4	$35
Rocking Horse 350QX128-1	General Line	1975	$4	$65
Rocking Horse 400QX128-1	General Line	1976	$4	$170
Rocking Horse 600QX148-3	General Line	1978	$6	$90
Rocking Horse, The 200QX340-7	General Line	1979	$2	$20
Rudolph & Santa 250QX213-1	General Line	1976	$2	$90
Santa & Sleigh 350QX129-1	Nostalgia	1975	$4	$150
Santa 150QX105-1	Yarn Ornaments	1974	$2	$18
Santa 175QX124-1	Yarn Ornaments	1975	$2	$25
Santa 175QX124-1	Yarn Ornaments	1976	$2	$24
Santa 175QX221-5	Cloth Doll Ornaments	1977	$2	$35
Santa 250QX135-6	Little Trimmers	1978	$2	$28
Santa 250QX155-1	Adorable Adornments	1975	$2	$100
Santa 300QX135-6	Little Trimmers	1979	$3	$28
Santa 300QX177-1	Tree Treats	1976	$3	$100
Santa 350QX307-6	Holiday Highlights	1978	$4	$80
Santa 450QX172-1	Twirl-Abouts	1976	$4	$43
Santa 500QX182-1	Yesteryears	1976	$5	$105
Santa With Elves 250XHD101-5	General Line	1973	$2	$80
Santa's Here 500QX138-7	Handcrafted Ornaments	1979	$5	$30
Santa's Motorcar 1st Ed. 900QX155-9	Here Comes Santa	1979	$9	$294
Schneeberg Bell 800QX152-3	Handcrafted Ornaments	1978	$8	$135
Seashore 250QX160-2	Beauty Of America Collection	1977	$2	$50
Shepherd 300QX175-1	Tree Treats	1976	$3	$70
Skating Raccoon 600QX142-3	Handcrafted Ornaments	1978	$6	$35
Skating Raccoon 650QX142-3	Handcrafted Ornaments	1979	$6	$35
Skating Snowman, The 500QX139-9	Handcrafted Ornaments	1979	$5	$30
Snowflake 350QX301-9	Holiday Highlights	1979	$4	$40
Snowflake 350QX308-3	Holiday Highlights	1978	$4	$65
Snowflake Collection (4) 500QX210-2	Metal Ornaments	1977	$5	$90
Snowgoose 250QX107-1	General Line	1974	$2	$70
Snowman 150QX104-1	Yarn Ornaments	1974	$2	$25
Snowman 450QX190-2	Twirl-Abouts	1977	$4	$78
Soldier 100XHD81-2	Yarn Ornaments	1973	$1	$16
Soldier 150QX102-1	Yarn Ornaments	1974	$2	$24
Soldier 450QX173-1	Twirl-Abouts	1976	$4	$45
Spencer Sparrow 350QX200-7	General Line	1979	$4	$25
Spencer Sparrow 350QX219-6	General Line	1978	$4	$50
Squirrel 250QX138-2	Decorative Ball Ornaments	1977	$2	$95
Stained Glass 350QX152-2	Decorative Ball Ornaments	1977	$4	$36
Star 350QX313-5	Holiday Highlights	1977	$4	$50
Star Chimes 450QX137-9	Holiday Chimes	1979	$4	$29
Star Over Bethlehem 350QX352-7	Colors Of Christmas	1979	$4	$44

Nativity, 1978, **$125.**

Betsey Clark, 1978, 6th in the Betsey Clark series, **$40.**

Santa's Motorcar, 1979, 1st in the Here Comes Santa series, **$294.**

Baby's First Christmas, 1979, **$28.**

Betsey Clark, 1979, 7th in the Betsey Clark series, **$19.**

Peanuts, 1978, **$70.**

Ornament Title	Series	Year	Issue Price	Current Value
Stuffed Full Stocking 200QX341-9	Sewn Trimmers	1979	$2	$24
Teacher 350QX213-9	Commemoratives	1979	$4	$21
Thimble Christmas Salute, A 2nd Ed. 400QX131-9	Thimble Series	1979	$4	$80
Thimble Series-Mouse 300QX133-6	Little Trimmers	1979	$3	$100
Thimble W/Mouse 1st Ed. 300QX133-6	Thimble Series	1978	$3	$120
Tiffany Angel Tree Topper 1000QX703 7	Tree Topper	1979	$10	$25
Toys 500QX183-5	Nostalgia	1977	$5	$67
Train 500QX181-1	Yesteryears	1976	$5	$78
Weather House 600QX191-5	Twirl-Abouts	1977	$6	$35
Wharf 250QX161-5	Beauty Of America Collection	1977	$2	$36
Winnie-The-Pooh 350QX206-7	General Line	1979	$4	$34
Words Of Christmas 350QX350-7	Colors Of Christmas	1979	$4	$78
Wreath 350QX156-2	Christmas Expressions Collection	1977	$4	$38
Wreath 350QX202-2	Colors Of Christmas	1977	$4	$60
Yesterday's Toys 350QX250-3	Decorative Ball Ornaments	1978	$4	$25

Christmas is for Children, 1979, $45.

Christmas Carousel, 1979, 2nd in the Carousel series, $115.

Ready for Christmas, 1979, **$50.**

Christmas Cheer, 1979, from the Holiday Highlights series, **$40.**

Mother, 1979, **$18.**

Peanuts: Time to Trim, 1979, **$45.**

Grandson, 1979, **$40.**

Joan Walsh Anglund, 1979, **$35.**

Angel Delight, 1979, from the Little Trimmers series, **$72.**

Christmas Tree, 1979, from the Holiday Highlights series, **$50.**

Skating Snowman, 1979, **$30.**

The Drummer Boy, 1979, **$75.**

Partridge in a Pear Tree, 1979, from the Colors of Christmas series, **$40.**

Christmas Heart, 1979, **$45.**

1980s

The 1980s was a busy decade for Hallmark. One of its best-known ornament series, the 27-year-long Frosty Friends series, debuted in 1980 and is still going strong. Another longtime favorite is the Nostalgic Houses and Shops series, which was introduced in 1984 and continues today. The Rocking Horse collection, which began in 1981, was another successful series. Other popular series introduced during the 1980s include: Chris Mouse in 1985, Mary's Angels in 1988, and Crayola Crayon in 1989.

The 1980s are also important for another reason: the founding of the Hallmark Keepsake Ornament Collector's Club in 1987, which was created in response to requests from collectors. The first club convention was held in Kansas City, Missouri, in 1991. Today the club boasts more than a quarter-million members. Membership offers many perks, including complimentary ornaments as well as the opportunity to purchase ornaments that are not available to the general public. Hundreds of local chapters of the national club are active in the United States and Canada. Local Hallmark retailers sponsor most of these independent clubs.

Other important firsts were noted during the 1980s: the first Magic Ornaments were offered to collectors in 1984, and the first miniature ornaments were introduced in 1988.

1980s Pricing

Ornament Title	Series	Year	Issue Price	Current Value
10th Christmas Together 650QX430-7	Commemoratives	1983	$6	$30
1983 450QX220-9	Decorative Ball Ornaments	1983	$4	$25
25 Years Together Photoholder 875QX485-5	Commemoratives	1989	$9	$5
25th Christmas Together 400QX206-1	Commemoratives	1980	$4	$18
25th Christmas Together 450QX211-6	Commemoratives	1982	$4	$14
25th Christmas Together 450QX224-7	Commemoratives	1983	$4	$18
25th Christmas Together 450QX707-5	Commemoratives	1981	$4	$11
25th Christmas Together 550QX504-2	Commemoratives	1981	$6	$4
40 Years Together Photoholder 875QX545-2	Commemoratives	1989	$9	$7
50 Years Together Photoholder 875QX486-2	Commemoratives	1989	$9	$17
50th Christmas Together 450QX212-3	Commemoratives	1982	$4	$10
50th Christmas Together QX708-2	Commemoratives	1981	$4	$4
Acorn Inn 850QX424-3	General Line	1986	$8	$25
Acorn Squirrel 450QXM568-2	Miniature Ornaments	1989	$4	$10
Airplane 5th Ed. 750QX404-1	Wood Childhood	1988	$8	$17
All Are Precious 800QLX704-1	Magic Ornaments	1984	$8	$26
All Are Precious 800QLX704-4	Magic Ornaments	1985	$8	$18
Alpine Elf 600QX452-1	General Line	1984	$6	$18
Amanda Doll 900QX432-1	General Line	1984	$9	$20
Americana Drum 775QX488-1	Handcrafted Ornaments	1988	$8	$27
And To All A Good Night 9th & Final Ed. 775QX370-4	Norman Rockwell	1988	$8	$20
Angel 300QX162-1	Yarn Ornaments	1980	$3	$12
Angel 400QX509-5	Frosted Images	1981	$4	$37
Angel 450QX507-5	Crown Classics Collection	1981	$4	$12
Angel 550QX309-6	Holiday Highlights	1982	$6	$80
Angel Bellringer 4th Ed. QX455-6	Bellringer Series	1982	$15	$75
Angel Chimes 550QX502-6	Holiday Chimes	1982	$6	$100
Angel Melody 950QLX720-2	Magic Ornaments	1989	$10	$22
Angel Messenger 650QX408-7	Handcrafted Ornaments	1983	$6	$55
Angel QX139-6	Handcrafted Ornaments	1981	$6	$90
Angel QX162-1	Yarn Ornaments	1981	$3	$11
Angel Tree Topper 2450QTT710-1	Tree Topper	1984	$25	$36
Angelic Messengers 1875QLX711-3	Magic Ornaments	1987	$19	$55
Angelic Minstrel 2950QX408-4	Collector's Club	1988	$30	$28
Angels 500QX219-7	Decorative Ball Ornaments	1983	$5	$15
Animals' Christmas, The 800QX150-1	Handcrafted Ornaments	1980	$8	$25
Animals Speak , The1350QLX723-2	Magic Ornaments	1989	$14	$48
Annunciation, The 450QX216-7	Decorative Ball Ornaments	1983	$4	$30
Arctic Penguin 400QX300-3	Ice Sculptures	1982	$4	$20
Arctic Tenor 400QX472-1	Handcrafted Ornaments	1988	$4	$20
Baby Locket 1500QX461-7	Commemoratives	1987	$15	$22
Baby Locket 1600QX401-2	Commemoratives	1985	$16	$38

A Cool Yule, 1980, 1st in the Frosty Friends series, **$350.**

Photo courtesy Hallmark

Ornament Title	Series	Year	Issue Price	Current Value
Baby Locket 1600QX412-3	Commemoratives	1986	$16	$15
Baby Partridge 675QX452-5	Artists' Favorites	1989	$7	$14
Baby Redbird 500QX410-1	Artists' Favorites	1988	$5	$14
Baby's 1st Xmas Photoholder 625QX468-2	Commemoratives	1989	$6	$29
Baby's 1st Xmas Photoholder 750QX461-9	Commemoratives	1987	$8	$30
Baby's 1st Xmas Photoholder QX300-1	Commemoratives	1984	$7	$12
Baby's 1st Xmas Photoholder QX302-9	Commemoratives	1983	$7	$19
Baby's Christening Keepsake 700BBY132-5	Baby Celebrations	1989	$7	$30
Baby's First Birthday 5500BBY172-9	Baby Celebrations	1989	$6	$31
Baby's First Christmas (Boy) 450QX216-3	Commemoratives	1982	$4	$30
Baby's First Christmas (Girl) 450QX207-3	Commemoratives	1982	$4	$34
Baby's First Christmas 1200QX156-1	Commemoratives	1980	$12	$20
Baby's First Christmas 1300QX440-2	Commemoratives	1981	$13	$38
Baby's First Christmas 1300QX455-3	Commemoratives	1982	$13	$38
Baby's First Christmas 1350QLX704-9	Magic Ornaments	1987	$14	$30
Baby's First Christmas 1400QX402-7	Commemoratives	1983	$14	$20
Baby's First Christmas 1400QX438-1	Commemoratives	1984	$14	$26
Baby's First Christmas 1500QX499-2	Commemoratives	1985	$15	$42
Baby's First Christmas 1600QMB900-7	General Line	1982	$16	$90
Baby's First Christmas 1600QMB903-9	General Line	1983	$16	$88
Baby's First Christmas 1600QX499-5	Commemoratives	1985	$16	$20
Baby's First Christmas 1600QX904-1	Commemoratives	1984	$16	$29
Baby's First Christmas 1650QLX700-5	Magic Ornaments	1985	$16	$34
Baby's First Christmas 1950QLX710-3	Lighted Ornaments Collection	1986	$20	$34
Baby's First Christmas 2400QLX718-4	Magic Ornaments	1988	$24	$30
Baby's First Christmas 3000QLX727-2	Magic Ornaments	1989	$30	$36
Baby's First Christmas 400QX200-1	Commemoratives	1980	$4	$28
Baby's First Christmas 450QX200-7	Commemoratives	1983	$4	$30
Baby's First Christmas 450QX200-9	Commemoratives	1983	$4	$18
Baby's First Christmas 500QX260-2	Commemoratives	1985	$5	$20
Baby's First Christmas 550QX271-3	Commemoratives	1986	$6	$30
Baby's First Christmas 550QX302-3	Commemoratives	1982	$6	$15
Baby's First Christmas 550QX516-2	Commemoratives	1981	$6	$32
Baby's First Christmas 575QX370-2	Commemoratives	1985	$6	$15
Baby's First Christmas 600QX372-1	Commemoratives	1988	$6	$20
Baby's First Christmas 600QX372-9	Commemoratives	1987	$6	$27
Baby's First Christmas 600QX380-3	Commemoratives	1986	$6	$24
Baby's First Christmas 600QXM573-2	Miniature Ornaments	1989	$6	$20
Baby's First Christmas 600QXM574-4	Miniature Ornaments	1988	$5	$12
Baby's First Christmas 675QX381-5	Commemoratives	1989	$7	$12
Baby's First Christmas 700QX478-2	Commemoratives	1985	$7	$16
Baby's First Christmas 725QX449-2	Commemoratives	1989	$7	$85
Baby's First Christmas 750QX301-9	Commemoratives	1983	$8	$10
Baby's First Christmas 850QX513-5	Commemoratives	1981	$8	$12
Baby's First Christmas 900QX412-6	Commemoratives	1986	$9	$40

Checking It Twice in its original box, 1980, **$180,** and 1981, **$85.**

Checking It Twice, 1980, **$180,** and 1981, **$85.**

The Animals' Christmas, 1980, **$25.**

Caroling Bear, 1980, **$63.**

Ornament Title	Series	Year	Issue Price	Current Value
Baby's First Christmas 975QX411-3	Commemoratives	1987	$10	$25
Baby's First Christmas 975QX470-1	Commemoratives	1988	$10	$20
Baby's First Christmas Photoholder 750QX470-4	Commemoratives	1988	$8	$15
Baby's First Christmas QX340-1	Commemoratives	1984	$6	$35
Baby's First Christmas-Black 450QX602-2	Commemoratives	1981	$4	$25
Baby's First Christmas-Boy 450QX240-4	Commemoratives	1984	$4	$28
Baby's First Christmas-Boy 450QX601-5	Commemoratives	1981	$4	$25
Baby's First Christmas-Boy 475BB145-3	Baby Celebrations	1989	$5	$22
Baby's First Christmas-Boy 475QX272-1	Commemoratives	1988	$5	$30
Baby's First Christmas-Boy 475QX272-5	Commemoratives	1989	$5	$22
Baby's First Christmas-Boy 475QX274-9	Commemoratives	1987	$5	$30
Baby's First Christmas-Girl 450QX600-2	Commemoratives	1981	$4	$25
Baby's First Christmas-Girl 475BBY155-3	Baby Celebrations	1989	$5	$22
Baby's First Christmas-Girl 475QX272-2	Commemoratives	1989	$5	$22
Baby's First Christmas-Girl 475QX272-4	Commemoratives	1988	$5	$30
Baby's First Christmas-Girl 475QX274-7	Commemoratives	1987	$5	$22
Baby's First Christmas-Girl QX240-1	Commemoratives	1984	$4	$30
Baby's First Xmas Photoholder 800QX379-2	Commemoratives	1986	$8	$20
Baby's First Xmas Photoholder 650QX312-6	Commemoratives	1982	$6	$30
Baby's Second Christmas 450QX226-7	Commemoratives	1983	$4	$18
Baby's Second Christmas 450QX241-1	Commemoratives	1984	$4	$38
Baby's Second Christmas 575QX460-7	Commemoratives	1987	$6	$22
Baby's Second Christmas 600QX471-1	Commemoratives	1988	$6	$32
Baby's Second Christmas 600QX478-5	Commemoratives	1985	$6	$26
Baby's Second Christmas 650QX413-3	Commemoratives	1986	$6	$15
Baby's Second Christmas 675QX449-5	Commemoratives	1989	$7	$25
Babysitter 450QX253-1	Commemoratives	1984	$4	$2
Baby-Sitter 475QX264-2	Commemoratives	1985	$5	$2
Baby-Sitter 475QX275-6	Commemoratives	1986	$5	$14
Babysitter 475QX279-1	Commemoratives	1988	$5	$7
Babysitter 475QX279-7	Commemoratives	1987	$5	$4
Backstage Bear 1350QLX721-5	Magic Ornaments	1989	$14	$37
Baker Elf 575QX491-2	General Line	1985	$6	$30
Balancing Elf 675QX489-5	General Line	1989	$7	$12
Baroque Angel 1500QX456-6	Handcrafted Ornaments	1982	$15	$100
Baroque Angels 1300QX422-9	Handcrafted Ornaments	1983	$13	$69
Bear-I-Tone 475QX454-2	Artists' Favorites	1989	$5	$14
Bearly Reaching 950QLX715-1	Magic Ornaments	1988	$10	$20
Beary Smooth Ride 650QX480-5	General Line	1986	$6	$24
Beary Special 475QX455-7	Artists' Favorites	1987	$5	$13
Beauty Of Friendship 400QX303-4	Commemoratives	1980	$4	$65
Bell Chimes 550QX494-3	Holiday Chimes	1982	$6	$25
Bell Ringer Squirrel 1000QX443-1	General Line	1984	$10	$20
Bell Wreath 650QX420-9	Handcrafted Ornaments	1983	$6	$25
Bellringers 2nd Ed. QX157-4	Bellringer Series	1980	$15	$75

Santa Mobile, 1980, from the Holiday Chimes series, also issued in 1981, **$30.**

Father, 1981, **$12.**

Frosty Friends, 1981, 2nd in the Frosty Friends series, **$325.**

A Heavenly Nap, 1980 and 1981, **$35.**

Christmas Dreams, 1981, **$110.**

Ornament Title	Series	Year	Issue Price	Current Value
Betsey Clark 10th Ed. QX215-6	Betsey Clark	1982	$4	$20
Betsey Clark 11th Ed. 450QX211-9	Betsey Clark	1983	$4	$30
Betsey Clark 12th Ed. 500QX249-4	Betsey Clark	1984	$5	$20
Betsey Clark 13th & Final Ed. 500QX263-2	Betsey Clark	1985	$5	$25
Betsey Clark 650QX307-4	General Line	1980	$6	$35
Betsey Clark 650QX404-7	General Line	1983	$6	$30
Betsey Clark 850QX305-6	General Line	1982	$8	$25
Betsey Clark 850QX508-5	General Line	1985	$8	$30
Betsey Clark 8th Ed. 400QX215-4	Betsey Clark	1980	$4	$22
Betsey Clark 900QX423-5	General Line	1981	$9	$75
Betsey Clark 900QX440-1	General Line	1983	$9	$35
Betsey Clark 9th Ed. 450QX802-2	Betsey Clark	1981	$4	$19
Betsey Clark Angel 900QX462-4	General Line	1984	$9	$15
Betsey Clark Blue Cameo QX512-2	General Line	1981	$8	$18
Betsey Clark: Home For Christmas 1st Ed. 500QX277-6	Betsey Clark: Home For Christmas	1986	$5	$25
Betsey Clark: Home For Christmas 2nd Ed. 500QX272-7	Betsey Clark: Home For Christmas	1987	$5	$22
Betsey Clark: Home For Christmas 3rd Ed. 500QX271-4	Betsey Clark: Home For Christmas	1988	$5	$20
Betsey Clark: Home For Christmas 4th Ed. 500QX230-2	Betsey Clark: Home For Christmas	1989	$5	$20
Betsey Clark's Christmas 750QX149-4	General Line	1980	$8	$20
Black Baby's First Christmas 400QX229-4	Commemoratives	1980	$4	$30
Black-Capped Chickadees 2nd Ed. 700QX309-9	Holiday Wildlife	1983	$7	$70
Bluebell 2nd Ed. 575QX454-5	Mary's Angels	1989	$6	$90
Bluebird 725QX428-3	General Line	1986	$7	$60
Bottlecap Fun Bunnies 775QX481-5	General Line	1985	$8	$20
Brass Angel 150QXM567-1	Miniature Ornaments	1988	$2	$16
Brass Bell 1200QX460-6	Brass Ornaments	1982	$12	$9
Brass Carousel 900QLX707-1	Magic Ornaments	1984	$9	$45
Brass Partridge 300QXM572-5	Miniature Ornaments	1989	$3	$8
Brass Promotional Ornament	General Line	1982	$4	$42
Brass Santa 900QX423-9	Handcrafted Ornaments	1983	$9	$6
Brass Snowflake 450QXM570-2	Miniature Ornaments	1989	$4	$9
Brass Star 150QXM566-4	Miniature Ornaments	1988	$2	$10
Brass Star Tree Toppers QX705-4	Tree Topper	1980	$25	$60
Brass Tree 150QXM567-4	Miniature Ornaments	1988	$2	$10
Bright Christmas Dreams QX473-7	General Line	1987	$7	$55
Bright Journey 1st Ed. 875QX-435-2	Crayola Crayon	1989	$9	$50
Bright Noel 700QLX705-9	Magic Ornaments	1987	$7	$25
British Soldier 1st Ed. 500QX458-3	Clothespin Soldier	1982	$5	$42
Brother 725QX445-2	Handcrafted Ornaments	1989	$7	$20
Bunny Hug 300QXM577-5	Miniature Ornaments	1989	$3	$6
Busy Beaver 1750QLX724-5	Magic Ornaments	1989	$18	$50

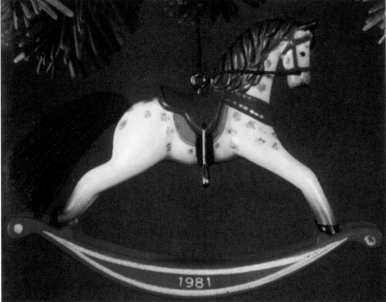

Photo courtesy Hallmark

Rocking Horse, 1981, 1st in the Rocking Horse series, **$425.**

The Ice Sculptor, 1981, **$90.** This ornament was re-iussed in 1982.

Topsy-Turvy Tunes, 1981, **$40.**

A Well-Stocked Stocking, 1981, **$18.**

Ornament Title	Series	Year	Issue Price	Current Value
Buttercup 1st Ed. 500QX407-4	Mary's Angels	1988	$5	$85
Cactus Cowboy 675QX411-2	General Line	1989	$7	$24
Calico Kitty 300QX403-5	Fabric Ornaments	1981	$3	$20
California Partridge 4th Ed. 750QX376-5	Holiday Wildlife	1985	$8	$30
Camera Claus 575QX546-5	General Line	1989	$6	$10
Canadian Mountie 3rd Ed. 500QX447-1	Clothespin Soldier	1984	$5	$18
Candle Cameo 675QX374-2	General Line	1985	$7	$8
Candy Apple Mouse 750QX470-5	General Line	1985	$6	$60
Candy Cane Elf 300QXM570-1	Miniature Ornaments	1988	$3	$19
Candyville Express 750QX418-2	Handcrafted Ornaments	1981	$8	$55
Cardinal Cutie 300QX400-2	Fabric Ornaments	1981	$3	$23
Cardinals 1st Ed. QX313-3	Holiday Wildlife	1982	$7	$195
Carolers, The 2nd Ed. 850QX511-5	Norman Rockwell	1981	$8	$30
Caroling Bear 750QX140-1	Handcrafted Ornaments	1980	$8	$63
Caroling Owl 450QX411-7	Handcrafted Ornaments	1983	$4	$20
Carousel Display Stand 629XPR972-3	Christmas Carousel Horse Collection	1989	$1	$8
Carousel Reindeer QXC581-7	Collector's Club	1987	$8	$30
Carousel Zebra 925QX451-5	Artists' Favorites	1989	$9	$9
Caught Napping 5th Ed. 750QX341-1	Norman Rockwell	1984	$8	$20
Cedar Waxwing 5th Ed. 750QX321-6	Holiday Wildlife	1986	$8	$20
Charlie Brown Christmas 475QX276-5	Peanuts Collection	1989	$5	$30
Charming Angel 975QX512-5	Heirloom Christmas Collection	1985	$10	$18
Chatty Penguin 575QX417-6	General Line	1986	$6	$18
Checking It Twice 2000QX158-4	Handcrafted Ornaments	1980	$20	$100
Checking It Twice 2250QX158-4	Handcrafted Ornaments	1981	$23	$85
Checking Up 7th Ed. 775QX321-3	Norman Rockwell	1986	$8	$25
Cherry Jubilee 500QX453-2	Artists' Favorites	1989	$5	$14
Chickadee 600QX451-4	General Line	1984	$6	$40
Children In The Shoe 950QX490-5	General Line	1985	$10	$34
Child's Fifth Christmas 675QX543-5	Commemoratives	1989	$7	$15
Child's Fourth Christmas 675QX543-2	Commemoratives	1989	$7	$12
Child's Third Christmas 450QX226-9	Commemoratives	1983	$4	$20
Child's Third Christmas 450QX261-1	Commemoratives	1984	$4	$12
Child's Third Christmas 575QX459-9	Commemoratives	1987	$6	$20
Child's Third Christmas 600QX471-4	Commemoratives	1988	$6	$12
Child's Third Christmas 600QX475-5	Commemoratives	1985	$6	$12
Child's Third Christmas 650QX413-6	Commemoratives	1986	$6	$12
Child's Third Christmas 675QX469-5	Commemoratives	1989	$7	$22
Chocolate Chipmunk 600QX456-7	General Line	1987	$6	$50
Chris Mouse 1st Ed. 1250QLX703-2	Chris Mouse	1985	$12	$55
Chris Mouse Cookout 5th Ed. 950QLX722-5	Chris Mouse	1989	$10	$50
Chris Mouse Dreams 2nd Ed. 1300QLX705-6	Chris Mouse	1986	$13	$70
Chris Mouse Glow 3rd Ed. 100QLX705-7	Chris Mouse	1987	$11	$65

Frosty Friends, 1982, 3rd in the Frosty Friends series, **$275.**

Pinecone Home, 1982, **$56.**

Promotional brass ornament, 1982, **$42.**

Right: Christmas Stocking, 1983, from the Holiday Highlights series, **$30.**

Grandparents, 1983, **$8.**

Ornament Title	Series	Year	Issue Price	Current Value
Chris Mouse Star 4th Ed. QLX715-4	Chris Mouse	1988	$9	$68
Christmas 1981-Schneeberg 450QX809-5	Decorative Ball Ornaments	1981	$4	$12
Christmas Angel 450QX220-6	Decorative Ball Ornaments	1982	$4	$28
Christmas At Home 400QX210-1	Commemoratives	1980	$4	$18
Christmas Beauty 600QX322-3	General Line	1986	$6	$10
Christmas Caboose 11th Ed. 1475QX458-5	Here Comes Santa	1989	$15	$35
Christmas Candy Shoppe 3rd Ed. 1375QX403-3	Nostalgic Houses & Shops	1986	$14	$250
Christmas Cardinal 475QX494-1	Handcrafted Ornaments	1988	$5	$14
Christmas Cardinals 400QX224-1	Decorative Ball Ornaments	1980	$4	$12
Christmas Carol, A 2nd Ed. 1600QLX702-9	Christmas Classics	1987	$16	$40
Christmas Choir 400QX228-1	Decorative Ball Ornaments	1980	$4	$80
Christmas Cuckoo 800QX480-1	Handcrafted Ornaments	1988	$8	$19
Christmas Cuddle 575QX453-7	General Line	1987	$6	$35
Christmas Dance 8th Ed. 775QX370-7	Norman Rockwell	1987	$8	$15
Christmas Dreams 1200QX437-5	Handcrafted Ornaments	1981	$12	$110
Christmas Eve Visit 1200QLX710-5	Magic Ornaments	1985	$12	$16
Christmas Fantasy 1300QX155-4	Handcrafted Ornaments	1982	$13	$50
Christmas Fantasy 1300QX155-4	Handcrafted Ornaments	1981	$13	$50
Christmas Fun Puzzle 800QX467-9	Christmas Pizzazz Collection	1987	$8	$16
Christmas Guitar 700QX512-6	Christmas Medley Collection	1986	$7	$18
Christmas In The Forest 450QX813-5	Decorative Ball Ornaments	1981	$4	$99
Christmas In The Forest 800QLX703-4	Magic Ornaments	1984	$8	$20
Christmas Is For Children 550QX135-9	Handcrafted Ornaments	1980	$6	$38
Christmas Is Gentle 1750QX444-9	General Line	1987	$18	$25
Christmas Is Magic 1200QLX717-1	Magic Ornaments	1988	$12	$27
Christmas Is Peaceful 1850QXC451-2	Collector's Club	1989	$19	$22
Christmas Is Sharing 1750QX407-1	Collector's Club	1988	$18	$28
Christmas Joy 450QX216-9	Decorative Ball Ornaments	1983	$4	$9
Christmas Keys 575QX473-9	General Line	1987	$6	$10
Christmas Kitten 400QX454-3	Little Trimmers	1982	$4	$22
Christmas Kitten 400QX454-3	Handcrafted Ornaments	1983	$4	$30
Christmas Kitten Test Ornament QX353-4	General Line	1980	$4	$260
Christmas Kitty 1st Ed. 1475QX544-5	Christmas Kitty	1989	$15	$15
Christmas Koala 400QX419-9	Handcrafted Ornaments	1983	$4	$25
Christmas Love 400QX207-4	Commemoratives	1980	$4	$15
Christmas Magic 450QX810-2	Decorative Ball Ornaments	1981	$4	$18
Christmas Magic 550QX311-3	Holiday Highlights	1982	$6	$20
Christmas Memories 650QX311-6	Commemoratives	1982	$6	$25
Christmas Memories Photoholder QX300-4	General Line	1984	$6	$10
Christmas Memories Photoholder QX372-4	Handcrafted Ornaments	1988	$6	$6
Christmas Morning 2450QLX701-3	Magic Ornaments	1987	$25	$45
Christmas Morning 2450QLX701-3	Magic Ornaments	1988	$25	$45
Christmas Owl 400QX131-4	Little Trimmers	1980	$4	$15
Christmas Owl 450QX131-4	Little Trimmers	1982	$4	$25
Christmas Owl 600QX444-1	General Line	1984	$6	$30

Jack Frost, 1983, **$31.**

Frosty Friends, 1983, 4th in the Frosty Friends series, **$200.**

Grandmother, 1983, **$20.**

Ring-Necked Pheasant, 1984, 3rd in the Holiday Wildlife series, **$30.**

Victorian Dollhouse, 1984, 1st in the Nostalgic Houses and Shops series, **$200.**

Ornament Title	Series	Year	Issue Price	Current Value
Christmas Prayer 450QX246-1	General Line	1984	$4	$22
Christmas Scenes 475QX273-1	General Line	1988	$5	$20
Christmas Sleigh 550QX309-3	Holiday Highlights	1982	$6	$70
Christmas Sleigh Ride 2450QLX701-2	Lighted Ornaments Collection	1986	$25	$60
Christmas Star 550QX501-5	Holiday Highlights	1981	$6	$30
Christmas Stocking 600QX303-9	Holiday Highlights	1983	$6	$30
Christmas Teddy 250QX135-4	Little Trimmers	1980	$2	$50
Christmas Teddy 500QX404-2	Plush Animals	1981	$6	$20
Christmas Time 400QX226-1	Decorative Ball Ornaments	1980	$4	$24
Christmas Time Mime 2750QX442-9	General Line	1987	$28	$15
Christmas Treat 550QX134-7	Handcrafted Ornaments	1980	$6	$80
Christmas Treats 550QX507-5	General Line	1985	$6	$9
Christmas Vigil 900QX144-1	Handcrafted Ornaments	1980	$9	$42
Christmas Wonderland 450QX221-9	Decorative Ball Ornaments	1983	$4	$80
Cinnamon Bear 1st Ed. 700QX428-9	Porcelain Bear	1983	$7	$50
Cinnamon Bear 2nd Ed. 700QX454-1	Porcelain Bear	1984	$7	$25
Cinnamon Bear 3rd Ed. 750QX479-2	Porcelain Bear	1985	$8	$55
Cinnamon Bear 4th Ed. 775QX405-6	Porcelain Bear	1986	$8	$25
Cinnamon Bear 5th Ed. 775QX442-7	Porcelain Bear	1987	$8	$18
Cinnamon Bear 6th Ed. 800QX404-4	Porcelain Bear	1988	$8	$18
Cinnamon Bear 7th Ed. 875QX461-5	Porcelain Bear	1989	$9	$18
Circling The Globe 1050QLX712-4	Magic Ornaments	1988	$10	$40
City Lights 1000QLX701-4	Magic Ornaments	1984	$10	$28
Classical Angel 2750QX459-1	General Line	1984	$28	$100
Glass Construction 775QX400-5	General Line	1989	$0	$10
Cloisonne Angel 1200QX145-4	Handcrafted Ornaments	1982	$12	$60
Clothespin Drummer Boy 450QX408-2	Little Trimmers	1981	$4	$22
Clothespin Soldier 350QX134-4	Little Trimmers	1980	$4	$30
Coca-Cola Santa QXO2796	General Line	1986	N/A	$5
Collect A Dream 900QXC428-5	Collector's Club	1989	$9	$24
Constitution, The 600QZ377-7	Collectible Series	1987	$6	$26
Cookie Mouse 450QX454-6	Little Trimmers	1982	$4	$23
Cookies For Santa 450QX414-6	General Line	1986	$4	$18
Cool Juggler 650QX487-4	Handcrafted Ornaments	1988	$6	$9
Cool Swing 625QX487-5	General Line	1989	$6	$18
Cool Yule, A 1st Ed. 650QX137-4	Frosty Friends	1980	$6	$350
Country Cat 625QX467-2	General Line	1989	$6	$12
Country Express 2450QLX721-1	Magic Ornaments	1988	$25	$40
Country Goose 775QX518-5	Country Christmas Collection	1985	$8	$9
Country Sleigh 1000QX511-3	Country Treasures Collection	1986	$10	$12
Country Wreath 400QXM573-1	Miniature Ornaments	1988	$4	$4
Country Wreath 450QXM573-1	Miniature Ornaments	1989	$4	$4
Country Wreath 575QX470-9	Old-Fashioned Christmas Collection	1987	$6	$20
Cowboy Snowman 800QX480-6	Handcrafted Ornaments	1982	$8	$28

Rocking Horse, 1984, 4th in the Rocking Horse series, **$85.**

Canadian Mountie, 1984, 3rd in the Clothespin Soldier series, **$18.**

Santa's Arrival, 1984, **$50.**

Ornament Title	Series	Year	Issue Price	Current Value
Cozy Skater 450QXM573-5	Miniature Ornaments	1989	$4	$9
Cranberry Bunny 575QX426-2	General Line	1989	$6	$14
Cuckoo Clock 1000QX455-1	General Line	1984	$10	$52
Currier & Ives 450QX201-3	Currier & Ives	1982	$4	$18
Currier & Ives 450QX215-9	Currier & Ives	1983	$4	$22
Currier & Ives 450QX250-1	Currier & Ives	1984	$4	$25
Currier & Ives: American Farm 475QX282-9	Currier & Ives	1987	$5	$35
Cycling Santa 2000QX435-5	Handcrafted Ornaments	1983	$20	$55
Cycling Santa 2000QX435-5	Handcrafted Ornaments	1982	$20	$55
Cymbals Of Christmas 550QX411-1	Artists' Favorites	1988	$6	$24
Dad 400QX214-1	Commemoratives	1980	$4	$18
Dad 600QX462-9	Commemoratives	1987	$6	$10
Dad 700QX414-1	Commemoratives	1988	$7	$19
Dad 725QX441-2	Commemoratives	1989	$7	$19
Dancer 2nd Ed. 750QX480-9	Reindeer Champs	1987	$8	$35
Dapper Penguin 500QX477-2	General Line	1985	$5	$25
Dappled 1st Ed. 450QXM562-4	Rocking Horse Miniatures	1988	$4	$29
Dasher 1st Ed. 750QX422-3	Reindeer Champs	1986	$8	$115
Daughter 400QX212-1	Commemoratives	1980	$4	$25
Daughter 450QX203-7	Commemoratives	1983	$4	$22
Daughter 450QX204-6	Commemoratives	1982	$4	$20
Daughter 450QX244-4	Commemoratives	1984	$4	$30
Daughter 450QX607-5	Commemoratives	1981	$4	$15
Daughter 550QX503-2	Commemoratives	1985	$6	$20
Daughter 575QX415-1	Commemoratives	1988	$6	$45
Daughter 575QX430-6	Commemoratives	1988	$6	$25
Daughter 575QX463-7	Commemoratives	1987	$6	$22
Daughter 625QX443-2	Commemoratives	1989	$6	$16
December Showers 550QX448-7	Artists' Favorites	1987	$6	$24
Deer Disguise 575QX426-5	General Line	1989	$6	$16
Diana Doll QX423-7	General Line	1983	$9	$14
Disney 400QX218-1	General Line	1980	$4	$25
Disney 450QX212-9	General Line	1983	$4	$55
Disney 450QX217-3	General Line	1982	$4	$20
Disney 450QX250-4	General Line	1984	$4	$40
Disney 450QX805-5	General Line	1981	$4	$15
Disney Christmas 475QX271-2	General Line	1985	$5	$35
Divine Miss Piggy, The 1200QX425-5	General Line	1982	$12	$50
Do Not Disturb Bear 775QX481-2	General Line	1985	$8	$32
Do Not Disturb Bear 775QX481-2	General Line	1986	$8	$32
Doc Holiday 800QX467-7	Christmas Pizzazz Collection	1987	$8	$24
Doggy In A Stocking 550QX474-2	General Line	1985	$6	$30
Dough Angel 550QX139-6	Handcrafted Ornaments	1981	$6	$60
Dove 400QX308-1	Frosted Images	1980	$4	$32
Dove Love 450QX462-3	Little Trimmers	1982	$4	$25
Dr. Seuss: Grinch's Christmas 475QX278-3	General Line	1987	$5	$100

Three Kittens in a Mitten, 1984, **$55.**

Village Church, 1984, re-issued in 1985, **$22-$28.**

The Gift of Music, 1984, **$60.**

Katybeth, 1984, **$21.**

Ornament Title	Series	Year	Issue Price	Current Value
Dress Rehearsal 4th Ed.N 750QX300-7	Norman Rockwell	1983	$8	$29
Drummer Boy 250QX148-1	Handcrafted Ornaments	1981	$2	$20
Drummer Boy 400QX309-4	Frosted Images	1980	$4	$30
Drummer Boy 550QX147-4	Handcrafted Ornaments	1980	$6	$50
Dutch 2nd Ed. 1000QX408-3	Windows Of The World	1986	$10	$12
Early American Soldier 2nd Ed. 500QX402-9	Clothespin Soldier	1983	$5	$25
Elfin Antics 900QX142-1	Handcrafted Ornaments	1980	$9	$100
Elfin Artist 6th & Final Ed. QX438-4	Bellringer Series	1984	$15	$26
Elfin Artist 900QX457-3	Handcrafted Ornaments	1982	$9	$25
Elves-Emil Painter Elf-Figure QSP930-9	General Line	1987	$10	$25
Elves-Hans Carpenter Elf-Figure QSP930-7	General Line	1987	$10	$8
Elves-Kurt Blue Print Elf Figure QSP931-7	General Line	1987	$10	$8
Embroidered Heart 650QX421-7	Handcrafted Ornaments	1983	$6	$25
Embroidered Heart 650QX421-7	General Line	1984	$6	$12
Embroidered Stocking 650QX479-6	Handcrafted Ornaments	1983	$6	$16
Embroidered Stocking 650QX479-6	General Line	1984	$6	$22
Embroidered Tree 650QX494-6	Handcrafted Ornaments	1982	$6	$14
Enameled Christmas Wreath 900QX311-9	Crown Classics Collection	1983	$9	$20
Engineering Mouse 550QX473-5	General Line	1985	$6	$15
Family Home Ist Ed. 850QXM563-4	Old English Village	1988	$8	$24
Father 450QX205-6	Commemoratives	1982	$4	$20
Father 450QX609-5	Commemoratives	1981	$4	$12
Father 600QX257-1	Commemoratives	1984	$6	$18
Father 650QX376-2	Commemoratives	1985	$6	$10
Father 650QX431-3	Commemoratives	1986	$6	$12
Favorite Santa 2250QX445-7	General Line	1987	$23	$19
Favorite Tin Drum 850QX514-3	Christmas Medley Collection	1986	$8	$18
Feliz Navidad 675QX416-1	Handcrafted Ornaments	1988	$7	$32
Feliz Navidad 675QX439-2	General Line	1989	$7	$35
Festive Angel 675QX463-5	General Line	1989	$7	$7
Festive Feeder 1150QLX720-4	Magic Ornaments	1988	$12	$50
Festive Treble Clef 875QX513-3	Christmas Medley Collection	1986	$9	$9
Festive Year 775QX384-2	Commemoratives	1989	$8	$18
Fifty Years Together 1000QX400-6	Commemoratives	1986	$10	$4
Fifty Years Together 675QX374-1	Commemoratives	1988	$7	$10
Fifty Years Together 800QX443-7	Commemoratives	1987	$8	$25
Filled With Fudge 475QX419-1	Handcrafted Ornaments	1988	$5	$32
Filling The Stockings 3rd Ed. 850QX305-3	Norman Rockwell	1982	$8	$20
First Christmas Together 1150QLX708-7	Magic Ornaments	1987	$12	$37
First Christmas Together 1200QLX702-7	Magic Ornaments	1988	$12	$35
First Christmas Together 1200QX409-6	Commemoratives	1986	$12	$12
First Christmas Together 1300QX493-5	Commemoratives	1985	$13	$15
First Christmas Together 1400QLX707-3	Lighted Ornaments Collection	1986	$14	$29
First Christmas Together 1500QX436-4	Commemoratives	1984	$15	$20
First Christmas Together 1500QX446-9	Commemoratives	1987	$15	$28

Frisbee Puppy, 1984, **$55.**

Daughter, 1984, **$30.**

Raccoon's Christmas, 1984, **$35.**

Cuckoo Clock, 1984, **$52.**

Ornament Title	Series	Year	Issue Price	Current Value
First Christmas Together 1600QMB901-9	Commemoratives	1982	$16	$45
First Christmas Together 1600QX400-3	Commemoratives	1986	$16	$12
First Christmas Together 1600QX904-4	Commemoratives	1984	$16	$20
First Christmas Together 1675QX400-5	Commemoratives	1985	$17	$20
First Christmas Together 1750QLX734-2	Magic Ornaments	1989	$18	$45
First Christmas Together 400QX205-4	Commemoratives	1980	$4	$30
First Christmas Together 400QX305-4	Commemoratives	1980	$4	$28
First Christmas Together 400QXM574-1	Miniature Ornaments	1988	$4	$12
First Christmas Together 450QX208-9	Commemoratives	1983	$4	$30
First Christmas Together 450QX211-3	Commemoratives	1982	$4	$24
First Christmas Together 450QX245-1	Commemoratives	1984	$4	$20
First Christmas Together 450QX706-2	Commemoratives	1981	$4	$28
First Christmas Together 475QX261-2	Commemoratives	1985	$5	$20
First Christmas Together 475QX270-3	Commemoratives	1986	$5	$15
First Christmas Together 475QX272-9	Commemoratives	1987	$5	$15
First Christmas Together 475QX273-2	Commemoratives	1989	$5	$20
First Christmas Together 475QX274-1	Commemoratives	1988	$5	$25
First Christmas Together 550QX302-6	Commemoratives	1982	$6	$15
First Christmas Together 550QX505-5	Commemoratives	1981	$6	$12
First Christmas Together 600QX306-9	Commemoratives	1983	$6	$19
First Christmas Together 600QX310-7	Commemoratives	1983	$6	$28
First Christmas Together 600QX342-1	Commemoratives	1984	$6	$12
First Christmas Together 650QX371-9	Commemoratives	1987	$6	$25
First Christmas Together 675QX370-5	Commemoratives	1985	$7	$12
First Christmas Together 675QX373-1	Commemoratives	1988	$7	$10
First Christmas Together 675QX383-2	Commemoratives	1989	$7	$12
First Christmas Together 675QX485-2	Commemoratives	1989	$10	$28
First Christmas Together 7000QX379-3	Commemoratives	1986	$7	$12
First Christmas Together 750QX301-7	Commemoratives	1983	$8	$25
First Christmas Together 750QX340-4	Commemoratives	1984	$8	$12
First Christmas Together 800QX445-9	Commemoratives	1987	$8	$29
First Christmas Together 800QX507-2	Commemoratives	1985	$8	$8
First Christmas Together 850QX306-6	Commemoratives	1982	$8	$24
First Christmas Together 850QXM564-2	Miniature Ornaments	1989	$8	$8
First Christmas Together 900QX489-4	Commemoratives	1988	$9	$19
First Christmas Together 950QX446-7	Commemoratives	1987	$10	$25
First Christmas, The 775QX547-5	General Line	1989	$8	$10
First Xmas Together-Locket 1500QX432-9	Commemoratives	1983	$15	$35
First Xmas Together-Locket 1500QX456-3	Commemoratives	1982	$15	$14
Five Golden Rings-5th Ed. 650QX371-4	Twelve Days Of Christmas	1988	$6	$22
Five Years Together 475QX273-5	Commemoratives	1989	$5	$7
Five Years Together 475QX274-4	Commemoratives	1988	$5	$10
Flights Of Fantasy 450QX256-4	General Line	1984	$4	$22
Folk Art Bunny 450QXM569-2	Miniature Ornaments	1989	$4	$12
Folk Art Lamb 250QXM568-1	Miniature Ornaments	1988	$3	$18
Folk Art Reindeer 250QXM568-4	Miniature Ornaments	1988	$3	$8

Frosty Friends, 1984, 5th in the Frosty Friends series, **$150.**

Nativity, 1984, **$20.**

Rocking Horse, 1985, 5th in the Rocking Horse series, **$68.**

Daughter, 1985, **$20.**

Santa Pipe, 1985, **$25.**

Trumpet Panda, 1985, **$20.**

Christmas Treats, 1985, **$9.**

Ornament Title	Series	Year	Issue Price	Current Value
Folk Art Santa 525QX474-9	Old-Fashioned Christmas Collection	1987	$5	$18
Forest Frolics 1st Ed. 2450QLX728-2	Forest Frolics	1989	$25	$55
Fortune Cookie Elf 450QX452-4	General Line	1984	$4	$30
Four Colly Birds 650QX370-9	Twelve Days Of Christmas	1987	$6	$25
Fraggle Rock Holiday 475QX265-5	General Line	1985	$5	$19
French Joyeaux Noel 4th Ed. 1000QX402-1	Windows Of The World	1988	$10	$15
French Officer 5th Ed. 550QX406-3	Clothespin Soldier	1986	$6	$25
Friendly Fiddler, The 800QX434-2	Handcrafted Ornaments	1981	$8	$45
Friends Are Fun 475QX272-3	Commemoratives	1986	$5	$30
Friends Share Joy 200QXM576-4	Miniature Ornaments	1988	$2	$9
Friendship 1600QMB904-7	General Line	1983	$16	$55
Friendship 400QX208-1	Commemoratives	1980	$4	$15
Friendship 450QX207-7	Commemoratives	1983	$4	$12
Friendship 450QX208-6	Commemoratives	1982	$4	$10
Friendship 450QX248-1	Commemoratives	1984	$4	$10
Friendship 450QX704-2	Commemoratives	1981	$4	$11
Friendship 550QX304-6	Commemoratives	1982	$6	$16
Friendship 550QX503-5	Commemoratives	1981	$6	$18
Friendship 600QX305-9	Commemoratives	1983	$6	$9
Friendship 675QX378-5	Commemoratives	1985	$7	$16
Friendship 775QX506-2	Commemoratives	1985	$8	$6
Friendship Greeting 800QX427-3	Commemoratives	1986	$8	$4
Friendship Time 975QX413-2	Commemoratives	1989	$10	$15
Friendship's Gift 600QX381-6	Commemoratives	1986	$6	$12
Frisbee Puppy 500QX444-4	General Line	1984	$5	$55
From Our Home To Yours 450QX248-4	Commemoratives	1984	$4	$50
From Our Home To Yours 475QX279-4	Commemoratives	1988	$5	$14
From Our Home To Yours 475QX279-9	Commemoratives	1987	$5	$18
From Our Home To Yours 600QX383-3	Commemoratives	1986	$6	$13
From Our Home To Yours 625QX384-5	Commemoratives	1989	$6	$20
From Our Home To Yours 775QX520-2	Commemoratives	1985	$8	$8
Frosty Friends 10th Ed. 925QX457-2	Frosty Friends	1989	$9	$40
Frosty Friends 2nd Ed. QX433-5	Frosty Friends	1981	$8	$325
Frosty Friends 3rd Ed. 800QX452-3	Frosty Friends	1982	$8	$275
Frosty Friends 4th Ed. 800QX400-7	Frosty Friends	1983	$8	$200
Frosty Friends 5th Ed. 800QX437-1	Frosty Friends	1984	$8	$150
Frosty Friends 6th Ed. 850QX482-2	Frosty Friends	1985	$8	$125
Frosty Friends 7th Ed. 850QX405-3	Frosty Friends	1986	$8	$95
Frosty Friends 8th Ed. 850QX440-9	Frosty Friends	1987	$8	$85
Frosty Friends 9th Ed. 875QX403-1	Frosty Friends	1988	$9	$90
Fudge Forever 500QX449-7	General Line	1987	$5	$35
Fun Of Friendship, The 600QX343-1	Commemoratives	1984	$6	$9
General Store 1575QLX705-3	Lighted Ornaments Collection	1986	$16	$50
Gentle Angel 200QXM577-1	Miniature Ornaments	1988	$2	$18

Old-Fashioned Toy Shop, 1985, 2nd in the Nostalgic Houses and Shops series, **$145.**

Scottish Highlander, 1985, 4th in the Clothespin Soldier series, **$22.**

Mexican, 1985, 1st in the Windows of the World series, **$65.**

Son, 1985, **$45.**

Ornament Title	Series	Year	Issue Price	Current Value
Gentle Blessings 1500QLX708-3	Lighted Ornaments Collection	1986	$15	$90
Gentle Fawn 775QX548-5	General Line	1989	$8	$20
George Washington Bicenten. 625QX386-2	General Line	1989	$6	$10
German 5th Ed. 1075QX462-5	Windows Of The World	1989	$11	$12
Gift Of Friendship 450QX260-4	Commemoratives	1984	$4	$15
Gift Of Love, The 450QX705-5	Commemoratives	1981	$4	$30
Gift Of Music 1500QX451-1	General Line	1984	$15	$60
Ginger 629XPR972-1	Christmas Carousel Horse Collection	1989	$4	$14
Gingham Dog 300QX402-2	Fabric Ornaments	1981	$3	$22
Glowing Christmas Tree 700QX428-6	General Line	1986	$7	$5
Glowing Wreath 600QX492-1	Handcrafted Ornaments	1988	$6	$15
Go For The Gold 800QX417-4	Handcrafted Ornaments	1988	$8	$15
Godchild 450QX201-7	Commemoratives	1983	$4	$14
Godchild 450QX222-6	Commemoratives	1982	$4	$18
Godchild 450QX242-1	Commemoratives	1984	$4	$18
Godchild 450QX603-5	Commemoratives	1981	$4	$16
Godchild 475QX271-6	Commemoratives	1986	$5	$15
Godchild 475QX276-7	Commemoratives	1987	$5	$22
Godchild 475QX278-4	Commemoratives	1988	$5	$16
Godchild 625QX311-2	Commemoratives	1989	$6	$8
Godchild 675QX380-2	Commemoratives	1985	$7	$4
Goin' Cross Country 850QX476-4	Handcrafted Ornaments	1988	$8	$15
Goin' South 425QX410-5	General Line	1989	$4	$8
Goldfinch 700QX464-9	General Line	1987	$7	$80
Gone Fishing 500QX479-4	Handcrafted Ornaments	1988	$5	$15
Gone Fishing 575QX479-4	General Line	1989	$6	$22
Good Cheer Blimp 1600QLX704-6	Magic Ornaments	1987	$16	$35
Good Friends 475QX265-2	Commemoratives	1985	$5	$30
Graceful Swan 675QX464-2	General Line	1989	$7	$9
Grandchild's First Christmas 1000QX411-6	Commemoratives	1986	$10	$10
Grandchild's First Christmas 1100QX495-5	Commemoratives	1985	$11	$10
Grandchild's First Christmas 110QX460-1	Commemoratives	1984	$11	$10
Grandchild's First Christmas 400q430-9	Commemoratives	1983	$14	$29
Grandchild's First Christmas 450QX257-4	Commemoratives	1984	$4	$10
Grandchild's First Christmas 500QX260-5	Commemoratives	1985	$5	$10
Grandchild's First Christmas 600QX312-9	Commemoratives	1983	$6	$24
Grandchild's First Christmas 900QX460-9	Commemoratives	1987	$9	$13
Granddaughter 400QX202-1	Commemoratives	1980	$4	$24
Granddaughter 450QX202-7	Commemoratives	1983	$4	$30
Granddaughter 450QX224-3	Commemoratives	1982	$4	$25
Granddaughter 450QX243-1	Commemoratives	1984	$4	$22
Granddaughter 450QX605-5	Commemoratives	1981	$4	$24
Granddaughter 475QX263-5	Commemoratives	1985	$5	$19
Granddaughter 475QX273-6	Commemoratives	1986	$5	$25

Santa's Workshop, 1985, **$34.**

Chris Mouse 1, 1985, from the Chris Mouse series, **$55.**

Children in the Shoe, 1985, **$34.**

Ornament Title	Series	Year	Issue Price	Current Value
Granddaughter 475QX277-4	Commemoratives	1988	$5	$38
Granddaughter 475QX278-2	Commemoratives	1989	$5	$10
Granddaughter 600QX374-7	Commemoratives	1987	$6	$22
Granddaughter's First Xmas 675QX382-2	Commemoratives	1989	$7	$10
Grandfather 400QX231-4	Commemoratives	1980	$4	$19
Grandfather 450QX207-6	Commemoratives	1982	$4	$16
Grandfather 450QX701-5	Commemoratives	1981	$4	$18
Grandmother 400QX204-1	Commemoratives	1980	$4	$19
Grandmother 450QX200-3	Commemoratives	1982	$4	$19
Grandmother 450QX205-7	Commemoratives	1983	$4	$20
Grandmother 450QX244-1	Commemoratives	1984	$4	$19
Grandmother 450QX702-2	Commemoratives	1981	$4	$18
Grandmother 475QX262-5	Commemoratives	1985	$5	$18
Grandmother 475QX274-3	Commemoratives	1986	$5	$16
Grandmother 475QX276-4	Commemoratives	1988	$5	$20
Grandmother 475QX277-5	Commemoratives	1989	$5	$10
Grandmother 475QX277-9	Commemoratives	1987	$5	$10
Grandparents 400QX213-4	Commemoratives	1980	$4	$40
Grandparents 450QX214-6	Commemoratives	1982	$4	$4
Grandparents 450QX256-1	Commemoratives	1984	$4	$10
Grandparents 450QX703-5	Commemoratives	1981	$4	$19
Grandparents 475QX277-1	Commemoratives	1988	$5	$10
Grandparents 475QX277-2	Commemoratives	1989	$5	$10
Grandparents 475QX277-7	Commemoratives	1987	$5	$15
Grandparents 650QX429-9	Commemoratives	1983	$6	$8
Grandparents 700QX380-5	Commemoratives	1985	$7	$5
Grandparents 750QX432-3	Commemoratives	1986	$8	$15
Grandson 400QX201-4	Commemoratives	1980	$4	$27
Grandson 450QX201-9	Commemoratives	1983	$4	$19
Grandson 450QX224-6	Commemoratives	1982	$4	$15
Grandson 450QX242-4	Commemoratives	1984	$4	$10
Grandson 450QX604-2	Commemoratives	1981	$4	$30
Grandson 475QX262-2	Commemoratives	1985	$5	$30
Grandson 475QX273-3	Commemoratives	1986	$5	$5
Grandson 475QX276-9	Commemoratives	1987	$5	$22
Grandson 475QX278-1	Commemoratives	1988	$5	$25
Grandson 475QX278-5	Commemoratives	1989	$5	$22
Grandson's First Christmas 675QX382-5	Commemoratives	1989	$7	$10
Gratitude 600QX344-4	Commemoratives	1984	$6	$15
Gratitude 600QX375-4	Commemoratives	1988	$6	$6
Gratitude 600QX432-6	Commemoratives	1986	$6	$10
Gratitude 675QX385-2	Commemoratives	1989	$7	$8
Gym Dandy 575QX418-5	General Line	1989	$6	$12
Hall Bros Card Shop 5th Ed. 1450QX401-4	Nostalgic Houses & Shops	1988	$14	$52
Hallis Star-Tree Topper EPCA	Tree Topper	1987	N/A	$70
Hang In There 525QX430-5	General Line	1989	$5	$22

Lamb in Legwarmers, 1985, **$24.**

Little Red Schoolhouse, 1985, **$45.**

Sister, 1985, **$12.**

Do Not Disturb Bear, 1985 and 1986, **$32.**

Heart Full of Love, 1985, **$8.**

Ornament Title	Series	Year	Issue Price	Current Value
Happy Bluebird 450QXM566-2	Miniature Ornaments	1989	$4	$11
Happy Christmas 400QX222-1	Decorative Ball Ornaments	1980	$4	$14
Happy Christmas To Owl 600QX418-3	General Line	1986	$6	$12
Happy Holidata 650QX471-7	Christmas Pizzazz Collection	1987	$6	$30
Happy Holidata QX471-4	Handcrafted Ornaments	1988	$6	$15
Happy Santa 450QXM561-4	Miniature Ornaments	1988	$4	$10
Happy Santa 475QX456-9	General Line	1987	$5	$30
Hark! It's Herald 1st Ed. 675QX455-5	Hark! It's Herald	1989	$7	$14
Hawaiian 3rd Ed. 1000QX482-7	Windows Of The World	1987	$10	$15
Heart 400QX307-9	Holiday Sculpture	1983	$4	$50
Heart Full Of Love 675QX378-2	Commemoratives	1985	$7	$8
Heart In Blossom 600QX372-7	Commemoratives	1987	$6	$12
Heartful Of Love 1000QX443-4	Commemoratives	1984	$10	$22
Heathcliff 750QX436-3	General Line	1986	$8	$16
Heavenly Dreamer 575QX417-3	General Line	1986	$6	$14
Heavenly Glow 1175QLX711-4	Magic Ornaments	1988	$12	$18
Heavenly Glow Tree Topper QXM566-1	Tree Topper	1989	$10	$14
Heavenly Harmony 1500QX465-9	General Line	1987	$15	$25
Heavenly Minstrel 15QX156-7	Handcrafted Ornaments	1980	$15	$125
Heavenly Nap 650QX139-4	Handcrafted Ornaments	1981	$6	$35
Heavenly Nap 650QX139-4	Handcrafted Ornaments	1980	$6	$35
Heavenly Sounds 750QX152-1	Handcrafted Ornaments	1980	$8	$36
Heavenly Trumpeter 2750QX405-2	General Line	1985	$28	$58
Heirloom Snowflake 675QX515-3	General Line	1986	$7	$9
Here Comes Santa 450QX217-7	Decorative Ball Ornaments	1983	$4	$54
Here's The Pitch 575QX545-5	General Line	1989	$6	$10
Hitchhiking Santa 800QX424-7	Handcrafted Ornaments	1983	$8	$10
Hoe-Hoe-Hoe 500QX422-1	Handcrafted Ornaments	1988	$5	$10
Hold On Tight QXC570-4	Collector's Club	1988	N/A	$36
Holiday Bell 1750QLX722-2	Magic Ornaments	1989	$18	$35
Holiday Deer 300QXM577-2	Miniature Ornaments	1989	$3	$8
Holiday Duet 4th Ed. 1325QX457-5	Mr. & Mrs. Claus	1989	$13	$35
Holiday Friendship 1300QX445-1	General Line	1984	$13	$28
Holiday Greetings 600QX375-7	Commemoratives	1987	$6	$12
Holiday Heart 800QX498-2	Commemoratives	1985	$8	$14
Holiday Heirloom 1st Ed. QX485-7	Holiday Heirloom	1987	$25	$25
Holiday Heirloom 2nd Ed. 2500QX406-4	Holiday Heirloom	1988	$25	$25
Holiday Heirloom 3rd & Final Ed. 2500QXC460-5	Holiday Heirloom	1989	$25	$30
Holiday Hero 500QX423-1	Handcrafted Ornaments	1988	$5	$11
Holiday Horn 800QX514-6	Christmas Medley Collection	1986	$8	$16
Holiday Hourglass 800QX470-7	Christmas Pizzazz Collection	1987	$8	$18
Holiday Jester 1100QX437-4	General Line	1984	$11	$19
Holiday Jingle Bell 1600QX404-6	General Line	1986	$16	$29
Holiday Puppy 350QX412-7	Handcrafted Ornaments	1983	$4	$20
Holiday Starburst 500QX253-4	General Line	1984	$5	$15

Mr. and Mrs. Santa, 1985, re-issued in 1986, **$40.**

The Statue of Liberty, 1986, **$22.**

Frosty Friends, 1985, 6th in the Frosty Friends series, **$125.**

Rocking Horse, 1986, 6th in the Rocking Horse series, **$58.**

Jolly St. Nick, 1986, **$38.**

Ornament Title	Series	Year	Issue Price	Current Value
Holly 629XPR972-2	Christmas Carousel Horse Collection	1989	$4	$14
Holy Family 850QXM561-1	Miniature Ornaments	1988	$8	$10
Holy Family 850QXM561-1	Miniature Ornaments	1989	$8	$7
Home 450QX709-5	Commemoratives	1981	$4	$18
Home Cooking 2nd Ed. 1325QX483-7	Mr. & Mrs. Claus	1987	$13	$55
Hoppy Holidays 775QX469-2	General Line	1989	$8	$16
Horse 4th Ed. 750QX441-7	Wood Childhood	1987	$8	$20
Horse Weathervane 575QX463-2	General Line	1989	$6	$10
Hot Dogger 650QX471-9	General Line	1987	$6	$20
House On Main St. 4th Ed. 1400QX483-9	Nostalgic Houses & Shops	1987	$14	$80
Hugga Bunch 500QX271-5	General Line	1985	$5	$15
Husband 700QX373-9	Commemoratives	1987	$7	$11
Husband 800QX383-6	Commemoratives	1986	$8	$8
I Remember Santa 475QX278-9	General Line	1987	$5	$35
Ice Fairy 650QX431-5	Handcrafted Ornaments	1981	$6	$88
Ice Sculptor, The 800QX432-2	Handcrafted Ornaments	1981	$8	$90
Ice-Skating Owl 500QX476-5	General Line	1985	$5	$23
Icy Treat 450QX450-9	General Line	1987	$4	$25
In A Nutshell 550QX469-7	Handcrafted Ornaments	1988	$6	$12
In A Nutshell 550QX469-7	Old-Fashioned Christmas Collection	1987	$6	$18
Jack Frost 900QX407-9	Handcrafted Ornaments	1983	$9	$31
Jack Frosting 700QX449-9	General Line	1987	$7	$40
Jammie Pies 475QX283-9	General Line	1987	$5	$20
Jingle Bell Clown 1500QX477-4	Handcrafted Ornaments	1988	$15	$17
Jingling Teddy 400QX477-6	Little Trimmers	1982	$4	$40
Joan Walsh Anglund 400QX217-4	General Line	1980	$4	$22
Joan Walsh Anglund 450QX219-3	General Line	1982	$4	$22
Joan Walsh Anglund 450QX804-2	General Line	1981	$4	$22
Jogging Santa 800QX457-6	Handcrafted Ornaments	1982	$8	$28
Jogging Through The Snow 725QX457-7	General Line	1987	$7	$16
Jolly Christmas Tree 650QX465-3	Handcrafted Ornaments	1982	$6	$70
Jolly Follies 850QX466-9	Christmas Pizzazz Collection	1987	$8	$35
Jolly Hiker 500QX483-2	General Line	1987	$5	$25
Jolly Hiker 500QX483-2	General Line	1986	$5	$12
Jolly Postman 6th Ed. 750QX374-5	Norman Rockwell	1985	$8	$32
Jolly Santa 350QX425-9	Handcrafted Ornaments	1983	$4	$20
Jolly Santa 400QX227-4	Decorative Ball Ornaments	1980	$4	$10
Jolly Snowman 350QX407-5	Little Trimmers	1981	$4	$59
Jolly St. Nick 2250QX429-6	General Line	1986	$23	$38
Jolly St. Nick 800QXM572-1	Miniature Ornaments	1988	$8	$15
Jolly Trolley 4th Ed. QX464-3	Here Comes Santa	1982	$15	$150
Jolly Walrus 450QX473-1	Handcrafted Ornaments	1988	$4	$24
Joy 400QX350-1	Colors Of Christmas	1980	$4	$30
Joy Of Friends 675QX382-3	Commemoratives	1986	$7	$4

Dasher, 1986, 1st in the Reindeer Champs series, **$115.**

Wynken, Blynken and Nod, 1986, **$25.**

Li'l Jinglers, 1986, re-issued in 1987, **$20.**

Sugarplum Cottage, 1986, re-issued in 1984 and 1985, **$25-$28.**

Ornament Title	Series	Year	Issue Price	Current Value
Joy Ride 1150QX440-7	General Line	1987	$12	$55
Joyful Carolers 975QX513-6	Christmas Medley Collection	1986	$10	$40
Joyful Trio 975QX437-2	General Line	1989	$10	$10
Joyous Angels 775QX465-7	General Line	1987	$8	$22
Joyous Carolers 3000QLX729-5	Magic Ornaments	1989	$30	$70
Joyous Heart 350QXM569-1	Miniature Ornaments	1988	$4	$16
Katybeth 1075QLX710-2	General Line	1985	$11	$21
Katybeth 700QX435-3	General Line	1986	$7	$21
Katybeth 900QX463-1	General Line	1984	$9	$21
Keep On Glowin! 1000QLX707-6	Lighted Ornaments Collection	1987	$10	$20
Keeping Cozy 1175QLX704-7	Magic Ornaments	1987	$12	$30
Keepsake Basket 1500QX514-5	Heirloom Christmas Collection	1985	$15	$12
Kermit The Frog 1100QX495-6	General Line	1982	$11	$79
Kermit The Frog 1100QX495-6	General Line	1983	$11	$75
Kermit The Frog 900QX424-2	General Line	1981	$9	$90
Kiss From Santa, A QX482-1	General Line	1989	$4	$14
Kiss From Santa, A QX482-1	General Line	1988	$5	$25
Kiss The Claus 500QX486-1	Handcrafted Ornaments	1988	$5	$12
Kit 550QX453-4	General Line	1984	$6	$16
Kit The Shepherd 575QX484-5	General Line	1985	$6	$20
Kitty Capers 1300QLX716-4	Magic Ornaments	1988	$13	$45
Kitty Cart 300QXM572-2	Miniature Ornaments	1989	$3	$10
Kitty Mischief 500QX474-5	General Line	1985	$5	$19
Kitty Mischief 500QX474-5	General Line	1986	$5	$19
Kringle Koach 10th Ed. 1400QX400-1	Here Comes Santa	1988	$14	$35
Kringle Moon 550QX495-1	Handcrafted Ornaments	1988	$6	$23
Kringle Portrait 750QX496-1	Handcrafted Ornaments	1988	$8	$20
Kringle Tree 650QX495-4	Handcrafted Ornaments	1988	$6	$29
Kringle's Kool Treats 8th Ed. 1400QX404-3	Here Comes Santa	1986	$14	$55
Kringle's Toy Shop 2450QLX701-7	Magic Ornaments	1989	$25	$28
Kringles, The 1st Ed. 600QXM562-2	Kringles, The	1989	$6	$15
Kristy Claus 575QX424-5	General Line	1989	$6	$12
Lacy Brass Snowflake 1150QLX709-7	Magic Ornaments	1987	$12	$12
Lacy Heart 875QX511-2	Heirloom Christmas Collection	1985	$9	$18
Lamb 1st Ed. 650QX439-4	Wood Childhood	1984	$6	$25
Lamb In Legwarmers 700QX480-2	General Line	1985	$7	$24
Language Of Love 625QX383-5	Commemoratives	1989	$6	$25
Last-Minute Hug 1950QLX718-1	Magic Ornaments	1988	$22	$48
Let It Snow 650QX458-9	General Line	1987	$6	$20
Let Us Adore Him 450QX811-5	Decorative Ball Ornaments	1981	$4	$25
Let's Play 725QX488-2	General Line	1989	$7	$14
Lighting The Tree 1st Ed. 2200QLX703-3	Santa & Sparky	1986	$22	$35
Li'L Jinglers 675QX419-3	General Line	1986	$7	$20

Christmas Candy Shoppe, 1986, 3rd in the Nostalgic Houses and Shops series, **$250.**

Nutcracker Santa, 1986, **$50.**

French Officer, 1986, 5th in the Clothespin Soldier series, **$25.**

Merry Mistletoe Time, 1986, 1st in the Mr. and Mrs. Claus series, **$70.**

Paddington Bear, 1986, **$19.**

Ornament Title	Series	Year	Issue Price	Current Value
Li'l Jingler 675QX419-3	General Line	1987	$7	$20
Little Drummer Boy 450QXM578-4	Miniature Ornaments	1988	$4	$18
Little Drummer Boy 4th Ed. 1350QLX724-2	Christmas Classics	1989	$14	$45
Little Drummers 1250QX511-6	Country Treasures Collection	1986	$12	$19
Little Jack Horner 800QX408-1	Artists' Favorites	1988	$8	$14
Little Red Schoolhouse 1575QLX711-2	Magic Ornaments	1985	$16	$45
Little Soldier 450QXM567-5	Miniature Ornaments	1989	$4	$9
Little Star Bringer 600QXM562-2	Miniature Ornaments	1989	$6	$20
Little Whittler 600QX469-9	Old-Fashioned Christmas Collection	1987	$6	$20
Load Of Cheer 600QXM574-5	Miniature Ornaments	1989	$6	$18
Locomotive 1st Ed. QXM576-2	Noel Railroad	1989	$8	$29
Love 1300QX422-7	Commemoratives	1983	$13	$24
Love 1600QMB900-9	General Line	1982	$16	$45
Love 400QX302-1	Commemoratives	1980	$4	$60
Love 450QX207-9	Commemoratives	1983	$4	$45
Love 450QX209-6	Commemoratives	1982	$4	$12
Love 450QX255-4	Commemoratives	1984	$4	$15
Love 550QX304-3	Commemoratives	1982	$6	$20
Love 550QX502-2	Commemoratives	1981	$6	$48
Love 600QX305-7	Commemoratives	1983	$6	$8
Love 600QX310-9	Commemoratives	1983	$6	$38
Love & Joy 900QX425-2	Handcrafted Ornaments	1981	$9	$29
Love At Christmas 575QX371-5	Commemoratives	1985	$6	$9
Love Fills The Heart 600QX374-4	Commemoratives	1988	$6	$14
Love Grows 475QX275-1	Commemoratives	1988	$5	$55
Love Is A Song 450QX223-9	Commemoratives	1983	$4	$40
Love Is Everywhere 475QX278-7	Commemoratives	1987	$5	$25
Love Is Forever 200QXM577-4	Miniature Ornaments	1988	$2	$14
Love Santa 500QX486-4	Handcrafted Ornaments	1988	$5	$10
Love Wreath 850QLX702-5	Magic Ornaments	1985	$8	$12
Lovebirds 600QXM563-5	Miniature Ornaments	1989	$6	$8
Love-The Spirit Of Christmas 450QX247-4	Commemoratives	1984	$4	$40
Loving Bear 475QX493-4	Handcrafted Ornaments	1988	$5	$18
Loving Holiday 2200QLX701-6	Magic Ornaments	1987	$22	$50
Loving Memories 900QX409-3	Commemoratives	1986	$9	$18
Loving Spoonful 1950QLX726-2	Magic Ornaments	1989	$20	$22
Madonna & Child With The Infant St. John 3rd & Final Ed. 675QX350-6	Art Masterpiece	1986	$7	$28
Madonna & Child 1200QX428-7	Handcrafted Ornaments	1983	$12	$28
Madonna & Child 1st Ed. 650QX349-4	Art Masterpiece	1984	$6	$10
Madonna & Child 600QX344-1	General Line	1984	$6	$42
Madonna Of The Pomegranate 2nd Ed. 675QX377-2	Art Masterpiece	1985	$7	$14
Magi, The 475QX272-6	General Line	1986	$5	$12
Magical Unicorn 2750QX429-3	General Line	1986	$28	$100

Snow Buddies, 1986, **$20.**

Treetop Trio, 1986, **$25.**

Katybeth, 1986, **$21.**

General Store, 1986, **$50.**

Joyful Carolers, 1986, **$40.**

Gentle Blessings, 1986, **$90.**

Ornament Title	Series	Year	Issue Price	Current Value
Mail Call 875QX452-2	Artists' Favorites	1989	$9	$13
Mailbox Kitten 650QX415-7	Handcrafted Ornaments	1983	$6	$35
Marathon Santa 800QX456-4	General Line	1984	$8	$22
Marty Links 400QX221-4	General Line	1980	$4	$10
Marty Links 450QX808-2	General Line	1981	$4	$5
Mary Emmerling 795QX275-2	American Country Collection	1986	$8	$25
Mary Hamilton 400QX219-4	General Line	1980	$4	$22
Mary Hamilton 450QX213-7	General Line	1983	$4	$55
Mary Hamilton 450QX217-6	General Line	1982	$4	$16
Mary Hamilton 450QX806-2	General Line	1981	$4	$18
Memories Are Forever Photo. 850QLX706-7	Magic Ornaments	1987	$8	$20
Memories To Cherish Photo. QX427-6	General Line	1986	$8	$14
Memories To Treasure 700QX303-7	Crown Classics Collection	1983	$7	$30
Meowy Christmas 1000QLX708-9	Magic Ornaments	1987	$10	$34
Merry Carousel 3rd Ed. 750QX141-4	Carousel Series	1980	$8	$100
Merry Christmas 450QX225-6	Designer Keepsakes	1982	$4	$22
Merry Christmas 450QX814-2	Decorative Ball Ornaments	1981	$4	$7
Merry Christmas Bell 850QLX709-3	Lighted Ornaments Collection	1986	$8	$22
Merry Koala 500QX415-3	General Line	1987	$5	$20
Merry Koala 500QX415-3	General Line	1986	$5	$20
Merry Mint Unicorn 850QX423-4	Artists' Favorites	1988	$8	$10
Merry Mistletoe Time 1st Ed. 1300QX402-6	Mr. & Mrs. Claus	1986	$13	$70
Merry Moose 550QX415-5	Little Trimmers	1982	$6	$28
Merry Mouse 450QX403-2	General Line	1986	$4	$30
Merry Mouse 450QX403-2	General Line	1985	$4	$17
Merry Redbird 350QX160-1	Little Trimmers	1980	$4	$55
Merry Seal 600QXM575-5	Miniature Ornaments	1989	$6	$14
Merry Shirt Tales 475QX267-2	General Line	1985	$5	$15
Merry-Go-Round Unicorn 1075QX447-2	Artists' Favorites	1989	$11	$16
Metro Express 2800QLX727-5	Magic Ornaments	1989	$28	$80
Mexican 1st Ed. QX490-2	Windows Of The World	1985	$10	$65
Midnight Snack 600QX410-4	Artists' Favorites	1988	$6	$16
Miniature Creche-1st Ed. 875QX4825	Miniature Creche	1985	$9	$14
Miniature Creche-2nd Ed. 900QX4076	Miniature Creche	1986	$9	$25
Miniature Creche-3rd Ed. 900QX4819	Miniature Creche	1987	$9	$20
Miniature Creche-4th Ed. 850QX4034	Miniature Creche	1988	$8	$16
Miniature Creche-5th & Final Ed. 925QX4592	Miniature Creche	1989	$9	$18
Miracle Of Love, The 600QX342-4	Commemoratives	1984	$6	$24
Miss Piggy & Kermit 450QX218-3	General Line	1982	$4	$28
Miss Piggy 1300QX405-7	General Line	1983	$13	$125
Mistletoad 700QX468-7	Handcrafted Ornaments	1988	$7	$24
Mistletoad 700QX468-7	Handcrafted Ornaments	1987	$7	$24
Mom & Dad 650QX429-7	Commemoratives	1983	$6	$8
Mom & Dad 975QX442-5	Commemoratives	1989	$10	$19

Bluebird, 1986, **$60.**

Frosty Friends, 1986, 7th in the Frosty Friends series, **$95.**

Village Express, 1986 and 1987, **$42.**

Snow Goose, 1987, 6th in the from the Holiday Wildlife series, **$22.**

Rocking Horse, 1987, 7th in the Rocking Horse series, **$67.**

Ornament Title	Series	Year	Issue Price	Current Value
Moments Of Love 450QX209-3	Commemoratives	1982	$4	$5
Moonlit Nap 875QLX713-4	Magic Ornaments	1989	$9	$15
Mother 300QXM572-4	Miniature Ornaments	1988	$3	$14
Mother 400QX203-4	Commemoratives	1980	$4	$18
Mother 400QX304-1	Commemoratives	1980	$4	$20
Mother 450QX205-3	Commemoratives	1982	$4	$22
Mother 450QX608-2	Commemoratives	1981	$4	$19
Mother 600QX306-7	Commemoratives	1983	$6	$20
Mother 600QX343-4	Commemoratives	1984	$6	$12
Mother 600QXM564-5	Miniature Ornaments	1989	$6	$10
Mother 650QX373-7	Commemoratives	1987	$6	$18
Mother 650QX375-1	Commemoratives	1988	$6	$16
Mother 675QX372-2	Commemoratives	1985	$7	$15
Mother 700QX382-6	Commemoratives	1986	$7	$20
Mother 975QX440-5	Commemoratives	1989	$10	$18
Mother & Child 750QX302-7	Crown Classics Collection	1983	$8	$40
Mother & Dad 400QX230-1	Commemoratives	1980	$4	$24
Mother & Dad 450QX222-3	Commemoratives	1982	$4	$16
Mother & Dad 450QX700-2	Commemoratives	1981	$4	$18
Mother & Dad 650QX258-1	Commemoratives	1984	$6	$12
Mother & Dad 700QX462-7	Commemoratives	1987	$7	$19
Mother & Dad 750QX431-6	Commemoratives	1986	$8	$26
Mother & Dad 775QX509-2	Commemoratives	1985	$8	$14
Mother & Dad 800QX414-4	Commemoratives	1988	$8	$22
Mother's Day-A Mother's Love MDQ340-7	Commemoratives	1983	$14	$75
Mountain Climbing Santa 650QX407-7	General Line	1984	$6	$20
Mountain Climbing Santa 650QX407-7	Handcrafted Ornaments	1983	$6	$30
Mouse 400QX508-2	Frosted Images	1981	$4	$25
Mouse In Bell 1000QX419-7	Handcrafted Ornaments	1983	$10	$30
Mouse In The Moon 550QX416-6	General Line	1987	$6	$18
Mouse In The Moon 550QX416-6	General Line	1986	$6	$16
Mouse On Cheese 650QX413-7	Handcrafted Ornaments	1983	$6	$18
Mouse Wagon 575QX476-2	General Line	1985	$6	$60
Mr. & Mrs. Claus Set 1200QX448-5	Handcrafted Ornaments	1981	$12	$88
Mr. & Mrs. Santa 1450QLX705-2	Magic Ornaments	1985	$14	$40
Mr. & Mrs. Santa 1450QLX705-2	Magic Ornaments	1986	$14	$40
Muffin 550QX442-1	General Line	1984	$6	$16
Muffin The Angel 575QX483-5	General Line	1985	$6	$12
Muppets 400QX220-1	General Line	1980	$4	$30
Muppets 450QX807-5	General Line	1981	$4	$15
Muppets Party 450QX218-6	General Line	1982	$4	$20
Muppets, The 450QX214-7	General Line	1983	$4	$28
Muppets, The 450QX251-4	General Line	1984	$4	$35
Musical Angel 550QX434-4	General Line	1984	$6	$42
Musical Angel 550QX459-6	Little Trimmers	1982	$6	$65
Napping Mouse 550QX435-1	General Line	1984	$6	$50

Santa at the Bat, 1987, **$20.**

Betsey Clark: Home for Christmas, 1987, 2nd in the Betsey Clark: Home for Christmas series, **$22.**

Wreath of Memories, 1987, from the Hallmark Keepsake Ornament Collector's Club, **$20.**

In a Nutshell, 1987, **$18,** and 1988, **$12.**

Ornament Title	Series	Year	Issue Price	Current Value
Nativity 1200QLX700-1	Magic Ornaments	1985	$12	$20
Nativity 1200QLX700-1	Magic Ornaments	1984	$12	$20
Nativity 1600QMB904-9	General Line	1983	$16	$125
Nativity 400QX225-4	Decorative Ball Ornaments	1980	$4	$44
Nativity 450QX308-3	Colors Of Christmas	1982	$4	$48
Nativity Scene 475QX264-5	General Line	1985	$5	$35
Nature's Decorations 475QX273-9	General Line	1987	$5	$35
Needlepoint Wreath 650QX459-4	General Line	1984	$6	$15
Nephew 675QX381-3	Commemoratives	1986	$6	$9
New Home 450QX210-7	Commemoratives	1983	$4	$15
New Home 450QX212-6	Commemoratives	1982	$4	$14
New Home 450QX245-4	Commemoratives	1984	$4	$60
New Home 475QX269-5	Commemoratives	1985	$5	$30
New Home 475QX274-6	Commemoratives	1986	$5	$60
New Home 475QX275-5	Commemoratives	1989	$5	$18
New Home 600QX376-1	Commemoratives	1988	$6	$22
New Home 600QX376-7	Commemoratives	1987	$6	$18
Nick The Kick 500QX422-4	Handcrafted Ornaments	1988	$5	$14
Niece 475QX275-9	Commemoratives	1987	$5	$12
Niece 575QX520-5	Commemoratives	1985	$6	$5
Niece 600QX426-6	Commemoratives	1986	$6	$7
Night Before Christmas 1300QX449-4	General Line	1985	$13	$30
Night Before Christmas 3rd Ed. 1500QLX716-1	Christmas Classics	1988	$15	$42
Night Before Christmas 650QX451-7	General Line	1987	$6	$32
Night Before Christmas QX451-7	Handcrafted Ornaments	1988	$6	$32
Noah's Ark 850QX490-4	Handcrafted Ornaments	1988	$8	$38
Noelle 1975QXC448-3	Collector's Club	1989	$20	$52
Norman Rockwell 450QX202-3	General Line	1982	$4	$25
Norman Rockwell 450QX215-7	General Line	1983	$4	$16
Norman Rockwell 475QX266-2	General Line	1985	$5	$15
Norman Rockwell 475QX276-2	General Line	1989	$5	$20
Norman Rockwell 475QX276-3	General Line	1986	$5	$30
Norman Rockwell QX251-1	General Line	1984	$4	$20
Norman Rockwell: Xmas Scenes 475QX282-7	General Line	1987	$5	$25
North Pole Jogger 575QX546-2	General Line	1989	$6	$10
North Pole Power & Light 627XPR933-3	Handcrafted Ornaments	1987	$3	$14
Nostalgic Lamb 675QX466-5	General Line	1989	$7	$4
Nostalgic Rocker 650QX468-9	Old-Fashioned Christmas Collection	1987	$6	$18
Nostalgic Sled 600QX442-4	General Line	1985	$6	$25
Nostalgic Sled 600QX442-4	General Line	1984	$6	$14
Nutcracker Ballet 1st Ed. 1750QLX704-3	Christmas Classics	1986	$18	$80
Nutcracker Santa 1000QX512-3	Country Treasures Collection	1986	$10	$50
Nutshell Dreams 575QX465-5	General Line	1989	$6	$12
Nutshell Holiday 575QX465-2	General Line	1989	$6	$14

Santa's Woody, 1987, 9th in the Here Comes Santa series, $52.

Heavenly Harmony, 1987, $25.

Dancer, 1987, 2nd in the Reindeer Champs series, $35.

Chris Mouse Glow, 1987, 3rd in the Chris Mouse series, $65.

Sailor, 1987, 6th and final edition in the Clothespin Soldier series, $18.

Ornament Title	Series	Year	Issue Price	Current Value
Nutshell Workshop 575QX487-2	General Line	1989	$6	$12
Old Fashioned Christmas 450QX217-9	Decorative Ball Ornaments	1983	$4	$20
Old Fashioned Christmas 450QX227-6	Designer Keepsakes	1982	$4	$45
Old Fashioned Rocking Horse 750QX346-4	General Line	1984	$8	$22
Old World Angels 450QX226-3	Designer Keepsakes	1982	$4	$25
Old-Fashioned Church 400QX498-1	Handcrafted Ornaments	1988	$4	$10
Old-Fashioned Doll 1450QX519 5	Country Christmas Collection	1985	$14	$40
Old-Fashioned Santa 1100QX409-9	Handcrafted Ornaments	1983	$11	$52
Old-Fashioned Santa QX0440-3	Open House Ornaments	1986	$13	$28
Old-Fashioned School House 400QX497-1	Handcrafted Ornaments	1988	$4	$22
Old-Fashioned Toy Shop 2nd Ed. 1375QX497-5	Nostalgic Houses & Shops	1985	$14	$145
Old-Fashioned Wreath 750QX373-5	General Line	1985	$8	$25
Old-World Gnome 775QX434-5	General Line	1989	$8	$11
Old-World Santa 300QXM569-5	Miniature Ornaments	1989	$3	$7
On The Links 575QX419-2	General Line	1989	$6	$20
On The Right Track QSP420-1	Gold Crown Exclusives	1986	$15	$27
On With The Show 3rd & Final Ed. 1950QLX719-1	Santa & Sparky	1988	$20	$22
Open Me First 725QX422-6	General Line	1986	$7	$32
Oreo Cookie 400QX481-4	Handcrafted Ornaments	1988	$4	$20
Oreo Cookie 400QX481-4	Handcrafted Ornaments	1989	$4	$16
Oriental Butterflies 450QX218-7	Decorative Ball Ornaments	1983	$4	$30
Ornament Express, The 2200QX580 5	Collector's Club	1989	$22	$25
Our Clubhouse QXC580-4	Collector's Club	1988	N/A	$18
Owliday Greetings 400QX165-5	General Line	1980	$4	$15
Owliday Wish QX455-9	Handcrafted Ornaments	1987	$6	$20
Owliday Wish QX455-9	Handcrafted Ornaments	1988	$6	$20
Paddington Bear 550QX472-7	General Line	1987	$6	$20
Paddington Bear 575QX429-2	General Line	1989	$6	$17
Paddington Bear 600QX435-6	General Line	1986	$6	$19
Palomino 2nd Ed. 450QXM560-5	Rocking Horse Miniatures	1989	$4	$22
Par For Santa 500QX479-1	Handcrafted Ornaments	1988	$5	$14
Parade Of The Toys 2200QLX719-4	Magic Ornaments	1988	$25	$30
Partridge In A Pear Tree 600QX348-4	Twelve Days Of Christmas	1984	$6	$235
Party Line 875QX476-1	General Line	1988	$9	$19
Party Line 875QX476-1	General Line	1989	$9	$30
Patterns Of Christmas 450QX226-6	Designer Keepsakes	1982	$4	$24
Peace On Earth 750QX341-4	General Line	1984	$8	$18
Peaceful Kingdom 575QX373-2	General Line	1985	$6	$25
Peanuts 400QX216-1	General Line	1980	$4	$25
Peanuts 450QX200-6	General Line	1982	$4	$25
Peanuts 450QX212-7	General Line	1983	$4	$30
Peanuts 450QX252-1	General Line	1984	$4	$30
Peanuts 450QX803-5	General Line	1981	$4	$30
Peanuts 475QX266-5	General Line	1985	$5	$38

Paddington Bear, 1987, **$20.**

House on Main Street, 1987, 4th in the Nostalgic Houses and Shops series, **$80.**

Wee Chimney Sweep, 1987, **$12.**

Carousel Reindeer, 1987, Hallmark Keep-sake Ornament Collector's Club, **$30.**

Twenty-Five Years Together, 1987, **$25.**

Ornament Title	Series	Year	Issue Price	Current Value
Peanuts 475QX276-6	General Line	1986	$5	$32
Peanuts 475QX280-1	Handcrafted Ornaments	1988	$5	$40
Peanuts 475QX281-9	General Line	1987	$5	$38
Peek-A-Boo Kitties 750QX487-1	General Line	1989	$8	$18
Peek-A-Boo Kitties 750QX487-1	General Line	1988	$8	$18
Peeking Elf 650QX419-5	Handcrafted Ornaments	1982	$6	$22
Penguin Pal 1st Ed. 375QXM563-1	Penguin Pals	1988	$4	$9
Penguin Pal 2nd Ed. 450QXM560-2	Penguin Pals	1989	$4	$10
Peppermint 1984 450QX456-1	General Line	1984	$4	$50
Peppermint Clown 2475QX450-5	General Line	1989	$25	$18
Peppermint Mouse 300QX401-5	Fabric Ornaments	1981	$3	$15
Peppermint Penguin 650QX408-9	Handcrafted Ornaments	1983	$6	$28
Perfect Portrait 2nd Ed. 1950QLX701-9	Santa & Sparky	1987	$20	$40
Perky Penguin 350QX409-5	Little Trimmers	1981	$4	$20
Perky Penguin 400QX409-5	Little Trimmers	1982	$4	$25
Pinecone Basket 450QXM573-4	Miniature Ornaments	1989	$4	$9
Pinecone Home 800QX461-3	Handcrafted Ornaments	1982	$8	$56
Playful Angel 675QX453-5	Artists' Favorites	1989	$7	$19
Playful Possum 1100QX425-3	General Line	1986	$11	$30
Polar Bear Drummer 450QX430-1	General Line	1984	$4	$30
Polar Bowler 500QX478-1	Handcrafted Ornaments	1988	$5	$12
Polar Bowler 575QX478-4	Handcrafted Ornaments	1989	$6	$12
Popcorn Mouse 675QX421-3	General Line	1986	$7	$25
Prancer 3rd Ed. 750QX405-1	Reindeer Champs	1988	$8	$29
Pretty Kitten 1100QX448 9	General Line	1987	$11	$32
Promise Of Peace 650QX374-9	General Line	1987	$11	$20
Puppy Cart 300QXM571-5	Miniature Ornaments	1989	$3	$8
Puppy Love 350QX406-2	Little Trimmers	1981	$4	$34
Puppy's Best Friend 650QX420-3	General Line	1986	$6	$15
Purple Finch 7th & Final Ed. 775QX371-1	Holiday Wildlife	1988	$8	$22
Purrfect Snuggle 625QX474-4	Handcrafted Ornaments	1988	$6	$18
Raccoon Biker 700QX458-7	General Line	1987	$7	$18
Raccoon Surprises 900QX479-3	Handcrafted Ornaments	1982	$9	$48
Raccoon Tunes 550QX405-5	Plush Animals	1981	$6	$10
Raccoon's Christmas 900QX-447-4	General Line	1984	$9	$35
Radiant Tree 1175QLX712-1	Magic Ornaments	1988	$12	$16
Rah Rah Rabbit 700QX421-6	General Line	1986	$7	$20
Rainbow Angel 550QX416-7	Handcrafted Ornaments	1983	$6	$65
Rainbow Brite & Friends 475QX268-2	General Line	1985	$5	$25
Reindeer 3rd Ed. 750QX407-3	Wood Childhood	1986	$8	$16
Reindeer Chimes 550QX320-3	Holiday Chimes	1980	$6	$35
Reindeer Racetrack 450QX254-4	General Line	1984	$4	$25
Reindoggy 575QX452-7	General Line	1987	$6	$15
Reindoggy 575QX452-7	General Line	1988	$6	$15
Rejoice 300QXM578-2	Miniature Ornaments	1989	$3	$7
Remembering Christmas 865QX510-6	Country Treasures Collection	1986	$9	$12

Jack Frosting, 1987, **$40.**

Frosty Friends, 1987, 8th in the Frosty Friends series, **$85.**

Bright Christmas Dreams, 1987, **$55.**

December Showers, 1987, **$24.**

Mouse in the Moon, 1987, **$18.**

Miniature Creche, 1988, 4th in the Miniature Creche series, **$16.**

Currier & Ives: American Farm Scene, 1987, **$35.**

Penguin Pal, 1988, 1st in the Penguin Pals series, **$9.**

Ornament Title	Series	Year	Issue Price	Current Value
Ring-Necked Pheasants 3rd Ed. 725QX347-4	Holiday Wildlife	1984	$7	$30
Rocking Horse 1st Ed. 900QX422-2	Rocking Horse	1981	$9	$425
Rocking Horse 2nd Ed. 1000QX502-3	Rocking Horse	1982	$10	$315
Rocking Horse 3rd Ed. 1000QX417-7	Rocking Horse	1983	$10	$223
Rocking Horse 4th Ed. 1000QX435-4	Rocking Horse	1984	$10	$85
Rocking Horse 5th Ed. 1075QX493-2	Rocking Horse	1985	$11	$68
Rocking Horse 6th Ed. 1075QX401-6	Rocking Horse	1986	$11	$58
Rocking Horse 7th Ed. 1075QX482-9	Rocking Horse	1987	$11	$67
Rocking Horse 8th Ed. 1075QX402-4	Rocking Horse	1988	$11	$52
Rocking Horse 9th Ed. 1075QX462-2	Rocking Horse	1989	$11	$45
Rocking Horse Memories 1000QX518-2	Country Christmas Collection	1985	$10	$7
Rocking Horse QX340-7	General Line	1980	$2	$20
Rodney Reindeer 675QX407-2	General Line	1989	$7	$10
Roller Skating Rabbit 500QX457-1	General Line	1984	$5	$20
Roller Skating Rabbit 500QX457-1	General Line	1985	$5	$20
Roly-Poly Pig 300QXM571-2	Miniature Ornaments	1989	$3	$8
Roly-Poly Ram 300QXM570-5	Miniature Ornaments	1989	$3	$12
Rooftop Deliveries 3rd Ed. 1300QX438-2	Here Comes Santa	1981	$13	$225
Rooster Weathervane 575QX467-5	General Line	1989	$6	$9
Rudolph Red-Nosed Reindeer 1950QLX725-2	Magic Ornaments	1989	$20	$24
Sailing Santa 1300QX439-5	Handcrafted Ornaments	1981	$13	$200
Sailing! Sailing! 850QX491-1	Handcrafted Ornaments	1988	$8	$19
Sailor 6th & Final Ed. 550QX480-7	Clothespin Soldier	1987	$6	$18
Santa & His Reindeer 975QX0440-6	Open House Ornaments	1986	$10	$15
Santa 1980 550QX146-1	Handcrafted Ornaments	1980	$6	$90
Santa 300QX161-4	Yarn Ornaments	1980	$3	$11
Santa 400QX308-7	Holiday Sculpture	1983	$4	$28
Santa 400QX310-1	Frosted Images	1980	$4	$20
Santa 450QX221-6	Decorative Ball Ornaments	1982	$4	$22
Santa 750QX458-4	General Line	1984	$8	$20
Santa & Reindeer 900QX467-6	Brass Ornaments	1982	$9	$45
Santa At The Bat 775QX457-9	General Line	1987	$8	$20
Santa Bell 1500QX148-7	Handcrafted Ornaments	1982	$15	$45
Santa Carousel 6th & Final Ed. 1100QX401-9	Carousel Series	1983	$11	$35
Santa Claus 675QX300-5	Santa Claus-The Movie	1985	$7	$7
Santa Flamingo 475QX483-4	Handcrafted Ornaments	1988	$5	$35
Santa Mobile 550QX136-1	Holiday Chimes	1981	$6	$30
Santa Mobile 550QX136-1	Holiday Chimes	1980	$6	$30
Santa Mouse 450QX433-4	General Line	1984	$4	$30
Santa QX161-4	Yarn Ornaments	1981	$3	$11
Santa Pipe 950QX494-2	General Line	1985	$10	$25
Santa Snoopy 5th & Final Ed. 1300QX416-9	Snoopy & Friends	1983	$13	$95
Santa Star 550QX450-4	General Line	1984	$6	$20
Santa Sulky Driver 900QX436-1	General Line	1984	$9	$18
Santa Tree Topper 1800qto700-6	Tree Topper	1986	$18	$35
Santa's Arrival 1300QLX702-4	Magic Ornaments	1984	$13	$50

North Pole Power & Light, 1987, **$14.**

Rocking Horse, 1988, 8th in the Rocking Horse series, **$52.**

Family Home, 1988, 1st in the Old English Village series, **$24**

Polar Bowler, 1988, **$12.**

And to All a Goodnight, 1988, 9th and final in the Norman Rockwell series, **$20.**

Ornament Title	Series	Year	Issue Price	Current Value
Santa's Coming 450QX812-2	Decorative Ball Ornaments	1981	$4	$28
Santa's Deliveries 6th Ed. 1300QX432-4	Here Comes Santa	1984	$13	$52
Santa's Express 2nd Ed. 1200QX143-4	Here Comes Santa	1980	$12	$150
Santa's Express 5th Ed. 1300QX403-7	Here Comes Santa	1983	$13	$225
Santa's Fire Engine 7th Ed. 1400QX496-5	Here Comes Santa	1985	$14	$50
Santa's Flight 450QX308-6	Colors Of Christmas	1982	$4	$40
Santa's Flight 550QX138 1	Handcrafted Ornaments	1980	$6	$62
Santa's Hot Tub 1200QX426-3	General Line	1986	$12	$60
Santa's Magic Ride 850QXM563-2	Miniature Ornaments	1989	$8	$14
Santa's Many Faces 600QX311-7	Handcrafted Ornaments	1983	$6	$30
Santa's On His Way 1000QX426-9	Handcrafted Ornaments	1983	$10	$35
Santa's On His Way 1500QLX711-5	Lighted Ornaments Collection	1986	$15	$70
Santa's Panda Pal 550QX0441-3	Open House Ornaments	1986	$5	$15
Santa's Roadster 600QXM566-5	Miniature Ornaments	1989	$6	$14
Santa's Ski Trip 1200QX496-2	General Line	1985	$12	$56
Santa's Sleigh 900QX478-6	Brass Ornaments	1982	$9	$30
Santa's Snack 1000QLX706-6	Lighted Ornaments Collection	1986	$10	$28
Santa's Surprise 450QX815-5	Decorative Ball Ornaments	1981	$4	$10
Santa's Villlage 675QX300-2	Santa Claus-The Movie	1985	$7	$10
Santa's Visitors 1st Ed. 650QX306-1	Norman Rockwell	1980	$6	$125
Santa's Woody 9th Ed. 1400QX484-7	Here Comes Santa	1987	$14	$52
Santa's Workshop 1000QX150 3	Handcrafted Ornaments	1983	$10	$40
Santa's Workshop 1000QX450-3	Handcrafted Ornaments	1982	$10	$40
Santa's Workshop 1300QLX700-4	Magic Ornaments	1984	$13	$79
Santa's Workshop 1300QLX700-4	Magic Ornaments	1985	$13	$34
Santa's Workshop 400QX223-4	Decorative Ball Ornaments	1980	$4	$10
Savior Is Born, A 450QX254-1	General Line	1984	$4	$32
Scooter 2nd Ed. 450QXM561-2	Kittens In Toyland	1989	$4	$18
Scottish Highlander 4th Ed. 550QX471-5	Clothespin Soldier	1985	$6	$22
Scrimshaw Reindeer 450QXM568-5	Miniature Ornaments	1989	$4	$6
Scrimshaw Reindeer 800QX424-9	Handcrafted Ornaments	1983	$8	$18
Sea Santa 575QX415-2	General Line	1989	$6	$22
Season For Caring 450QX221-3	Decorative Ball Ornaments	1982	$4	$25
Season For Friendship 850QLX706-9	Magic Ornaments	1987	$8	$22
Season Of Beauty 800QLX712-2	Magic Ornaments	1985	$8	$22
Season Of The Heart 475QX270-6	Commemoratives	1986	$5	$8
Seasoned Greetings 625QX454-9	General Line	1987	$6	$16
Season's Greeting 450QX219-9	Decorative Ball Ornaments	1983	$4	$26
Sewn Photoholder 700QX379-5	General Line	1985	$7	$5
Shall We Dance? 3rd Ed. 1300QX401-1	Mr. & Mrs. Claus	1988	$13	$40
Sharing A Ride 850QXM576-5	Miniature Ornaments	1989	$8	$15
Sharing Friendship 850QLX706-3	Lighted Ornaments Collection	1986	$8	$25
Sheep At Christmas 825QX517-5	Country Christmas Collection	1985	$8	$19

Frosty Friends, 1988, 9th in the Frosty Friends series, **$90.**

Daughter, 1988, **$45.**

Dad, 1988, **$19.**

Our Clubhouse, 1988, Hall-mark Keepsake Ornament Collectors Club, **$18.**

The Town Crier, 1988, **$14.**

Little Jack Horner, 1988, **$14.**

Ornament Title	Series	Year	Issue Price	Current Value
Shepherd Scene 550QX500-2	Holiday Highlights	1981	$6	$20
Shining Star 1750QLT709-6	Tree Topper	1986	$18	$20
Shiny Sleigh 575QX492-4	Handcrafted Ornaments	1988	$6	$9
Shirt Tales 450QX214-9	General Line	1983	$4	$24
Shirt Tales 450QX252-4	General Line	1984	$4	$17
Shirt Tales Parade 475QX277-3	General Line	1986	$5	$15
Silver Bell QX110-9	General Line	1983	$12	$31
Sister 450QX206-9	Commemoratives	1983	$4	$25
Sister 450QX208-3	Commemoratives	1982	$4	$16
Sister 475QX279-2	Commemoratives	1989	$5	$20
Sister 600QX474-7	Commemoratives	1987	$6	$18
Sister 650QX259-4	Commemoratives	1984	$6	$28
Sister 675QX380-6	Commemoratives	1986	$7	$9
Sister 725QX506-5	Commemoratives	1985	$7	$12
Sister 800QX499-4	Commemoratives	1988	$8	$10
Sitting Purrty QXC581-2	Collector's Club	1989	N/A	$15
Six Geese A-Laying 675QX381-2	Twelve Days Of Christmas	1989	$7	$19
Skateboard Raccoon 650QX473-2	General Line	1985	$6	$35
Skateboard Raccoon 650QX473-2	General Line	1986	$6	$40
Skater Carousel 4th Ed. 900QX427-5	Carousel Series	1981	$9	$80
Skater's Waltz 2450QLX720-1	Magic Ornaments	1988	$25	$35
Skater's Waltz 700QXM560-1	Miniature Ornaments	1988	$7	$11
Skating Rabbit 800QX409-7	Handcrafted Ornaments	1983	$8	$55
Skating Snowman, The 550QX139-9	Handcrafted Ornaments	1980	$6	$30
Ski Holiday 2nd Ed. 900QX154-1	Snoopy & Friends	1980	$9	$165
Ski Lift Santa 800QX410-7	Handcrafted Ornaments	1984	$8	$33
Ski Tripper 675QX420-6	General Line	1986	$7	$13
Skiing Fox 800QX420-7	Handcrafted Ornaments	1983	$8	$25
Sleepy Santa 625QX450-7	General Line	1987	$6	$40
Sleighful Of Dreams 800QXC580-1	Collector's Club	1988	$8	$15
Slipper Spaniel 450QX472-4	Handcrafted Ornaments	1988	$4	$12
Slow Motion 600QXM575-2	Miniature Ornaments	1989	$6	$10
Sneaker Mouse 400QXM571-1	Miniature Ornaments	1988	$4	$20
Sneaker Mouse 450QX400-9	Handcrafted Ornaments	1983	$4	$12
Snoopy & Friends 3rd Ed. 1200QX436-2	Snoopy & Friends	1981	$12	$90
Snoopy & Friends 4th Ed. 1300QX480-3	Snoopy & Friends	1982	$13	$115
Snoopy & Woodstock 600QX474-1	Handcrafted Ornaments	1988	$6	$32
Snoopy & Woodstock 675QX433-2	General Line	1989	$7	$25
Snoopy & Woodstock 750QX439-1	General Line	1984	$8	$98
Snoopy & Woodstock 434-6	Handcrafted Ornaments	1986	$8	$55
Snoopy & Woodstock 725QX472-9	General Line	1987	$7	$38
Snoopy & Woodstock 750QX491-5	General Line	1985	$8	$60
Snoopy & Woodstock 800QX438-3	General Line	1986	$8	$55
Snow 929XPR971-9	Christmas Carousel Horse Collection	1989	$4	$20
Snow Buddies 800QX423-6	General Line	1986	$8	$20

Hall Bros' Card Shop, 1988, 5th in the Nostalgic Houses and Shops series, **$52.**

Festive Feeder, 1988, **$50.**

Baby's Second Christmas, 1988, **$32.**

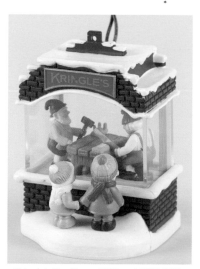

Kringle's Toy Shop, 1988 and 1989, **$28.**

Ornament Title	Series	Year	Issue Price	Current Value
Snow Goose 6th Ed. 750QX371-7	Holiday Wildlife	1987	$8	$22
Snowflake 650QX510-5	Heirloom Christmas Collection	1985	$6	$4
Snowflake Chimes 550QX165-4	Holiday Chimes	1980	$6	$30
Snowflake Chimes 550QX165-4	Holiday Chimes	1981	$6	$30
Snowflake Swing, The 400QX133-4	Handcrafted Ornaments	1980	$4	$30
Snowman 300QX163-4	Yarn Ornaments	1980	$3	$11
Snowman 400QX510-2	Frosted Images	1981	$4	$26
Snowman Carousel 5th Ed. 1000QX478-3	Carousel Series	1982	$10	$95
Snowman Chimes 550QX445-5	Holiday Chimes	1981	$6	$30
Snowman QX163-4	Yarn Ornaments	1981	$3	$10
Snowmobile Santa 650QX431-4	General Line	1984	$6	$25
Snow-Pitching Snowman 450QX470-2	General Line	1985	$4	$18
Snow-Pitching Snowman 450QX470-2	General Line	1986	$4	$18
Snowplow Santa 575QX420-5	General Line	1989	$6	$22
Snowshoe Penguin 650QX453-1	General Line	1984	$6	$35
Snowy Seal 400QX300-6	Ice Sculptures	1982	$4	$20
Snowy Seal 400QX450-1	General Line	1985	$4	$20
Snowy Seal 400QX450-1	General Line	1984	$4	$20
Snuggly Skater 450QXM571-4	Miniature Ornaments	1988	$4	$18
Soccer Beaver 650QX477-5	General Line	1985	$6	$12
Soccer Beaver 650QX477-5	General Line	1986	$6	$12
Soft Landing 700QX475-1	Handcrafted Ornaments	1988	$7	$10
Soldier 300QX164-1	Yarn Ornaments	1980	$3	$10
Soldier QX164-1	Yarn Ornaments	1981	$3	$10
Son 300QX211-4	Commemorative School	1980	$3	$30
Son 450QX202-9	Commemoratives	1983	$4	$38
Son 450QX204-3	Commemoratives	1982	$4	$26
Son 450QX243-4	Commemoratives	1984	$4	$30
Son 450QX606-2	Commemoratives	1981	$4	$10
Son 550QX502-5	Commemoratives	1985	$6	$45
Son 575QX415-4	Commemoratives	1988	$6	$11
Son 575QX430-3	Commemoratives	1986	$6	$19
Son 575QX463-9	Commemoratives	1987	$6	$36
Son 625QX444-5	Commemoratives	1989	$6	$10
Song Of Christmas 850QLX711-1	Magic Ornaments	1988	$8	$14
Space Santa 650QX430-2	Handcrafted Ornaments	1981	$6	$59
Sparkling Snowflake 775QX547-2	General Line	1989	$8	$22
Sparkling Tree 600QX483-1	Handcrafted Ornaments	1988	$6	$9
Special Delivery 500QX415-6	General Line	1986	$5	$14
Special Delivery 525QX432-5	General Line	1989	$6	$22
Special Friend 450QXM565-2	Miniature Ornaments	1989	$4	$8
Special Friends 575QX372-5	Commemoratives	1985	$6	$6
Special Memories Photoholder 675QX464-7	General Line	1987	$7	$25
Spencer Sparrow, Esq. 675QX431-2	General Line	1989	$7	$12
Spirit Of Christmas 475QX276-1	Commemoratives	1988	$5	$9

Party Line, 1988, **$19.**

Peek-a-Boo Kitties, 1988, **$18.**

Chris Mouse Star, 1988, 4th in the Chris Mouse series, **$68.**

Miniature Creche, 1989, 5th and final edition in the Miniature Creche series, **$18.**

Teacher, 1988, **$22.**

Ornament Title	Series	Year	Issue Price	Current Value
Spirit Of Christmas, The 1000QX452-6	Handcrafted Ornaments	1982	$10	$90
Spirit Of Santa Claus, The 2250QX498-5	General Line	1985	$23	$100
Spirit Of St. Nick 2450QLX728-5	Magic Ornaments	1989	$25	$65
Spot Of Christmas Cheer 800QX153-4	Handcrafted Ornaments	1980	$8	$60
Spots 'N Stripes 550QX452-9	General Line	1987	$6	$20
Squeaky Clean 675QX475-4	Handcrafted Ornaments	1988	$7	$25
St. Louie Nick 775QX453-9	Christmas Pizzazz Collection	1987	$8	$22
St. Louie Nick QX453-9	Handcrafted Ornaments	1988	$8	$22
St. Nicholas 1st Ed. 550QX279-5	Gift Bringers	1989	$5	$10
St. Nicholas 550QX446-2	Handcrafted Ornaments	1981	$6	$50
Stained Glass 450QX228-3	Designer Keepsakes	1982	$4	$10
Stained Glass 800QLX703-1	Magic Ornaments	1984	$8	$20
Star 629XPR972-0	Christmas Carousel Horse Collection	1989	$4	$22
Star Brighteners 600QX322-6	General Line	1986	$6	$18
Star Of Peace 600QX304-7	Holiday Highlights	1983	$6	$25
Star Swing 550QX421-5	Handcrafted Ornaments	1981	$6	$20
Stardust Angel 575QX475-2	General Line	1985	$6	$22
Starlit Mouse 450QXM565-5	Miniature Ornaments	1989	$4	$12
Starry Angel 475QX494-4	Handcrafted Ornaments	1988	$5	$10
Statue Of Liberty, The 600QX384-3	General Line	1986	$6	$22
Stocking Kitten 675QX456-5	General Line	1989	$7	$11
Stocking Mouse, The 450QX412-2	Little Trimmers	1981	$4	$45
Stocking Pal 450QXM567-2	Miniature Ornaments	1989	$4	$7
Strollin' Snowman 450QXM574-2	Miniature Ornaments	1989	$4	$16
Sugarplum Cottage 1100QLX701-1	Magic Ornaments	1986	$11	$25
Sugarplum Cottage 1100QLX701-1	Magic Ornaments	1985	$11	$25
Sugarplum Cottage 1100QLX701-1	Magic Ornaments	1984	$11	$28
Sun & Fun Santa 775QX492-2	General Line	1985	$8	$22
Sweet Dreams 700QXM560-4	Miniature Ornaments	1988	$7	$18
Sweet Memories Photoholder 675QX438-5	General Line	1989	$7	$10
Sweet Shop 2nd Ed. 850QXM561-5	Old English Village	1989	$8	$20
Sweet Star 500QX418-4	Handcrafted Ornaments	1988	$5	$33
Sweetheart 1100QX408-6	Commemoratives	1986	$11	$35
Sweetheart 1100QX447-9	Commemoratives	1987	$11	$25
Sweetheart 975QX486-5	Commemoratives	1989	$10	$35
Sweetheart 975QX490-1	Commemoratives	1988	$10	$20
Swingin' Bellringer 3rd. Ed. QX441-5	Bellringer Series	1981	$15	$75
Swingin' On A Star 400QX130-1	Little Trimmers	1980	$4	$38
Swinging Angel Bell 1100QX492-5	General Line	1985	$11	$22
Swiss Cheese Lane 1300QLX706-5	Magic Ornaments	1985	$13	$49
Teacher 400QX209-4	Commemoratives	1980	$4	$12
Teacher 450QX214-3	Commemoratives	1982	$4	$8
Teacher 450QX224-9	Commemoratives	1983	$4	$5
Teacher 450QX249-1	Commemoratives	1984	$4	$5
Teacher 450QX800-2	Commemoratives	1981	$4	$5

Prancer, 1988, 3rd in the Reindeer Champs series, **$29.**

Reindoggy, 1988, also issued in 1987, **$15.**

Vixen, 1989, 4th in the Reindeer Champs series, **$15.**

Rocking Horse, 1989, 9th in the Rocking Horse series, **$45.**

Cinnamon Bear, 1989, 7th in the Porcelain Bear series, **$18.**

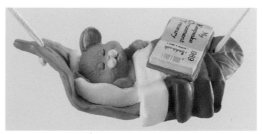

Collect a Dream, 1989, **$24.**

Ornament Title	Series	Year	Issue Price	Current Value
Teacher 475QX275-3	Commemoratives	1986	$5	$15
Teacher 575QX412-5	Commemoratives	1989	$6	$8
Teacher 575QX466-7	Commemoratives	1987	$6	$24
Teacher 600QX304-9	Commemoratives	1983	$6	$15
Teacher 625QX417-1	Commemoratives	1988	$6	$22
Teacher 650QX312-3	Commemoratives	1982	$6	$15
Teacher, Owl 600QX505-2	Commemoratives	1985	$6	$15
Teacher-Apple 550QX301-6	Commemoratives	1982	$6	$15
Teddy Bellringer 5th Ed. QX403-9	Bellringer Series	1983	$15	$55
Teeny Taster 475QX418-1	General Line	1988	$5	$17
Teeny Taster 475QX418-1	General Line	1989	$5	$17
Ten Years Together 475QX274-2	Commemoratives	1989	$5	$25
Ten Years Together 475QX275-1	Commemoratives	1988	$5	$20
Ten Years Together 650QX258-4	Commemoratives	1984	$6	$15
Ten Years Together 700QX444-7	Commemoratives	1987	$7	$22
Ten Years Together 750QX401-3	Commemoratives	1986	$8	$15
Thimble Angel 4th Ed. 450QX413-5	Thimble Series	1981	$4	$100
Thimble Angel 7th Ed. 500QX430-4	Thimble Series	1984	$5	$40
Thimble Drummer 10th Ed. 575QX441-9	Thimble Series	1987	$6	$19
Thimble Elf 3rd Ed. 400QX132-1	Thimble Series	1980	$4	$70
Thimble Elf 6th Ed. 500QX401-7	Thimble Series	1983	$5	$14
Thimble Mouse 5th Ed. 500QX451-3	Thimble Series	1982	$5	$30
Thimble Partridge 9th Ed. 575QX406-6	Thimble Series	1986	$6	$16
Thimble Puppy 12th & Final Ed. 575QX455-2	Thimble Series	1989	$6	$14
Thimble Santa 8th Ed. QX472-5	Thimble Series	1985	$6	$22
Thimble Snowman 11th Ed. 575QX405-4	Thimble Series	1988	$6	$20
Three French Hens 650QX378-6	Twelve Days Of Christmas	1986	$6	$28
Three Kings 850QX307-3	Handcrafted Ornaments	1982	$8	$25
Three Kittens In A Mitten 800QX431-1	General Line	1984	$8	$55
Three Kittens In A Mitten 800QX431-1	General Line	1985	$8	$48
Three Little Kittens 600QXM569-4	Miniature Ornaments	1988	$6	$12
Three Little Kittens 600QXM569-4	Miniature Ornaments	1989	$6	$12
Three Men In A Tub 800QX454-7	Artists' Favorites	1987	$8	$12
Three Wise Men 400QX300-1	Holiday Highlights	1980	$4	$32
Time For Friends 475QX280-7	Commemoratives	1987	$5	$22
Time For Sharing 600QX307-7	Holiday Highlights	1983	$6	$30
Timeless Love 600QX379-6	Commemoratives	1986	$6	$30
Tin Locomotive 1st Ed. 1300QX460-3	Tin Locomotive	1982	$13	$400
Tin Locomotive 2nd Ed. 1300QX404-9	Tin Locomotive	1983	$13	$225
Tin Locomotive 3rd Ed. 1400QX440-4	Tin Locomotive	1984	$14	$50
Tin Locomotive 4th Ed. 1475QX497-2	Tin Locomotive	1985	$15	$47
Tin Locomotive 5th Ed. 1475QX403-6	Tin Locomotive	1986	$15	$40
Tin Locomotive 6th Ed. 1475QX484-9	Tin Locomotive	1987	$15	$35
Tin Locomotive 7th Ed. 1475QX400-4	Tin Locomotive	1988	$15	$38
Tin Locomotive 8th & Final Ed. 1475QX460-2	Tin Locomotive	1989	$15	$38
Tin Rocking Horse 650QX414-9	Handcrafted Ornaments	1983	$6	$48

Paddington Bear, 1989, **$17.**

Baby's First Christmas, 1989, **$29.**

Tiny Tinker, 1989, **$50.**

Holiday Duet, 1989, 4th in the Mr. and Mrs. Claus series, **$35.**

Ornament Title	Series	Year	Issue Price	Current Value
Tin Soldier 650QX483-6	Handcrafted Ornaments	1982	$6	$38
Tiny Tinker 1950QLX717-4	Magic Ornaments	1989	$20	$50
Tipping The Scales 675QX418-6	General Line	1986	$7	$12
Topsy-Turvy Tunes 750QX429-5	Handcrafted Ornaments	1981	$8	$40
Touchdown Santa 800QX423-3	General Line	1986	$8	$20
Town Crier, The 550QX473-4	Handcrafted Ornaments	1988	$6	$14
Traditional (Black Santa) 450QX801-5	Decorative Ball Ornaments	1981	$4	$98
Train 1st Ed. 500QXM562-1	Kittens In Toyland	1988	$5	$14
Train 2nd Ed. 700QX472-2	Wood Childhood	1985	$7	$24
Train Station 1275QLX703-9	Magic Ornaments	1987	$13	$31
Travels With Santa 1000QX477-1	Handcrafted Ornaments	1988	$10	$29
Tree Chimes 550QX484-6	Holiday Chimes	1982	$6	$30
Tree Of Friendship 850QLX710-4	Magic Ornaments	1988	$8	$25
Tree Photoholder 550QX515-5	Crown Classics Collection	1981	$6	$28
Treetop Dreams QX459-7	Handcrafted Ornaments	1988	$7	$22
Treetop Trio 1100QX424-6	General Line	1987	$11	$25
Treetop Trio 1100QX425-6	General Line	1986	$11	$25
Truck 6th & Final Ed. 775QX459-5	Wood Childhood	1989	$8	$10
Trumpet Panda 450QX471-2	General Line	1985	$4	$20
Tufted Titmouse QX479-5	General Line	1985	$6	$26
TV Break 625QX409-2	General Line	1989	$6	$9
Twelve Days Of Christmas 1500QMB415-9	General Line	1983	$15	$75
Twelve Days Of Christmas 1500QX415-9	General Line	1984	$15	$80
Twelve Days Of Christmas 450QX203-6	Designer Keepsakes	1982	$4	$18
Twenty-Five Years Together 650QX259-1	Commemoratives	1984	$6	$22
Twenty-Five Years Together 675QX373-4	Commemoratives	1988	$7	$16
Twenty-Five Years Together 750QX443-9	Commemoratives	1987	$8	$25
Twenty-Five Years Together 800QX410-3	Commemoratives	1986	$8	$22
Twenty-Five Years Together 800QX500-5	Commemoratives	1985	$8	$15
Two Turtledoves 650QX371-2	Twelve Days Of Christmas	1985	$6	$74
U.S. Post Office 6th Ed. 1425QX458-2	Nostalgic Houses & Shops	1989	$14	$58
Uncle Sam 600QX449-1	General Line	1984	$6	$50
Uncle Sam Nutcracker 700QX488-4	Handcrafted Ornaments	1988	$7	$22
Unicorn 1000QX426-7	Handcrafted Ornaments	1983	$10	$30
Unicorn 850QX516-5	Crown Classics Collection	1981	$8	$23
Unicorn Fantasy 950QLX723-5	Magic Ornaments	1989	$10	$22
Very Strawbeary 475QX409-1	Artists' Favorites	1988	$5	$20
Victorian Dollhouse 1st Ed. 1300QX448-1	Nostalgic Houses & Shops	1984	$13	$200
Victorian Lady 950QX513-2	Heirloom Christmas Collection	1985	$10	$24
Village Church 1500QLX702-1	Magic Ornaments	1984	$15	$28
Village Church 1500QLX702-1	Magic Ornaments	1985	$15	$22
Village Express 2450QLX707-2	Lighted Ornaments Collection	1987	$25	$42
Village Express 2450QLX707-2	Lighted Ornaments Collection	1986	$25	$42

Frosty Friends, 1989, 10th in the Frosty Friends series, **$40.**

U.S. Post Office, 1989, 6th in the Nostalgic Houses and Shops series, **$58.**

On the Links, 1989, from the Holiday Highlights series, **$20.**

Loving Spoonful, 1989, **$22.**

Dad, 1989, **$19.**

Ornament Title	Series	Year	Issue Price	Current Value
Visit From Santa QXC580-2	Collector's Club	1989	N/A	$44
Vixen 4th Ed. 775QX456-2	Reindeer Champs	1989	$8	$15
Walnut Shell Rider 600QX419-6	General Line	1987	$6	$25
Walnut Shell Rider 600QX419-6	General Line	1986	$6	$25
Warmth Of Friendship 600QX375-9	Commemoratives	1987	$6	$11
Wee Chimney Sweep 625QX451-9	Artists' Favorites	1987	$6	$12
Welcome Christmas 825QX510-3	Country Treasures Collection	1986	$8	$30
Well-Stocked Stocking 900QX154-7	Handcrafted Ornaments	1981	$9	$18
Whirligig Santa 1250QX519-2	Country Christmas Collection	1985	$12	$18
White Christmas 1600QX905-1	General Line	1984	$16	$90
Wiggly Snowman 675QX489-2	General Line	1989	$7	$25
Winter Fun 850QX478-1	Handcrafted Ornaments	1988	$8	$12
Winter Surprise 1st Ed. 1075QX427-2	Winter Surprise	1989	$11	$10
Wise Men, The 450QX220-7	Decorative Ball Ornaments	1983	$4	$40
With Appreciation 675QX375-2	Commemoratives	1985	$7	$8
Wonderful Santacycle, The 225QX411-4	Handcrafted Ornaments	1988	$23	$30
Word Of Love 800QX447-7	Commemoratives	1987	$8	$20
World Of Love 475QX274-5	Commemoratives	1989	$5	$30
Wreath 400QX301-4	Holiday Highlights	1980	$4	$35
Wreath Of Memories QXC580-9	Collector's Club	1987	N/A	$20
Wynken, Blynken & Nod 975QX424-6	General Line	1986	$10	$25
Year To Remember 700QX416-4	Commemoratives	1988	$7	$20

The Ornament Express, 1989, from the Hallmark Keepsake Ornament Collector's Club, $25.

1990s

During the 1990s, Hallmark emerged as an indisputable leader in the surging contemporary collectibles hobby. As proof of this, the company announced even more collectible ornament series, including Classic American Cars and Star Trek, both introduced in 1991; All-American Trucks in 1995; and Lionel Trains in 1996.

The first Easter ornaments were offered to collectors in 1991, and the Kiddie Car Classics line of miniature pedal cars followed suit in 1992. (The Kiddie Car Classics line of ornaments debuted in 1994.)

Perhaps one of the most famous ornaments issued in the 1990s is Starship Enterprise from 1991, the first edition in the Star Trek series. This is one of the most valuable Hallmark ornaments ever produced.

Several American icons made it into the Hallmark line during the 1990s: Barbie, Looney Tunes, The Lion King, the Wizard of Oz, Star Wars, Lionel trains, and others.

Of course, no summarization of the 1990s for Hallmark is complete without the celebration of the ornament line's milestone 25th anniversary in 1998.

1990s Pricing

Ornament Title	Series	Year	Issue Price	Current Value
#1 Student QX6646	General Line	1998	$8	$8
1917 Curtiss JN-4D Jenny 2nd Ed. QX6286	Sky's The Limit	1998	$15	$29
1931 Ford Model A Roadster 1st Ed. 1495QEO8416	Vintage Roadsters	1998	$15	$12
1932 Chevrolet Sports Roadster 2nd Ed. QEO8379	Vintage Roadsters	1999	$15	$14
1935 Steelcraft By Murray QXC4496	Kiddie Car Classics	1998	$16	$44
1935 Steelcraft Streamline Velocipede 1st Ed. QEO8632	Sidewalk Cruisers	1997	$13	$20
1937 Ford V-8 4th Ed. QX6263	All-American Trucks	1998	$14	$23
1937 Steelcraft Airflow By Murray 2nd Ed. QXM4477	Miniature Kiddie Car Luxury Edition	1999	$7	$9
1937 Steelcraft Airflow By Murray QXC5185	Kiddie Car Classics	1997	$16	$30
1937 Steelcraft Auburn 1st Ed. QXM4143	Miniature Kiddie Car Luxury	1998	N/A	$9
1937 Steelcraft Auburn QXC4174	Collector's Club	1996	$16	$40
1939 Garton Ford Station Wagon QXC4509	Kiddie Car Classics	1999	$16	$19
1939 Mobo Horse 2nd Ed. QEO8393	Sidewalk Cruisers	1998	$13	$20
1949 Cadillac Coupe Deville QX6429	General Line	1999	$15	$28
1950 Garton Delivery Cycle 3rd Ed. QEO8367	Sidewalk Cruisers	1999	$13	$20
1950 Lionel Santa Fe F3 Diesel Locomotive QBG6119	Crown Reflections	1999	$35	$42
1950 Santa Fe F3 Diesel Locomotive 2nd Ed.	Lionel Trains	1997	$19	$26
1953 GMC 3rd Ed. QX610-5	All-American Trucks	1997	$14	$23
1955 Chevrolet Cameo 2nd Ed. QX524-1	All-American Trucks	1996	$14	$18
1955 Chevrolet Nomad Wagon 9th Ed. QX6367	Classic American Cars	1999	$14	$9
1955 Murray Fire Truck QBG6909	General Line	1998	$35	$45
1955 Murray Ranch Wagon QBG6077	Crown Reflections	1999	$35	$19
1955 Murray Tractor & Trailer 5th Ed. QX637-6	Kiddie Car Classics	1998	$17	$16
1955 Murray Tractor & Trailer 5th Ed. QXM4479	Miniature Kiddie Car Classics	1999	$7	$12
1956 Ford Thunderbird 3rd Ed.1275QX527-5	Classic American Cars	1993	$13	$19
1956 Ford Truck 1st Ed. QX552-7	All-American Trucks	1995	$14	$25
1956 Garton Hot Rod Racer 1st Ed. QEO8479	Winner's Circle	1999	$14	$15
1957 Chevrolet Bel Air 4th Ed. 1275QX542-2	Classic American Cars	1994	$13	$16
1957 Corvette 1st Ed. 1275QX431-9	Classic American Cars	1991	$13	$80
1957 Dodge Sweptside D100 5th Ed. QX6269	All-American Trucks	1999	$14	$19
1958 Ford Edsel Citation Convertible QXC416-7	Classic American Cars	1995	$13	$50
1959 Cadillac DeVille 6th Ed. QX538-4	Classic American Cars	1996	$13	$21
1966 Mustang 2nd Ed. 1275QX428-4	Classic American Cars	1992	$13	$30

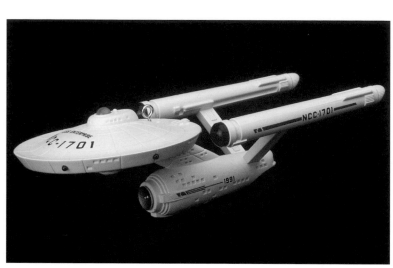

Starship Enterprise, 1991, from the Star Trek Series, **$285.**

Frosty Friends, 1990, 11th in the Frosty Friends series, **$30.**

Holiday Home, 1990, 7th in the Nostalgic Houses and Shops series, **$58.**

Ornament Title	Series	Year	Issue Price	Current Value
1968 Murray Jolly Roger Flagship 6th Ed. QX6279	Kiddie Car Classics	1999	$14	$14
1969 Chevrolet Camaro 5th Ed. QX523-9	Classic American Cars	1995	$13	$13
1969 Hurst Oldsmobile 442 7th Ed. QX6102	Classic American Cars	1997	$14	$15
1970 Plymouth Hemi 'Cuda 8th Ed. QX6256	Classic American Cars	1998	$14	$10
1988 Happy Holidays Barbie Doll Ornament 1st Ed. QXC4181	Happy Holidays Barbie	1996	$15	$35
1989 Happy Holidays Barbie Doll Ornament 2nd Ed. QXC5162	Happy Holidays Barbie	1997	$16	$30
1990 Happy Holidays Barbie Doll Ornament 3rd Ed. QXC4493	Happy Holidays Barbie	1998	$16	$39
1991 Happy Holidays Barbie Doll Ornament 4th Ed.	Happy Holidays Barbie	1999	$16	$35
1997 Corvette Miniature QXI4322	Special Issues	1997	$7	$5
1997 Corvette QXI6455	Special Issues	1997	$14	$9
1998 Corvette Convertible QX6416	General Line	1998	$14	$14
1998 Corvette QXL7605	General Line	1998	$24	$28
25 Years Together 1000AGA711-3	Anniversary Ornaments	1992	$10	$20
25 Years Together 1000AGA768-6	Anniversary Ornaments	1993	$10	$20
25 Years Together Ann. Bell 800AGA713-4	Anniversary Ornaments	1992	$10	$16
25 Years Together Ann. Bell 800AGA768-7	Anniversary Ornaments	1993	$10	$24
25 Years Together Photoholder QX493-7	Commemoratives	1991	$9	$10
40 Years Together 1000AGA731-6	Anniversary Ornaments	1992	$10	$20
40 Years Together 1000AGA786-8	Anniversary Ornaments	1993	$10	$24
40th Anniversary Barbie QXI8049	Barbie	1999	$16	$24
50 Years Together 1000AGA721-4	Anniversary Ornaments	1992	$10	$17
50 Years Together 1000AGA778-7	Anniversary Ornaments	1993	$10	$17
50 Years Together Ann. Bell 800AGA723-5	Anniversary Ornaments	1992	$10	$17
50 Years Together Ann. Bell 800AGA778-8	Anniversary Ornaments	1993	$10	$17
700E Hudson Steam Locomotive 1st Ed. QX553-1	Lionel Trains	1996	$19	$70
746 Norfolk & Western Steam Locomotive 4th Ed. QX6377	Lionel Trains	1999	$19	$22
A+ Teacher 375QXM551-1	Miniature Ornaments	1992	$4	$6
Abearnathy/Son 495XPR974-7	Bearingers Of Victoria Circle	1993	$5	$5
Accessories For Nostalgic Houses & Shops QX508-9	Nostalgic Houses & Shops	1995	$9	$15
Acorn 500 QX592-9	Handcrafted Ornaments	1995	$11	$5
Acorn Wreath 600QXM568-6	Miniature Ornaments	1990	$6	$8
Across The Miles 675QX304-4	Commemoratives	1992	$7	$6
Across The Miles 675QX315-7	Commemoratives	1991	$7	$15
Across The Miles 675QX317-3	Commemoratives	1990	$7	$4
Across The Miles 875QX591-2	Commemoratives	1993	$9	$15
Across The Miles QX5656	Commemoratives	1994	N/A	$10
Across The Miles QX584-7	Commemoratives	1995	$9	$15
Adding The Best Part QX6569	General Line	1999	$8	$18

Little Frosty Friends Memory Wreath, 1990, from the Little Frosty Friends series, **$8.**

Club Hollow, 1990, **$10.**

Mr. Ashbourne, 1990, from the Dickens Caroler Bell series, **$20.**

Rocking Horse, 1990, 10th in the Rocking Horse series, **$98.**

Stitches of Joy, 1990, **$8.**

Ornament Title	Series	Year	Issue Price	Current Value
African Elephants QXM422-4	Miniature Ornaments-Noah's Ark	1996	$6	$19
African-American Holiday Barbie QX6936	Holiday Barbie Collection	1998	$16	$20
African-American Millennium Princess BarbieQXI6449	Barbie	1999	$16	$25
Air Express QX5977	Handcrafted Ornaments	1995	$8	$9
Air Santa 450QXM565-6	Miniature Ornaments	1990	$4	$9
Airmail For Santa	Collector's Club	1996	$9	$18
Airplane 4th Ed. 450QXM563-9	Kittens In Toyland	1991	$4	$14
Alice In Wonderland 1st Ed. QXM4777	Alice In Wonderland	1995	$7	$12
All Aboard 450QXM586-9	Miniature Ornaments	1991	$4	$9
All Pumped Up 895QX592-3	General Line	1994	$9	$9
All Sooted Up QX6837	General Line	1999	$10	$10
All Star 675QX532-9	General Line	1991	$7	$9
All-Round Sports Fan QX6392	General Line	1997	$9	$24
All-Weather Walker	General Line	1997	$9	$9
Angel Friend QX6762	General Line	1997	$15	$17
Angel Hare 895QX589-6	General Line	1994	$9	$12
Angel In Disguise QX6629	General Line	1999	$9	$18
Angel In Flight 1575QK105-2	Folk Art Americana	1993	$16	$39
Angel Kitty 875QX474-6	Artists' Favorites	1990	$9	$20
Angel Of Hope QXI6339	General Line	1999	$15	$18
Angel Of Light 3000QLX723-9	Magic Ornaments	1991	$30	$60
Angel Of Light 3000QLX723-9	Magic Ornaments	1992	$30	$37
Angel Of Light QK115-9	All Is Bright	1995	$12	$12
Angel Of The Nativity 2nd Ed. QX6419	Madame Alexander Holiday Angels	1999	$15	$30
Angel Song QX6939	General Line	1999	$19	$19
Angelic Flight QXI4146	25th Anniversary Edition	1998	$85	$55
Angelic Harpist 450QXM552-4	Miniature Ornaments	1992	$4	$16
Angelic Messenger 1375QK103-2	Holiday Enchantment	1993	$14	$12
Angelic Messenger QLZ4287	Laser Creations	1999	$8	$12
Anniversary Year Photoholder QX597-2	General Line	1993	$10	$3
Anniversary Year Photoholder 975QX485-1	General Line	1992	$10	$3
Anniversary Year Photoholder QX581-9	General Line	1995	$9	$5
Anniversary Year Photoholder 1095QX568-3	General Line	1994	$11	$24
Antique Tractors 1st Ed. QXM4185	Antique Tractors	1997	$7	$16
Antique Tractors 2nd Ed. QXM4166	Antique Tractors	1998	$7	$16
Antique Tractors 3rd Ed. QXM4567	Antique Tractors	1999	$7	$11
Antlers Aweigh! QX590-1	General Line	1996	$10	$18
Apollo Lunar Module 3rd Ed. QLX754-3	Journeys Into Space	1998	$24	$32
Appaloosa 6th Ed. 450QXM511-2	Rocking Horse Miniatures	1993	$4	$12
Apple Blossom Lane 1st Ed. QEO820-7	Apple Blossom Lane	1995	$9	$12
Apple Blossom Lane 2nd Ed. QEO808-4	Apple Blossom Lane	1996	$9	$10
Apple Blossom Lane 3rd Ed. QEO8662	Apple Blossom Lane	1997	$9	$10
Apple For Teacher 775QX590-2	General Line	1993	$8	$11

Christmas Memories, 1990, **$55.**

Comet, 1990, 5th in the Reindeer Champs series, **$29.**

Fabulous Decade, 1990, **$24.**

Hop 'N Pop Popper, 1990, **$30.**

Chris Mouse Wreath, 1990, 6th in the Chris Mouse series, **$39.**

Ornament Title	Series	Year	Issue Price	Current Value
Apple For Teacher QX612-1	General Line	1996	$8	$8
April Showers QEO826-3	Easter Ornaments	1995	$7	$5
Arctic Artist QXC4527	Collector's Club	1999	N/A	$9
Arctic Dome 2500QLX711-7	Magic Ornaments	1991	$25	$34
Ariel, The Little Mermaid QXI4072	General Line	1997	$13	$11
Arizona Cardinals QSR5505	NFL Collection	1997	$10	$10
Arizona Cardinals QSR6484	NFL Collection	1996	$10	$9
Arizona Wildcats QSR2429	Collegiate Collection	1999	$10	$5
Armful Of Joy 975QXC445-3	Collector's Club	1990	$10	$20
Atlanta Falcons QSR5305	NFL Collection	1997	$10	$10
Atlanta Falcons QSR6364	NFL Collection	1996	$10	$9
Away In A Manger 1600QLX738-3	Magic Ornaments	1994	$16	$34
Away In A Manger QK109-7	Holiday Enchantment	1995	$14	$25
Away To The Window QXC5135	Collector's Club	1997	N/A	$8
Babe Ruth 1st Ed. 1295QX532-3	Baseball Heroes	1994	$13	$20
Babs Bunny 575QXM411-6	Tiny Toon Adventure	1994	$6	$7
Baby Bear QP615-7	Personalized Ornaments	1995	$13	$14
Baby Block Photoholder 1495QP603-5	Personalized Ornaments	1994	$15	$16
Baby Block Photoholder QP603-5	Personalized Ornaments	1993	$15	$16
Baby Mickey's Sweet Dreams QXD4087	Mickey & Co.	1999	$11	$11
Baby Sylvester QXM415-4	Looney Tunes Lovables	1996	$6	$10
Baby Tweety QXM401-4	Looney Tunes Lovables	1996	$6	$16
Baby Unicorn 975QX548-6	General Line	1990	$10	$10
Baby's 1st Christmas Photoholder BBY147-0	Baby Celebrations	1993	$10	$9
Baby's 1st Christmas Photoholder QX464-1	Commemoratives	1992	$8	$12
Baby's Christening 1000BBY132-6	Baby Celebrations	1990	$10	$8
Baby's Christening 1200BBY291-7	Baby Celebrations	1993	$12	$9
Baby's Christening Lamb 1000BBY131-7	Baby Celebrations	1991	$10	$8
Baby's Christening Photoholder BBY 133-5	Baby Celebrations	1993	$10	$9
Baby's Christening-White Heart BBY133-1	Baby Celebrations	1992	$8	$14
Baby's First Christmas 1075QX551-5	General Line	1993	$11	$12
Baby's First Christmas 1295QX574-3	General Line	1994	$13	$18
Baby's First Christmas 1775QX510-7	Commemoratives	1991	$18	$18
Baby's First Christmas 1875QX458-1	Commemoratives	1992	$19	$20
Baby's First Christmas 1875QX551-2	General Line	1993	$19	$28
Baby's First Christmas 1895QX563-3	General Line	1994	$19	$22
Baby's First Christmas 2000QLX746-6	Magic Ornaments	1994	$20	$19
Baby's First Christmas 2200QLX728-1	Magic Ornaments	1992	$22	$55
Baby's First Christmas 2200QLX736-5	Magic Ornaments	1993	$22	$25
Baby's First Christmas 2800QLX724-6	Magic Ornaments	1990	$28	$35
Baby's First Christmas 3000QLX724-7	Magic Ornaments	1991	$30	$55
Baby's First Christmas 450QXM5494	Miniature Ornaments	1992	$4	$20
Baby's First Christmas 575QXM400-3	Miniature Ornaments	1994	$6	$10
Baby's First Christmas 575QXM514-5	Miniature Ornaments	1993	$6	$10
Baby's First Christmas 600QXM579-9	Miniature Ornaments	1991	$6	$12
Baby's First Christmas 675QX303-6	Commemoratives	1990	$7	$12

Popcorn Party, 1990, 5th in the Mr. and Mrs. Claus series, **$40.**

Elfin Whittler, 1990, **$25.**

Gentle Dreamers, 1990, **$24.**

Ornament Title	Series	Year	Issue Price	Current Value
Baby's First Christmas 775QX464-4	Commemoratives	1992	$8	$25
Baby's First Christmas 775QX485-6	Commemoratives	1990	$8	$40
Baby's First Christmas 775QX488-9	Commemoratives	1991	$8	$35
Baby's First Christmas 775QX552-5	General Line	1993	$8	$25
Baby's First Christmas 795QX571-3	Baby's First Christmas	1994	$8	$35
Baby's First Christmas 850QXM570-3	Miniature Ornaments	1990	$8	$6
Baby's First Christmas 975QX485-3	Commemoratives	1990	$10	$15
Baby's First Christmas Moon 1400BBY291-9	Baby Celebrations	1993	$14	$17
Baby's First Christmas Musical QLX731-7	Baby's First Christmas	1995	$22	$20
Baby's First Christmas Photoholder QX552 2	General Line	1993	$8	$18
Baby's First Christmas QLX740-4	Magic Ornaments	1996	$22	$23
Baby's First Christmas QX554-7	Handcrafted Ornaments	1995	$19	$34
Baby's First Christmas QX555-7	Handcrafted Ornaments	1995	$10	$12
Baby's First Christmas QX555-9	Teddy Bear Years Collection	1995	$8	$22
Baby's First Christmas QX574-4	General Line	1996	$19	$13
Baby's First Christmas QX575-4	General Line	1996	$10	$20
Baby's First Christmas QX576-1 Photoholder	General Line	1996	$8	$8
Baby's First Christmas QX576-4	General Line	1996	$8	$31
Baby's First Christmas QX6233	General Line	1998	$10	$10
Baby's First Christmas QX6482	General Line	1997	$8	$18
Baby's First Christmas QX6485	General Line	1997	$10	$18
Baby's First Christmas QX6492	General Line	1997	$10	$10
Baby's First Christmas QX6495	General Line	1997	$8	$18
Baby's First Christmas QX6535	General Line	1997	$15	$14
Baby's First Christmas QX6586	General Line	1998	$10	$15
Baby's First Christmas QX6596	General Line	1998	$9	$10
Baby's First Christmas QX6603	Child's Age Collection	1998	$8	$35
Baby's First Christmas QX6647	General Line	1999	$19	$19
Baby's First Christmas QX6649	General Line	1999	$8	$15
Baby's First Christmas QX6657	General Line	1999	$9	$15
Baby's First Christmas QX6659	General Line	1999	$10	$15
Baby's First Christmas QX6667	General Line	1999	$8	$18
Baby's First Christmas QXM4027	Miniature Ornaments	1995	$5	$7
Baby's First Christmas Rabbit BBY291-8	Baby Celebrations	1993	$12	$17
Baby's First Christmas: Baby Boy QX206-3	Commemoratives	1990	$5	$15
Baby's First Christmas: Baby Girl QX206-6	Commemoratives	1990	$5	$15
Baby's First Christmas: Photoholder QX554-9	General Line	1995	$8	$15
Baby's First Christmas-Baby Boy QX231-9	General Line	1995	$5	$15
Baby's First Christmas-Baby Girl QX231-7	General Line	1995	$5	$15
Baby's First Christmas-Blue Pony BBY145-6	Baby Celebrations	1992	$8	$19
Baby's First Christmas-Boy 475QX219-1	Commemoratives	1992	$5	$15
Baby's First Christmas-Boy 475QX221-7	Commemoratives	1991	$5	$15
Baby's First Christmas-Boy 500QX243-6	Baby's First Christmas	1994	$5	$20
Baby's First Christmas-Boy Pony BBY141-6	Baby Celebrations	1991	$10	$18

Santa Special, 1991, **$40.**

Cinnamon Bear, 1990, 8th in the Porcelain Bear series, **$14.**

Fire Station, 1991, 8th in the Nostalgic Houses and Shops series, **$55.**

Mrs. Beaumont, 1991, from the Dickens Caroler Bells series, **$30.**

Ornament Title	Series	Year	Issue Price	Current Value
Baby's First Christmas-Boy Pony BBY145-4	Baby Celebrations	1990	$10	$25
Baby's First Christmas-Boy QX210-5	General Line	1993	$5	$15
Baby's First Christmas-Bunny 850BBY155-7	Baby Celebrations	1992	$8	$19
Baby's First Christmas-Girl 475QX209-2	General Line	1993	$5	$15
Baby's First Christmas-Girl 475QX220-4	Commemoratives	1992	$5	$14
Baby's First Christmas-Girl 475QX222-7	Commemoratives	1991	$5	$15
Baby's First Christmas-Girl 500QX243-3	Baby's First Christmas	1994	$5	$15
Baby's First Christmas-Girl Bunny BBY151	Baby Celebrations	1991	$10	$25
Baby's First Christmas-Girl Bunny BBY155	Baby Celebrations	1990	$10	$28
Baby's First Easter 675QEO815-3	Easter Ornaments	1994	$7	$10
Baby's First Easter 675QEO834-5	Easter Ornaments	1993	$7	$10
Baby's First Easter 675QEO927-1	Easter Ornaments	1992	$7	$11
Baby's First Easter 875QEO518-9	Easter Ornaments	1991	$9	$18
Baby's First Easter QEO823-7	Easter Ornaments	1995	$8	$10
Baby's First Xmas Photoholder 775QX484-3	Commemoratives	1990	$8	$19
Baby's First Xmas-Photoholder 775QX486-9	Commemoratives	1991	$8	$6
Baby's Second Christmas 675QX465-1	Commemoratives	1992	$7	$24
Baby's Second Christmas 675QX486-3	Commemoratives	1990	$7	$22
Baby's Second Christmas 675QX489-7	Commemoratives	1991	$7	$25
Baby's Second Christmas 675QX599-2	General Line	1993	$7	$19
Baby's Second Christmas 795QX571-6	Teddy Bear Years Collection	1994	$8	$25
Baby's Second Christmas QX556-7	Teddy Bear Years Collection	1995	$8	$17
Baby's Second Christmas QX577-1	General Line	1996	$8	$10
Baby's Second Christmas QX6502	General Line	1997	$8	$15
Baby's Second Christmas QX6606	Child's Age Collection	1998	$8	$20
Baby's Second Christmas QX6609	General Line	1999	$0	$15
Backyard Bunny 675QEO840-5	Easter Ornaments	1993	$7	$12
Backyard Orchard QK106-9	Nature's Sketchbook	1995	$19	$28
Baking Tiny Treats QXM403-3 Set Of Six	Miniature Ornaments	1994	$29	$44
Balthasar-The Magi QX8037	Blessed Nativity Collection	1999	$13	$10
Balthazar (Frankincense) QK1174	Magi Bells	1996	$14	$20
Baltimore Ravens QSR5352	NFL Collection	1997	$10	$7
Bandleader Mickey 1st Ed. QXD4022	Mickey's Holiday Parade	1997	$14	$15
Barbie 1st In Ed. QX500-6	Barbie	1994	$15	$17
Barbie & Ken Wedding Day QXI6815	Barbie	1997	$35	$38
Barbie Anniversary Edition Lunchbox QEO8399	Easter Ornaments	1999	$13	$13
Barbie As Rapunzel #1 QEO8635	Barbie	1997	$15	$16
Barbie Doll Dreamhouse Playhouse QXI8047	Barbie	1999	$15	$19
Barbie: Brunette Debut 1959 QXC539-7	Collector's Club	1995	$15	$39
Barbie: Enchanted Evening 3rd In Ed. QXI654-1	Barbie	1996	$15	$16
Barbie: Solo In Spotlight 2nd In Ed. QXI504-9	Barbie	1995	$15	$15
Barney 2400QLX750-6	Magic Ornaments	1994	$24	$45
Barney 995QX596-6	General Line	1994	$10	$14

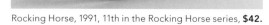

Rocking Horse, 1991, 11th in the Rocking Horse series, **$42.**

Cupid, 1991, 6th in the Reindeer Champs series, **$22.**

1957 Corvette, 1991, 1st in the Classic American Cars series, **$80.**

Beary Artistic, 1991, Hallmark Keepsake Ornament Collectors Club, **$19.**

Snow Twins, 1991, **$15.**

Ornament Title	Series	Year	Issue Price	Current Value
Barrel-Back Rider QX518-9	Handcrafted Ornaments	1995	$10	$12
Barrow Of Giggles 875QEO840-2	Easter Ornaments	1993	$9	$12
Bashful Gift-Set Of Two 1195QEO8446	Easter Ornaments	1998	$12	$8
Basket Bell Players 775QX537-7	General Line	1991	$8	$9
Basket Buddy 600QXM569-6	Miniature Ornaments	1990	$6	$12
Batman 1295QX585-3	Batman	1994	$13	$20
Batmobile QX573-9	Batman	1995	$15	$17
Batter Up! QEO8389	Peanuts Collection	1999	$13	$14
Bear Bell Champ 775QX507-1	General Line	1992	$8	$24
Bear Hug 600QXM563-3	Miniature Ornaments	1990	$6	$8
Bearback Rider 975QX548-3	General Line	1990	$10	$10
Bearnadette/Daughter 495XPR974-8	Bearingers Of Victoria Circle	1993	$5	$6
Beary Artistic 1000QXC725-9	Collector's Club	1991	$10	$19
Beary Gifted 775QX576-2	General Line	1993	$8	$10
Beary Good Deal 675QX473-3	General Line	1990	$7	$12
Beary Perfect Tree 475QXM407-6	Miniature Ornaments	1994	$5	$7
Beary Short Nap 1000QLX732-6	Magic Ornaments	1990	$10	$30
Bearymores, The 1st Ed. 575QXM554-4	Bearymores	1992	$6	$8
Bearymores, The 2nd Ed. 575QXM512-5	Bearymores	1993	$6	$9
Bearymores, The 3rd & Final Ed. 575QXM513-3	Bearymores	1994	$6	$16
Beatles Gift Set QX537-3	Handcrafted Ornaments	1994	$48	$63
Beautiful Memories Photoholder 675QEO836-2	Easter Ornaments	1993	$7	$5
Belle Bunny 975QEO935-4	Easter Ornaments	1992	$10	$18
Bells Are Ringing 2800QLX740-2	Magic Ornaments	1993	$28	$58
Benjamin Bunny 3rd Ed. 895QEO8383	Beatrix Potter	1998	$9	$15
Best Pals QX6879	General Line	1999	$19	$44
Best-Dressed Turtle 575QEO839-2	Easter Ornaments	1993	$6	$12
Betsey Clark: Home For Christmas 5th Ed. 500QX203-3	Betsey Clark: Home For Christmas	1990	$5	$12
Betsey Clark: Home For Christmas 6th & Final Ed. 500QX210-9	Betsey Clark: Home For Christmas	1991	$5	$10
Betsey's Country Christmas 1st Ed. 500QX210-4	Betsy's Country Christmas	1992	$5	$14
Betsey's Country Christmas 2nd Ed. 500QX206-2	Betsy's Country Christmas	1993	$5	$10
Betsey's Country Christmas 3rd Ed. 500QX240-3	Betsy's Country Christmas	1994	$5	$12
Betsey's Perfect 10 QXM4609	Miniature Ornaments	1999	$5	$8
Betsey's Prayer QXM4263	Miniature Ornaments	1998	$5	$6
Betty & Wilma QX541-7	Flintstones	1995	$15	$15
Beverly & Teddy QX525-9	Special Edition	1995	$22	$18
Big Cheese, The 675QX532-7	Commemoratives	1991	$7	$8
Big On Gardening 975QX584-2	General Line	1993	$10	$10
Big Roller 875QX535-2	General Line	1993	$9	$8
Big Shot 795QX587-3	Handcrafted Ornaments	1994	$8	$10

Chris Mouse Mail, 1991, 7th in the Chris Mouse series, **$34.**

Checking His List, 1991, 6th in the Mr. and Mrs. Claus series, **$20.**

Piglet and Eeyore, 1991, Winnie the Pooh, **$25.**

Polar Circus Wagon, 1991, from the Artists' Favorites series, **$10.**

Ornament Title	Series	Year	Issue Price	Current Value
Biking Buddies QX6682	General Line	1997	$13	$15
Bill Elliott 3rd & Final Ed. QXI4039	Stock Car Champions	1999	$16	$21
Billboard Bunny 775QX519-6	General Line	1990	$8	$10
Bingo Bear QX591-9	Handcrafted Ornaments	1995	$8	$10
Bird Watcher 975QX525-2	General Line	1993	$10	$9
Birds' Christmas Tree, The QK111-4	Nature's Sketchbook	1996	$19	$19
Birthday Celebration QEO8409	World Of Wishes	1999	$9	$0
Black-Capped Chickadee 300QXM548-4	Miniature Ornaments	1992	$3	$14
Bless You 675QEO929-1	Easter Ornaments	1992	$7	$14
Blessings Of Love 1400QLX736-3	Magic Ornaments	1990	$14	$35
Blitzen 8th & Final Ed. 875QX433-1	Reindeer Champs	1993	$9	$13
Bob Cratchit 1375QX499-7	Christmas Carol Collection, A	1991	$14	$15
Boba Fett QXI4053	General Line	1998	$15	$13
Bobbin' Along QX587-9	Handcrafted Ornaments	1995	$9	$19
Book Of The Year QX6645	General Line	1997	$8	$15
Born To Dance 775QX504-3	General Line	1990	$8	$10
Bounce Pass QX603-1	General Line	1996	$8	$6
Bouncy Baby Sitter QXD4096	General Line	1998	$13	$14
Bouquet Of Memories 795QEO8456	Easter Ornaments	1998	$8	$9
Bowl'Em Over QX601-4	General Line	1996	$8	$8
Bowling For Zzzs 775QX556-5	General Line	1993	$8	$12
Bowling's A Ball QX6577	General Line	1999	$8	$12
Box Car 4th Ed. QXM5441	Noel Railroad	1992	$7	$12
Brass Bells 300QXM597-7	Miniature Ornaments	1991	$3	$5
Brass Bouquet 600QXM577-6	Miniature Ornaments	1990	$6	$5
Brass Church 300QXM597-9	Miniature Ornaments	1991	$3	$6
Brass Horn 300QXM579-3	Miniature Ornaments	1990	$3	$5
Brass Peace 300QXM579-6	Miniature Ornaments	1990	$3	$9
Brass Santa 300QXM578-6	Miniature Ornaments	1990	$3	$6
Brass Soldier 300QXM598-7	Miniature Ornaments	1991	$3	$10
Brass Year 300QXM583-3	Miniature Ornaments	1990	$3	$4
Breezin' Along QX6722	General Line	1997	$9	$14
Bright Blazing Colors 4th Ed. 975QX426-4	Crayola Crayon	1992	$10	$25
Bright Boxers 450QXM587-7	Miniature Ornaments	1991	$4	$9
Bright Flying Colors 8th Ed. QX539-1	Crayola Crayon	1996	$11	$16
Bright Moving Colors 2nd Ed. 875QX458-6	Crayola Crayon	1990	$9	$35
Bright N'sunny Tepee 7th Ed. QX524-7	Crayola Crayon	1995	$11	$12
Bright Playful Colors 6th Ed. 1095QX527-3	Crayola Crayon	1994	$11	$20
Bright Rocking Colors 9th Ed. QX6235	Crayola Crayon	1997	$13	$16
Bright Shining Castle 5th Ed. 1075QX442-2	Crayola Crayon	1993	$11	$16
Bright Sledding Colors 10th & Final Ed. QX6166	Crayola Crayon	1998	$13	$16
Bright Stringers 375QXM584-1	Miniature Ornaments	1992	$4	$14
Bright Vibrant Carols 3rd Ed. 975QX421-9	Crayola Crayon	1991	$10	$25
Bringing Home The Tree 1375QK104-2	Holiday Enchantment	1993	$14	$10
Bringing Home The Tree 2800QLX724-9	Magic Ornaments	1991	$28	$60

Tigger, 1991, Winnie the Pooh, **$50.**

Rabbit, 1991, Winnie the Pooh, **$20.**

Christopher Robin, 1991, Winnie the Pooh, **$20.**

Winnie-the-Pooh, 1991, **$25.**

Kanga and Roo, 1991, Winnie the Pooh, **$20.**

Ornament Title	Series	Year	Issue Price	Current Value
British Soldier 1st Ed. QXM4097	Miniature Clothespin Soldier	1995	$4	$12
Brother 575QX449-3	Commemoratives	1990	$6	$9
Brother 675QX468-4	Commemoratives	1992	$7	$9
Brother 675QX547-9	Commemoratives	1991	$7	$12
Brother 675QX554-2	General Line	1993	$7	$5
Brother 695QX551-6	Handcrafted Ornaments	1994	$7	$6
Brother QX567-9	Handcrafted Ornaments	1995	$7	$7
Brown Spotted 8th Ed. QXM4827	Rocking Horse Miniatures	1995	$5	$9
Browns QSR639-1	NFL Collection	1996	$10	$9
Brownspotted Rocker 5th Ed. 4500XM5454	Rocking Horse Miniatures	1992	$4	$9
Buck-A-Roo 450QXM581-4	Miniature Ornaments	1992	$4	$7
Bucket Brigade QX6382	General Line	1997	$9	$8
Buffalo Bills QSR5312	NFL Collection	1997	$10	$10
Buffalo Bills QSR637-1	NFL Collection	1996	$10	$9
Bugs Bunny 875QX541-2	Looney Tunes	1993	$10	$15
Bugs Bunny QEO827-9	Easter Ornaments	1995	$9	$10
Bugs Bunny QX501-9	Looney Tunes	1995	$9	$12
Bugs Bunny QX644-3	Looney Tunes	1998	$14	$5
Building A Snowman QXD4133	Disney Collection	1998	$15	$16
Bumper Crop QEO8735	Tender Touches	1997	N/A	$12
Buster Bunny 575QXM516-3	Tiny Toon Adventure	1994	$6	$6
Busy Batter 795QX587-6	Handcrafted Ornaments	1994	$8	$14
Busy Bear 450QXM593-9	Miniature Ornaments	1991	$4	$11
Busy Carver 450QXM567-3	Miniature Ornaments	1990	$4	$6
Buzz Lightyear QXD4066	Toy Story	1998	$15	$24
C-3PO & R2-D2 QXI1426 6	Miniature Ornaments	1997	$13	$23
Caboose 10th & Final Ed. QXM4216	Noel Railroad	1998	$7	$12
Caboose 395XPR973-3	Claus & Co. R.R. Ornaments	1991	$4	$10
Caboose 5th & Final Ed. QX6373	Yuletide Central	1998	$19	$19
Caboose 975QX532-1	Christmas Sky Line Collection	1992	$10	$15
Cafe 14th Ed. QX6245	Nostalgic Houses & Shops	1997	$17	$19
Cal Ripken Jr. QXI4033	At The Ballpark	1998	$15	$23
Camellia 8th Ed. QX514-9	Mary's Angels	1995	$7	$25
Canadian Mountie 3rd Ed. QXM4155	Miniature Clothespin Soldier	1997	$5	$7
Candy Cane Lookout 1800QLX737-6	Magic Ornaments	1994	$18	$59
Candy Caper 895QX577-6	Handcrafted Ornaments	1994	$9	$12
Candy Car 9th Ed. QXM417-5	Noel Railroad	1997	$7	$14
Captain James T. Kirk QXI553-9	Star Trek	1995	$14	$16
Captain Jean-Luc Picard QXI573-7	Star Trek	1995	$14	$14
Captain John Smith & Meeko QXI617-9	Pocahontas	1995	$13	$10
Captain Kathryn Janeway QXI4046	Star Trek	1998	$15	$20
Cardinal Cameo 600QXM595-7	Miniature Ornaments	1991	$6	$9
Caring Doctor 895QX582-3	Handcrafted Ornaments	1994	$9	$5
Caring Nurse 675QX578-5	General Line	1993	$7	$18
Caring Shepherd 600QXM594-9	Miniature Ornaments	1991	$6	$16
Carmen QK116-4	Cookie Jar Friends	1996	$16	$12

Santa Claus, 1992, from the Santa and His Reindeer Collection, **$9.**

Comet & Cupid, 1992, from the Santa and His Reindeer Collection, **$14.**

Prancer & Vixen, 1992, from the Santa and His Reindeer Collection, **$15.**

Dasher & Dancer, 1992, from the Santa and His Reindeer Collection, **$20.**

Donder & Blitzen, 1992, from the Santa and His Reindeer Collection, **$25.**

Santa and His Reindeer Collection set, 1992, **$83.**

Ornament Title	Series	Year	Issue Price	Current Value
Carole QX114-7	Angel Bells	1995	$13	$18
Carolina Panthers QSR6227	Football Helmet Collection	1995	$10	$9
Carolina Panthers QSR5026	NFL Collection	1998	$10	$10
Carolina Panthers QSR5217	NFL Collection	1999	$11	$8
Carolina Panthers QSR5315	NFL Collection	1997	$10	$10
Carolina Panthers QSR637-4	NFL Collection	1996	$10	$9
Caroling Angel QK113-4	Folk Art Americana	1996	$17	$15
Casablanca Set Of 3 QXM4272	Miniature Ornaments	1997	$20	$19
Caspar (Myrrh) QK118-4	Magi Bells	1996	$14	$13
Caspar-The Magi QX8039	Blessed Nativity Collection	1999	$13	$13
Cat In The Hat 1st Ed. QX16457	Dr. Seuss Books	1999	$15	$14
Cat Naps 1st Ed. 795QX531-3	Cat Naps	1994	$8	$20
Cat Naps 2nd Ed. QX509-7	Cat Naps	1995	$8	$15
Cat Naps 3rd Ed. QX564-1	Cat Naps	1996	$8	$16
Cat Naps 4th Ed. QX620-5	Cat Naps	1997	$9	$14
Cat Naps 5th Ed. QX6373	Cat Naps	1998	$9	$12
Catch Of The Day QX6712	General Line	1997	$10	$13
Catch Of The Season QX6786	General Line	1998	$15	$18
Catch The Spirit QX589-9	Handcrafted Ornaments	1995	$8	$14
Catching 40 Winks 1675QK118-3	Folk Art Americana	1994	$17	$20
Celebration Of Angels, A 1st Ed. QX5077	Celebration Of Angels	1995	$13	$15
Celebration Of Angels, A 2nd Ed. QX5634	Celebration Of Angels	1996	$13	$10
Celebration Of Angels, A 3rd Ed. QX6175	Celebration Of Angels	1997	$14	$15
Celebration Of Angels, A 4th Ed. QX6366	Celebration Of Angels	1998	$14	$12
Celestial Kitty QXM4639	Miniature Ornaments	1999	$7	$9
Centennial Games Atlanta 1996 QX316-9	Olympic Spirit Collection	1995	$8	$5
Centuries Of Santa 1st Ed. QXM5153	Centuries Of Santa	1994	$6	$18
Centuries Of Santa 2nd Ed. QXM4789	Centuries Of Santa	1995	$6	$11
Centuries Of Santa 3rd Ed. QXM4091	Centuries Of Santa	1996	$6	$9
Centuries Of Santa 4th Ed. QXM4295	Centuries Of Santa	1997	$6	$9
Centuries Of Santa 5th Ed. QXM4206	Centuries Of Santa	1998	$6	$8
Centuries Of Santa 6h & Final Ed. QXM4589	Centuries Of Santa	1999	$6	$10
Champ, The QP604-6	Personalized Ornaments	1995	$13	$14
Champion Teacher 695QX583-6	Handcrafted Ornaments	1994	$7	$14
Charlie Brown QRP420-7	A Charlie Brown Christmas	1995	$4	$24
Charlotte Hornets QSR1057	NBA Collection	1999	$11	$4
Charlotte Hornets QSR1222	NBA Collection	1997	$10	$4
Chatty Chipmunk QX6716	General Line	1998	$10	$12
Checking His List 6th Ed. 1375QX433-9	Mr. & Mrs. Claus	1991	$14	$20
Checking Santa's Files QX6806	General Line	1998	$9	$6
Cheerful Santa 975QX515-4	General Line	1992	$10	$24
Cheers To You! 1095QX579-6	Handcrafted Ornaments	1994	$11	$10
Cheery Cyclists 1295QX578-6	Handcrafted Ornaments	1994	$13	$15
Cheese Please 375QXM407-2	Miniature Ornaments	1993	$4	$6
Cheshire Cat 4th & Final Ed. QXM4186	Alice In Wonderland	1998	$10	$8
Chewbacca QXI4009	General Line	1999	$15	$15

Child's Fourth Christmas, 1992, **$12.**

Granddaughter's First Christmas, 1992, **$10.**

Santa Maria, 1992, **$9.**

Gift Exchange, 1992, 7th in the Mr. & Mrs. Claus series, **$20.**

Owl, 1992, Winnie the Pooh, **$20.**

Sew, Sew Tiny set of six ornaments, 1992, **$25.**

Ornament Title	Series	Year	Issue Price	Current Value
Chicago Bears QSR6237	Football Helmet Collection	1995	$10	$24
Chicago Bears QSR5033	NFL Collection	1998	$10	$10
Chicago Bears QSR5219	NFL Collection	1999	$11	$8
Chicago Bears QSR5322	NFL Collection	1997	$10	$10
Chicago Bears QSR638-1	NFL Collection	1996	$10	$9
Chicago Bulls QSR1019	NBA Collection	1999	$11	$4
Chicago Bulls QSR1232	NBA Collection	1997	$10	$4
Chicken Coop Chorus QLX749-1	Magic Ornaments	1996	$25	$30
Chicks-On-A-Twirl 775QEO837-5	Easter Ornaments	1993	$8	$8
Child Care Giver 675QX316-6	Commemoratives	1990	$7	$8
Child Care Giver 795QX590-6	Handcrafted Ornaments	1994	$8	$6
Child Care Giver QX607-1	General Line	1996	$9	$4
Child Is Born, A QX617-6	General Line	1998	$13	$26
Child Of Wonder QX6817	General Line	1999	$15	$28
Childhood Treasures QBG4237	Crown Reflections	1999	$30	$19
Children's Express 2800QLX724-3	Magic Ornaments	1990	$28	$45
Child's Christmas 975QX457-4	Commemoratives	1992	$10	$17
Child's Christmas 975QX488-7	Commemoratives	1991	$10	$9
Child's Christmas, A QX588-2	Handcrafted Ornaments	1993	$10	$9
Child's Fifth Christmas 675QX466-4	Commemoratives	1992	$7	$12
Child's Fifth Christmas 675QX487-6	Commemoratives	1990	$7	$15
Child's Fifth Christmas 675QX490-9	Commemoratives	1991	$7	$12
Child's Fifth Christmas 675QX522-2	General Line	1993	$7	$12
Child's Fifth Christmas 695QX573-3	Teddy Bear Years Collection	1994	$7	$6
Child's Fifth Christmas QX563-7	Teddy Bear Years Collection	1995	$7	$13
Child's Fifth Christmas QX678-4	General Line	1996	$7	$10
Child's Fifth Christmas QX6515	General Line	1997	$8	$11
Child's Fifth Christmas QX6623	Child's Age Collection	1998	$8	$15
Child's Fifth Christmas QX6679	General Line	1999	$8	$15
Child's Fourth Christmas 675QX466-1	Commemoratives	1992	$7	$12
Child's Fourth Christmas 675QX487-3	Commemoratives	1990	$7	$12
Child's Fourth Christmas 675QX490-7	Commemoratives	1991	$7	$12
Child's Fourth Christmas 675QX521-5	General Line	1993	$7	$12
Child's Fourth Christmas 695QX572-6	Teddy Bear Years Collection	1994	$7	$9
Child's Fourth Christmas QX562-9	Teddy Bear Years Collection	1995	$7	$16
Child's Fourth Christmas QX578-1	General Line	1996	$8	$12
Child's Fourth Christmas QX6512	General Line	1997	$8	$13
Child's Fourth Christmas QX6616	Child's Age Collection	1998	$8	$15
Child's Fourth Christmas QX6687	General Line	1999	$8	$15
Child's Gifts, A QXM423-4	Miniature Ornaments	1996	$7	$6
Child's Third Christmas 675QX465-4	Commemoratives	1992	$7	$20
Child's Third Christmas 675QX486-6	Commemoratives	1990	$7	$20
Child's Third Christmas 675QX489-9	Commemoratives	1991	$7	$15
Child's Third Christmas 675QX599-5	General Line	1993	$7	$15
Child's Third Christmas 695QX572-3	Teddy Bear Years Collection	1994	$7	$16
Child's Third Christmas QX562-7	Teddy Bear Years Collection	1995	$8	$16

Five and Ten Cent Store, 1992, 9th in the Nostalgic Houses and Shops series, **$32.**

Frosty Friends, 1992, 13th in the Frosty Friends series, **$30.**

Baby's First Christmas, 1992, **$12.**

Chris Mouse Tales, 1992, 8th in the Chris Mouse series, **$15.**

Ornament Title	Series	Year	Issue Price	Current Value
Child's Third Christmas QX577-4	General Line	1996	$8	$11
Child's Third Christmas QX6505	General Line	1997	$8	$12
Child's Third Christmas QX6613	Child's Age Collection	1998	$8	$15
Child's Third Christmas QX6677	General Line	1999	$8	$10
Chilly Chap 675QX533-9	General Line	1991	$7	$15
Chiming In 975QX436-6	General Line	1990	$10	$15
Chinese Barbie 2nd Ed. QX6162	Dolls Of The World	1997	$15	$18
Chipmunk Parcel Service QXC519-4	Collector's Club	1992	$7	$10
Chris Mouse Flight 9th Ed. 1200QLX715-2	Chris Mouse	1993	$12	$17
Chris Mouse Inn 12th Ed. QLX737-1	Chris Mouse	1996	$14	$20
Chris Mouse Jelly 10th Ed. 1200QLX739-3	Chris Mouse	1994	$12	$15
Chris Mouse Luminaria 13th & Final Ed. QLX752-5	Chris Mouse	1997	$15	$18
Chris Mouse Mail 7th Ed. 1000QLX720-7	Chris Mouse	1991	$10	$34
Chris Mouse Tales 8th Ed. 1200QLX707-4	Chris Mouse	1992	$12	$15
Chris Mouse Tree 11th Ed. QLX730-7	Chris Mouse	1995	$12	$16
Chris Mouse Wreath 6th Ed. 1000QLX729-6	Chris Mouse	1990	$10	$39
Christkindl 2nd Ed. QX563-1	Christmas Visitors	1996	$15	$13
Christkindl 3rd Ed. 500QX211-7	Gift Bringers	1991	$5	$10
Christmas Bear QXM424-1	Miniature Ornaments	1996	$5	$6
Christmas Bells 1st Ed. QXM4007	Christmas Bells	1995	$5	$25
Christmas Bells 2nd Ed. QXM4071	Christmas Bells	1996	$5	$19
Christmas Bells 3rd Ed. QXM4162	Christmas Bells	1997	$5	$12
Christmas Bells 4th Ed. QXM4196	Christmas Bells	1998	$5	$10
Christmas Bells 5th Ed. QXM4489	Christmas Bells	1999	$5	$8
Christmas Donus 300QXM501-1	Miniature Ornaments	1992	$3	$5
Christmas Break 775QX582-5	General Line	1993	$8	$12
Christmas Bunny QK110-4	Nature's Sketchbook	1996	$19	$29
Christmas Cardinal QK107-7	Nature's Sketchbook	1995	$19	$34
Christmas Castle 575QXM408-5	Miniature Ornaments	1993	$6	$9
Christmas Checkup QX6385	General Line	1997	$8	$14
Christmas Copter 575QXM584-4	Miniature Ornaments	1992	$6	$8
Christmas Croc 775QX437-3	General Line	1990	$8	$14
Christmas Dove 450QXM563-6	Miniature Ornaments	1990	$4	$15
Christmas Eve Bake-Off QXC4049	Collector's Club	1995	$55	$75
Christmas Eve Kiss 10th & Final Ed. QX515-7	Mr. & Mrs. Claus	1995	$15	$15
Christmas Eve Story: Becky Kelly QX6873	General Line	1998	$14	$16
Christmas Feast 1575QK115-2	Portraits In Bisque	1993	$16	$9
Christmas Fever QX596-7	Handcrafted Ornaments	1995	$8	$6
Christmas In Bloom QLZ4257	Laser Creations	1999	$9	$8
Christmas Joy QX624-1	Collector's Choice	1996	$15	$14
Christmas Kitty 2nd Ed. 1475QX450-6	Christmas Kitty	1990	$15	$12
Christmas Kitty 3rd Ed. 1475QX437-7	Christmas Kitty	1991	$15	$24
Christmas Limited 1975QXC476-6	Collector's Club	1990	$20	$100
Christmas Memories 2500QLX727-6	Magic Ornaments	1990	$25	$55
Christmas Morning QX599-7	Handcrafted Ornaments	1995	$11	$9

1966 Mustang, 1992, 2nd in the Classic American Cars series, **$30.**

Rodney Takes Flight, 1992, **$15.**

Donder, 1992, 7th in the Reindeer Champs series, **$21.**

Fabulous Decade, 1992, **$45.**

Ornament Title	Series	Year	Issue Price	Current Value
Christmas Parade 3000QLX727-1	Magic Ornaments	1992	$30	$29
Christmas Partridge 775QX524-6	General Line	1990	$8	$10
Christmas Patrol QX595-9	Handcrafted Ornaments	1995	$8	$10
Christmas Request QX6193	General Line	1998	$15	$9
Christmas Sleigh Ride QX6556	General Line	1998	$13	$10
Christmas Snowman QX621-4	Marjolein Bastin	1996	$10	$19
Christmas Story, The QX6897	Collector's Choice	1999	$22	$28
Christmas Treasures 2200QXC546-4	Collector's Club	1992	$22	$100
Christmas Welcome 975QX529-9	General Line	1991	$10	$10
Christopher Robin 975QX557-9	General Line	1991	$10	$20
Christy QX556-4	All God's Children	1996	$13	$15
Church 5th Ed. 700QXM5384	Old English Village	1992	$7	$20
Cincinnati Bengals QSR5325	NFL Collection	1997	$10	$10
Cincinnati Bengals QSR638-4	NFL Collection	1996	$10	$9
Cinderella 1st Ed. QX631-1	Madame Alexander	1996	$15	$20
Cinderella 1st Ed. QXD4045	Enchanted Memories Collection	1997	$30	$30
Cinderella 3rd & Final Ed. QEO8327	Children's Collector Barbie	1999	$15	$20
Cinderella's Coach QXD4083	General Line	1998	$15	$22
Cinderellla At The Ball QXD7576	General Line	1998	$24	$68
Cinnamon Bear 8th & Final Ed. 875QX442-6	Porcelain Bear	1990	$9	$14
Classic Batman & Robin QXM4659	Miniature Ornaments	1999	$13	$28
Classic Cross QX6805	General Line	1997	$14	$50
Claus Construction 775QX488-5	Collectible Series	1990	$8	$8
Claus Mobile 19th Ed. QX6262	Here Comes Santa	1997	$15	$15
Clauses On Vacation 1st Ed. QX6112	Clauses On Vacation	1997	$15	$10
Clauses On Vacation 2nd Ed. QX6276	Clauses On Vacation	1998	$15	$10
Clauses On Vacation 3rd & Final Ed. QX6399	Clauses On Vacation	1999	$13	$15
Clever Camper QX6445	General Line	1997	$8	$10
Clever Cookie 775QX566-2	General Line	1993	$8	$15
Cloisonne Medallion QXE404-1	Olympic Spirit Collection	1996	$10	$10
Cloisonne Partridge QXM4017	Miniature Ornaments	1995	$10	$10
Cloisonne Poinsettia 1050QXM553-3	Miniature Ornaments	1990	$10	$9
Cloisonne Snowflake 975QXM401-2	Miniature Ornaments	1993	$10	$9
Close-Knit Friends QX587-4	General Line	1996	$10	$15
Clownin' Around Crayola Crayon QX6487	General Line	1999	$11	$11
Club Hollow QXC445-6	Collector's Club	1990	N/A	$10
Clyde QK116-1	Cookie Jar Friends	1996	$16	$12
Coach 675QX593-5	General Line	1993	$7	$5
Coach 795QX593-3	Handcrafted Ornaments	1994	$8	$9
Coal Car 2nd Ed. QXM575-6	Noel Railroad	1990	$8	$17
Coal Car 975QX540-1	Christmas Sky Line Collection	1992	$10	$8
Coca-Cola Santa 575QXM588-4	Miniature Ornaments	1992	$6	$12
Coca-Cola Time QXM4296	Miniature Ornaments	1998	$7	$10
Cock-A-Doodle Christmas QX539-6	Handcrafted Ornaments	1994	$9	$24

Winnie the Pooh, 1993, Winnie the Pooh, **$25.**

Kanga and Roo, 1993, Winnie the Pooh, **$15.**

Owl, 1993, Winnie the Pooh, **$11.**

Eeyore, 1993, Winnie the Pooh, **$15.**

Rabbit, 1993, Winnie the Pooh, **$15.**

Tigger and Piglet, 1993, Winnie the Pooh, **$28.**

Ornament Title	Series	Year	Issue Price	Current Value
Cocoa Break, Hershey's QX8009	General Line	1999	$11	$15
Collecting Memories QXC411-7	Collector's Club	1995	$20	$10
Colonial Church 2nd Ed. QXL7387	Candlelight Services	1999	$19	$22
Colorful Coal Car 2nd Ed. QEO8652	Cottontail Express	1997	$9	$9
Colorful Spring 775QEO816-6	Easter Ornaments	1994	$8	$15
Colors Of Joy 795QX589-3	Handcrafted Ornaments	1994	$8	$10
Come All Ye Faithful QX624-4	Collector's Choice	1996	$13	$14
Comet & Cupid 495XPR973-7	Santa & His Reindeer Collection	1992	$5	$14
Comet 5th Ed. 775QX443-3	Reindeer Champs	1990	$8	$29
Coming To See Santa QLX736-9	Magic Ornaments	1995	$32	$60
Commander Data QXI6345	General Line	1997	$15	$15
Commander William T. Riker QXI1555-1	Star Trek	1996	$15	$19
Compact Skater QX6766	General Line	1998	$10	$9
Computer Cat 'N' Mouse 1295QP604-6	Personalized Ornaments	1994	$13	$13
Continental Express 3200QLX726-4	Magic Ornaments	1992	$32	$76
Conversation W/Santa 2800QLX742-6	Magic Ornaments	1994	$28	$45
Cookie Car 8th Ed. QXM411-4	Noel Railroad	1996	$7	$14
Cookie Time 1295QP607-3	Personalized Ornaments	1994	$13	$13
Cookie Time QP607-3	Personalized Ornaments	1995	$13	$14
Cool Delivery Coca-Cola QXM402-1	Miniature Ornaments	1996	$6	$8
Cool Fliers 1075QX547-4	General Line	1992	$11	$10
Cool 'N' Sweet 450QXM586-7	Miniature Ornaments	1991	$4	$14
Cool Santa QXC4457	Collector's Club	1995	$6	$10
Cool Snowman 875QP605-2	Personalized Ornaments	1993	$9	$9
Cool Uncle Sam 300QXM556-1	Miniature Ornaments	1992	$3	$10
Copy Of Cheer 775QX448-6	Commemoratives	1990	$8	$9
Corny Elf 450QXM406-3	Miniature Ornaments	1994	$4	$7
Corvette Miniature QXM1433-2	Miniature Ornaments	1997	$7	$10
Cosmic Rabbit 775QEO936-4	Easter Ornaments	1992	$8	$14
Counting On Success QX6707	General Line	1999	$8	$5
Country Angel 675QX504-6	General Line	1990	$7	$120
Country Church, The 795XPR945-0	Sarah, Plain & Tall Collection	1994	$8	$15
Country Fiddling 375QXM406-2	Miniature Ornaments	1993	$4	$6
Country Heart 450QXM569-3	Miniature Ornaments	1990	$4	$5
Country Home QX5172	Nature's Sketchbook	1998	$11	$12
Country Showtime 2200QLX741-6	Magic Ornaments	1994	$22	$22
Country Sleigh 450QXM599-9	Miniature Ornaments	1991	$4	$14
Courier Turtle 450QXM585-7	Miniature Ornaments	1991	$4	$8
Cowardly Lion, The 995QX544-6	Wizard Of Oz Collection	1994	$10	$40
Cows Of Bali QX599-9	Handcrafted Ornaments	1995	$9	$4
Coyote Carols 875QX499-3	General Line	1990	$9	$9
Cozy Christmas QXC4119	Santa's Club Soda	1995	$9	$12
Cozy Cottage Teapot QK112-7	Invitation To Tea	1995	$16	$25
Cozy Goose 575QX496-6	General Line	1990	$6	$8
Cozy Home 10th Ed. 1475QX417-5	Nostalgic Houses & Shops	1993	$15	$41

Look for the Wonder, 1993, **$15.**

Frosty Friends Anniversary Edition, 1993, from the Frosty Friends series, **$29.**

Frosty Friends, 1993, 14th in the Frosty Friends series, **$29.**

The Lamplighter, 1993, **$20.**

1956 Ford Thunderbird, 1993, 3rd in the Classic American Cars series, **$19.**

Ornament Title	Series	Year	Issue Price	Current Value
Cozy Kayak 375QXM555-1	Miniature Ornaments	1992	$4	$7
Crayola Bunny 775QEO930-4	Easter Ornaments	1992	$8	$25
Crayola QX551-9	Colorful World	1995	$11	$13
Cross Of Faith QEO8467	Easter Ornaments	1999	$14	$14
Cross Of Hope QX6557	Collector's Choice	1999	$10	$18
Cross Of Peace QX6856	General Line	1998	$10	$16
Crown Prince QXC560-3	Collector's Club	1990	N/A	$15
Cruella De Vil 1st Ed. QXD4063	Unforgettable Villains	1998	$15	$19
Cruising Into Christmas QX6196	General Line	1998	$17	$14
Crystal Angel 975QXM401-5	Miniature Ornaments	1993	$10	$29
Crystal Claus QXM4637	Miniature Ornaments	1999	$10	$11
Cuddly Lamb 675QX519-9	General Line	1991	$7	$18
Cultivated Gardener 575QEO935-1	Easter Ornaments	1992	$6	$9
Cupid 6th Ed. 775QX434-7	Reindeer Champs	1991	$8	$22
Curious Raccoons Mark Newman 3rd Ed. QX6287	Majestic Wilderness	1999	$13	$13
Curly 'N' Kingly 1075QX528-5	General Line	1993	$11	$14
Curtiss R3C-2 Seaplane 3rd Ed. QX6387	Sky's The Limit	1999	$15	$38
Cute As A Button 375QXM410-3	Miniature Ornaments	1994	$4	$8
Cycling Santa QX6425	General Line	1997	$15	$22
Dad 675QX453-3	Commemoratives	1990	$7	$6
Dad 775QX467-4	Commemoratives	1992	$8	$16
Dad 775QX512-7	Commemoratives	1991	$8	$20
Dad 775QX585-5	General Line	1993	$8	$10
Dad 795QX546-3	Handcrafted Ornaments	1994	$8	$10
Dad QX564-9	Handcrafted Ornaments	1995	$8	$18
Dad QX573-1	General Line	1996	$8	$12
Dad QX6532	General Line	1997	$9	$8
Dad QX6663	General Line	1998	$9	$6
Dad QX6719	General Line	1999	$9	$10
Dad-To-Be 575QX487-9	Commemoratives	1991	$6	$9
Dad-To-Be 575QX491-3	Commemoratives	1990	$6	$10
Dad-To-Be 675QX461-1	Commemoratives	1992	$7	$11
Dad-To-Be 675QX553-2	General Line	1993	$7	$5
Dad-To-Be 795QX547-3	Handcrafted Ornaments	1994	$8	$18
Dad-To-Be QX566-7	Handcrafted Ornaments	1995	$8	$8
Daffy Duck 895QX541-6	Looney Tunes	1994	$9	$14
Daffy Duck QEO815-4	Easter Ornaments	1996	$9	$20
Daisy 10th Ed. QX6242	Mary's Angels	1997	$8	$16
Daisy Days 995QX598-6	Garden Elves Collection	1994	$10	$5
Dallas Cowboys QSR6217	Football Helmet Collection	1995	$10	$24
Dallas Cowboys QSR5046	NFL Collection	1998	$10	$10
Dallas Cowboys QSR5227	NFL Collection	1999	$11	$8
Dallas Cowboys QSR5355	NFL Collection	1997	$10	$10
Dallas Cowboys QSR639-4	NFL Collection	1996	$10	$9
Dan Marino 5th Ed. QXI4029	Football Legends	1999	$15	$20

Humpty-Dumpty, 1993, 1st in the Mother Goose series, **$17.**

Fabulous Decade, 1993, **$10.**

Tannenbaum's Department Store, 1993, from the Nostalgic Houses and Shops series, **$45.**

Cozy Home, 1993, 10th in the Nostalgic Houses and Shops series, **$41.**

Ornament Title	Series	Year	Issue Price	Current Value
Dance For The Season QX6587	General Line	1999	$10	$15
Dancing Angels Tree Topper QXM589-1	Tree Topper	1992	$10	$18
Dancing Angels Tree Topper QXM589-1	Tree Topper	1994	$10	$9
Dancing Angels Tree-Topper QXM589-1	Tree Topper	1993	$10	$13
Dancing Nutcracker, The 3000QLX726-1	Magic Ornaments	1992	$30	$60
Daphne 11th Ed. QX615-3	Mary's Angels	1998	$8	$12
Dapper Snowman 1375QK105-3	General Line	1994	$14	$20
Darth Vader QXI753-1	General Line	1997	$24	$19
Darth Vader's TIE Fighter QXI7399	General Line	1999	$24	$35
Dasher & Dancer 495XPR973-5	Santa & His Reindeer Collection	1992	$5	$20
Daughter 575QEO517-9	Easter Ornaments	1991	$6	$22
Daughter 575QEO815-6	Easter Ornaments	1994	$6	$7
Daughter 575QEO834-2	Easter Ornaments	1993	$6	$11
Daughter 575QEO928-4	Easter Ornaments	1992	$6	$12
Daughter 575QX449-6	Commemoratives	1990	$6	$6
Daughter 575QX547-7	Commemoratives	1991	$6	$15
Daughter 675QX503-1	Commemoratives	1992	$7	$12
Daughter 675QX587-2	General Line	1993	$7	$14
Daughter 695QX562-3	Handcrafted Ornaments	1994	$7	$5
Daughter QEO823-9	Easter Ornaments	1995	$6	$7
Daughter QX567-7	Handcrafted Ornaments	1995	$7	$12
Daughter QX607-7	General Line	1996	$9	$13
Daughter QX6612	General Line	1997	$8	$16
Daughter QX6673	General Line	1998	$9	$10
Daughter QX6729	General Line	1999	$9	$15
David & Goliath 1st Ed. QX6447	Favorite Bible Stories	1999	$14	$19
Daydreams QXD4136	Disney Collection	1998	$14	$13
Dazzling Reindeer 975QXM402-6	Miniature Ornaments	1994	$10	$9
Dear Santa Mouse 1495QX580-6	Handcrafted Ornaments	1994	$15	$14
Deck The Hogs 875QX520-4	General Line	1992	$9	$15
Decorating Maxine-Style QXE6883	General Line	1998	$11	$9
Decorator Taz QXL7502	Magic Ornaments	1997	$30	$40
Deer Crossing 1800QLX721-3	Magic Ornaments	1990	$18	$45
Delivering Kisses QX410-7	Handcrafted Ornaments	1995	$11	$24
Denver Broncos QSR5053	NFL Collection	1998	$10	$10
Denver Broncos QSR5229	NFL Collection	1999	$11	$8
Denver Broncos QSR5362	NFL Collection	1997	$10	$10
Denver Broncos QSR641-1	NFL Collection	1996	$10	$7
Detroit Lions QSR5365	NFL Collection	1997	$10	$10
Detroit Lions QSR641-4	NFL Collection	1996	$10	$9
Detroit Pistons QSR1027	NBA Collection	1999	$11	$4
Detroit Pistons QSR1242	NBA Collection	1997	$10	$4
Digging In QEO8712	Easter Ornaments	1997	$8	$8
Dinoclaus 775QX527-7	General Line	1991	$8	$11
Divine Duet 675QEO818-3	Easter Ornaments	1994	$7	$12

Winnie the Pooh, 1993, **$24.**

A Fitting Moment, 1993, 8th in the Mr. and Mrs. Claus series, **$20.**

Great Connections, 1993, **$16.**

Peek-A-Boo Tree, 1993, **$25.**

Ornament Title	Series	Year	Issue Price	Current Value
Dizzy Devil 575QXM413-3	Tiny Toon Adventure	1994	$6	$7
Dog's Best Friend 1200QLX717-2	Magic Ornaments	1993	$12	$18
Dollhouse Dreams 2200QLX737-2	Magic Ornaments	1993	$22	$45
Donald & Daisy In Venice 1st Ed. QXD4103	Romantic Vacations	1998	$15	$18
Donald Plays The Cymbals 3rd Ed. QXD4057	Mickey's Holiday Parade	1999	$14	$29
Donald's Surprising Gift 1st Ed. QXD4025	Hallmark Archives	1997	$13	$14
Donder & Blitzen 495XPR973-8	Santa & His Reindeer Collection	1992	$5	$25
Donder 7th Ed. 875QX528-4	Reindeer Champs	1992	$9	$21
Donder's Diner 1375QX482-3	Artists' Favorites	1990	$14	$12
Don'T Open Till 2000 QLZ4289	Laser Creations	1999	$9	$10
Dorothy & Glinda, The Good Witch QX6509	Wizard Of Oz Collection	1999	$24	$29
Dorothy & Toto 1095QX543-3	Wizard Of Oz Collection	1994	$11	$43
Dorothy's Ruby Slippers 1st Ed. QXM4599	Wonders Of Oz	1999	$6	$26
Dove Of Peace 2475QXC447-6	Collector's Club	1990	$25	$45
Downhill Dash	Tender Touches	1993	$23	$23
Downhill Dash QX6776	General Line	1998	$14	$22
Downhill Double QXM4837	Miniature Ornaments	1995	$5	$7
Downhill Run QX6702	General Line	1997	$10	$20
Down-Under Holiday 775QX514-4	General Line	1992	$8	$9
Dr. Leonard H. McCoy QXI1635-2	Star Trek	1997	$15	$16
Dream On QX600-7	Handcrafted Ornaments	1995	$11	$14
Duck QEO8377	Easter Egg Surprise	1999	$15	$15
Dudley The Dragon QX620-9	Handcrafted Ornaments	1995	$11	$10
Duke Blue Devils QSR2437	Collegiate Collection	1999	$10	$5
Dumbo's First Flight QXD1117	Disney Collection	1999	$14	$22
Dunkin' Roo 775QX557-5	General Line	1993	$8	$6
Eager For Christmas 1500QX533-6	Tender Touches	1994	$15	$10
Eagle Has Landed, The 2400QLX768-6	Magic Ornaments	1994	$24	$30
Early American Soldier 2nd Ed. QXM4144	Miniature Clothespin Soldier	1996	$5	$7
Ears To Pals 375QXM407-5	Miniature Ornaments	1993	$4	$6
Easter Art Show 775QEO819-3	Easter Ornaments	1994	$8	$12
Easter Egg Nest QEO8427	Easter Ornaments	1999	$8	$8
Easter Eggspressions QEO826-9	Easter Ornaments	1995	$5	$12
Easter Memories Photoholder QEO513-7	Easter Ornaments	1991	$8	$8
Easter Morning QEO816-4	Easter Ornaments	1996	$8	$21
Easter Parade 1st Ed. 675QEO930-1	Easter Parade	1992	$7	$15
Easter Parade 2nd Ed. 675QEO832-5	Easter Parade	1993	$7	$12
Easter Parade 3rd & Final Ed. 675QEO813-6	Easter Parade	1994	$7	$14
Ebenezer Scrooge 1375QX498-9	Christmas Carol Collection, A	1991	$14	$46
Eeyore 975-QX571-2	General Line	1993	$10	$15
Egg Nog Nest 775QX512-1	General Line	1992	$8	$14
Eggs In Sports 1st Ed. 675QEO934-1	Eggs In Sports	1992	$7	$22
Eggs In Sports 2nd Ed. 675QEO833-2	Eggs In Sports	1993	$7	$5
Eggs In Sports 3rd & Final Ed. 675QEO813-3	Eggs In Sports	1994	$7	$10
Eggs-Pert Artist, Crayola Crayon QEO8695	Easter Ornaments	1997	$9	$9

Blitzen, 1993, 8th and final edition in the Reindeer Champs series, **$13.**

Rocking Horse, 1993, 13th in the Rocking Horse series, **$30.**

The Pink Panther, 1993, **$18.**

Julianne and Teddy, 1993, **$19.**

It's in the Mail, 1993, **$10.**

Ornament Title	Series	Year	Issue Price	Current Value
Eggspert Painter 675QEO936-1	Easter Ornaments	1992	$7	$15
Eggstra Special Surprise QEO816-1	Easter Ornaments	1996	$9	$10
Eight Maids-A-Milking 675QX308-9	Twelve Days Of Christmas	1991	$7	$10
Electra-Glide 1st Ed. QXI6137	Mini Harley-Davidson Motorcycles	1999	$8	$28
Elegance On Ice QX6432	General Line	1997	$10	$10
Elegant Lily QEO826-7	Easter Ornaments	1995	$7	$5
Eleven Pipers Piping 695QX318-3	Twelve Days Of Christmas	1994	$7	$19
Elf Of The Year 1000QLX735-6	Magic Ornaments	1990	$10	$22
Elfin Engineer 1000QLX720-9	Magic Ornaments	1991	$10	$16
Elfin Marionette 1175QX593-1	Artists' Favorites	1992	$12	$10
Elfin Whittler 2000QLX726-5	Magic Ornaments	1990	$20	$25
Elmer Fudd 875QX549-5	Looney Tunes	1993	$9	$12
Elvis QX5624	General Line	1992	N/A	$14
Emerald City QLX745-4	Wizard Of Oz Collection	1996	$32	$45
Emmitt Smith 4th Ed. QXI403-6	Football Legends	1998	$15	$15
Enchanted Clock 3000QLX727-4	Magic Ornaments	1992	$30	$60
Eric The Baker 875QX524-4	North Pole Nutcrackers	1992	$9	$12
Esmeralda & Djalo QXI635-1	Hunchback Of Notre Dame	1996	$15	$21
Etch-A-Sketch 1295QP600-6	Personalized Ornaments	1994	$13	$13
Etch-A-Sketch QP601-5	Personalized Ornaments	1995	$13	$14
European Castle QK112-9	Invitation To Tea	1995	$16	$25
Evergreen Inn 875QX538-9	Matchbox Memories	1991	$9	$10
Evergreen Santa QX571-4	Special Edition	1996	$22	$40
Everything's Ducky! 675QEO933-1	Easter Ornaments	1992	$7	$15
Ewalia QXI1223	General Line	1990	$17	$17
Expressly For Teacher QX6375	General Line	1997	$8	$3
Extra-Special Delivery 795QX583-3	Handcrafted Ornaments	1994	$8	$12
Extra-Special Friends 475QX2279	Commemoratives	1991	$5	$5
Fabulous Decade 10th Ed. QX6357	Fabulous Decade	1999	$8	$25
Fabulous Decade 1st Ed. 775QX446-6	Fabulous Decade	1990	$8	$24
Fabulous Decade 2nd Ed. 775QX411-9	Fabulous Decade	1991	$8	$28
Fabulous Decade 3rd Ed. 775QX424-4	Fabulous Decade	1992	$8	$45
Fabulous Decade 4th Ed. 775QX447-5	Fabulous Decade	1993	$8	$10
Fabulous Decade 5th Ed. 795QX526-3	Fabulous Decade	1994	$8	$10
Fabulous Decade 6th Ed. QX514-7	Fabulous Decade	1995	$8	$10
Fabulous Decade 7th Ed. QX566-1	Fabulous Decade	1996	$8	$17
Fabulous Decade 8th Ed. QX623-2	Fabulous Decade	1997	$8	$10
Fabulous Decade 9th Ed. QX6393	Fabulous Decade	1998	$8	$34
Faithful Fan QX589-7	Handcrafted Ornaments	1995	$9	$10
Faithful Fire Fighter 775QX578-2	General Line	1993	$8	$9
Family Portrait QXD4149	Lady & The Tramp	1999	$15	$22
Famous Flying Ace 2nd Ed. QX6409	Spotlight On Snoopy	1999	$10	$15
Fancy Footwork QX6536	General Line	1998	$9	$9
Fancy Wreath 450QXM591-7	Miniature Ornaments	1991	$4	$3
Fanfare Bear 875QX533-7	Tender Touches	1991	$9	$10

The Bearingers of Victoria Circle, 1993, **$30 for the set.** Fireplace Hearth, **$7**; Abearnathy/Son, **$5**; Bearnadette/Daughter, **$6**; Papa Bearinger, **$7**; and Mama Bearinger, **$5**.

Ornament Title	Series	Year	Issue Price	Current Value
Fan-Tastic Season QX592-4	General Line	1996	$10	$12
Farm House 1st Ed. QX6439	Town & Country	1999	$16	$18
Farmer's Market, Tender Touches QXC5182	Collector's Club	1997	$15	$10
Fast Finish 375QXM530-1	Miniature Ornaments	1992	$4	$9
Father Christmas 1400QLX714-7	Magic Ornaments	1991	$14	$14
Father Time QLX739-1	Magic Ornaments	1996	$25	$28
Feathered Friends 1400QLX709-1	Magic Ornaments	1992	$14	$32
Feeding Time 575QXM548-1	Miniature Ornaments	1992	$6	$12
Feelin' Groovy 795QX595-3	Handcrafted Ornaments	1994	$8	$18
Feline Of Christmas, A 895QX581-6	General Line	1994	$9	$15
Feliz Navidad 2800QLX743-3	Magic Ornaments	1994	$28	$65
Feliz Navidad 600QXM588-7	Miniature Ornaments	1991	$6	$9
Feliz Navidad 675QX517-3	General Line	1990	$7	$22
Feliz Navidad 675QX518-1	General Line	1992	$7	$21
Feliz Navidad 675QX527-9	General Line	1991	$7	$29
Feliz Navidad 875QX536-5	General Line	1993	$9	$12
Feliz Navidad 895QX579-3	Handcrafted Ornaments	1994	$9	$22
Feliz Navidad QX586-9	Handcrafted Ornaments	1995	$8	$9
Feliz Navidad QX6173	General Line	1998	$9	$9
Feliz Navidad QX630-4	General Line	1996	$10	$11
Feliz Navidad QX6665	General Line	1997	$9	$28
Feliz Navidad Santa QX6999	General Line	1999	$9	$12
Festival Of Fruit 2nd Ed. QBG6069	Crown Reflections/General Line	1999	$35	$35
Festive Album Photoholder 1295QP602-5	Personalized Ornaments	1994	$13	$13
Festive Album Photoholder QP602-5	Personalized Ornaments	1993	$13	$13
Festive Angel Tree Topper 975QXM578-3	Tree Topper	1990	$10	$24
Festive Brass Church 1400QLX717-9	Magic Ornaments	1991	$14	$35
Festive Locomotive QBG6903	General Line	1998	$35	$45
Festive Surrey 12th Ed. 1475QX492-3	Here Comes Santa	1990	$15	$42
Fetching The Firewood QKI105-7	Folk Art Americana	1995	$17	$20
Fiddlin' Around 775QX438-7	Artists' Favorites	1991	$8	$6
Fifty Years Together 975QX490-6	Commemoratives	1990	$10	$1
Fifty Years Together Photoholder 875QX494-7	Commemoratives	1991	$9	$8
Filled W/Cookies 1275QP604-2	Personalized Ornaments	1993	$13	$11
Filling The Stockings 1575QK115-5	General Line	1993	$16	$15
Fills The Bill 875QX557-2	General Line	1993	$9	$14
Final Putt-Minnie Mouse QEO8349	Easter Ornaments	1999	$11	$11
Fire Station 8th Ed. 1475QX413-9	Nostalgic Houses & Shops	1991	$15	$55
Fireman, The First Ed. QK102-7	Turn Of The Century Parade	1995	$17	$15
Fireplace Hearth XPR974-9	Bearingers Of Victoria Circle	1993	$5	$7
First Christmas Together 600QXM553-6	Miniature Ornaments	1990	$6	$14
First Christmas Together Photo. QX469-4	Commemoratives	1992	$9	$12
First Christmas Together Photoholder QX491-7	Commemoratives	1991	$9	$12

Locomotive, 1994, 1st in the Yuletide Central series, **$16.**

Holiday Barbie, 1994, 2nd in the Holiday Barbie Collection, **$25.**

Our Family photo holder, 1994, **$20.**

Murray Champion, 1994, 1st in the Kiddie Car Classics series, **$30.**

Grandparents, 1994, **$12.**

1957 Chevrolet Bel Air, 1994, 4th in the Classic American Cars series, **$16.**

Ornament Title	Series	Year	Issue Price	Current Value
First Christmas Together QLX725-5	Magic Ornaments	1990	$18	$45
First Christmas Together QX222-9	Commemoratives	1991	$5	$12
First Christmas Together QX313-9	Commemoratives	1991	$7	$12
First Christmas Together QX491-9	Commemoratives	1991	$9	$15
First Christmas Together QX713-7	Magic Ornaments	1991	$25	$25
First Christmas Together QXM581-9	Miniature Ornaments	1991	$6	$10
First Class Thank You	Artists on Tour	1997	N/A	$19
First Contact USS Enterprise NCC-1710-E QXI7633	Star Trek	1998	$24	$50
Fishing For Fun QXC520-7	Collector's Club	1995	$11	$10
Fishing Party QK103-9	Folk Art Americana	1995	$16	$20
Fitting Moment, A 8th Ed. 1475QX420-2	Mr. & Mrs. Claus	1993	$15	$20
Five Years Together 475QX210-3	Commemoratives	1990	$5	$20
Five Years Together 775QX492-7	Commemoratives	1991	$8	$18
Five Years Together QXC315-9	Collector's Club	1991	N/A	$19
Five-&-Ten-Cent Store 9th Ed. 1475QX425-4	Nostalgic Houses & Shops	1992	$15	$32
Flag Of Liberty 675QX524-9	Commemoratives	1991	$7	$10
Flame-Fighting Friends QX6619	General Line	1999	$15	$11
Flash, The QX6469	General Line	1999	$13	$15
Flatbed Car 4th Ed. QEO8387	Cottontail Express	1999	$10	$8
Flatbed Car 5th Ed. QXM510-5	Noel Railroad	1993	$7	$14
Flight At Kitty Hawk 1st Ed. QX5574	Sky's The Limit	1997	$15	$19
Flik QXD4153	General Line	1998	$13	$22
Florida State Seminoles QSR2439	Collegiate Collection	1999	$10	$5
Flowerpot Friends QEO822-9	Easter Ornaments	1995	$15	$15
Fly By 450QXM586-9	Miniature Ornaments	1991	$4	$16
Foghorn Leghorn & Henery Hawk QX544-4	Looney Tunes	1996	$14	$17
Folk Art Reindeer 875QX535-9	General Line	1991	$9	$10
Follow The Leader QXC4503	Peanuts Collection	1998	$17	$30
Follow The Sun 895QX584-6	Handcrafted Ornaments	1994	$9	$9
Following The Star QK109-9	Holiday Enchantment	1995	$14	$12
For My Grandma Photoholder QX518-4	Commemoratives	1992	$8	$2
For My Grandma QX6747	General Line	1999	$8	$9
For My Grandma Photoholder 695QX561-3	Handcrafted Ornaments	1994	$7	$12
For My Grandma Photoholder QX572-9	Handcrafted Ornaments	1995	$9	$10
For The One I Love 975QX484-4	Commemoratives	1992	$10	$11
Forecast For Fun QX6869	General Line	1999	$15	$19
Forest Frolics 2nd Ed. 2500QLX723-6	Forest Frolics	1990	$25	$44
Forest Frolics 3rd Ed. 2500QLX721-9	Forest Frolics	1991	$25	$35
Forest Frolics 4th Ed. 2800QLX725-4	Forest Frolics	1992	$28	$28
Forest Frolics 5th Ed. 2500QLX716-5	Forest Frolics	1993	$25	$22
Forest Frolics 6th Ed. 2800QLX743-6	Forest Frolics	1994	$28	$34
Forest Frolics 7th & Final Ed. 2800QLX729-9	Forest Frolics	1995	$28	$38
Forever Friends Bear QX525-8	Handcrafted Ornaments	1995	$9	$9
Forever Friends Bear QX6303	General Line	1998	$9	$9
Forever Friends QEO8423	Easter Ornaments	1998	$10	$10

Mufasa and Simba, 1994, from the Lion King series, **$15.**

Timon and Pumbaa, 1994, from the Lion King series, **$10.**

Simba and Nala, 1994, from the Lion King series, **$20/set of two.**

Mistletoe Surprise, 1994, **$15.**

Road Runner and Wile E. Coyote, 1994, from the Looney Tunes series, **$18.**

Ornament Title	Series	Year	Issue Price	Current Value
Forty Winks QXC5294	Santa's Club Soda	1993	N/A	$15
Forty Years Together 775QX493-9	Commemoratives	1991	$8	$5
Forty Years Together 975QX490-3	Commemoratives	1990	$10	$1
Frankincense QBG6896	Crown Reflections	1998	$22	$28
Frankincense QBG6896	Crown Reflections	1999	$22	$19
Franz The Artist 875QX526-1	North Pole Nutcrackers	1992	$9	$16
Fred & Barney 1495QX500-3	Flintstones	1994	$15	$19
Fred & Dino QLX728-9	Flintstones	1995	$28	$50
Freedom / 1st Ed. QLX752-4	Journeys Into Space	1996	$24	$45
French Officer 5th Ed. QXM4579	Miniature Clothespin Soldier	1999	$5	$8
Frieda The Animals' Friend 875QX526-4	North Pole Nutcrackers	1992	$9	$22
Friend Of My Heart QX672-3	General Line	1998	$15	$14
Friendly Boost QX582-7	Handcrafted Ornaments	1995	$9	$15
Friendly Delivery QEO8419	Mary's Bears	1999	$13	$13
Friendly Fawn 600QXM594-7	Miniature Ornaments	1991	$6	$15
Friendly Greetings 775QX504-1	Commemoratives	1992	$8	$7
Friendly Push 895QX568-6	Handcrafted Ornaments	1994	$9	$9
Friendly Tin Soldier 450QXM587-4	Miniature Ornaments	1992	$4	$12
Friends Are Fun 975QX528-9	Commemoratives	1991	$10	$15
Friends Are Tops 450QXM552-1	Miniature Ornaments	1992	$4	$6
Friends Need Hugs 450QXM401-6	Miniature Ornaments	1994	$4	$4
Friends Share Fun QLX734-9	Magic Ornaments	1995	$16	$18
Friendship 7 2nd Ed. QLX753-2	Journeys Into Space	1997	$24	$42
Friendship Blend QX6655	General Line	1997	$10	$18
Friendship Duet QXM4019	Miniature Ornaments	1995	$5	$7
Friendship Kitten 675QX4144-3	Commemoratives	1990	$7	$25
Friendship Line 975QX503-4	Commemoratives	1992	$10	$8
Friendship Sundae 1095QX476-6	Handcrafted Ornaments	1994	$11	$19
Friendship Tree 1000QLX716-9	Magic Ornaments	1991	$10	$20
From Our Home To Yours 475QX213-1	Commemoratives	1992	$5	$10
From Our Home To Yours 475QX216-6	Commemoratives	1990	$5	$18
From Our Home To Yours 475QX228-7	Commemoratives	1991	$5	$20
From The Heart 1495QP603-6	Personalized Ornaments	1994	$25	$25
From The Heart QP603-6	Personalized Ornaments	1995	$15	$15
Frosty Friends 11th Ed. 975QX439-6	Frosty Friends	1990	$10	$30
Frosty Friends 12th Ed. 975QX432-7	Frosty Friends	1991	$10	$39
Frosty Friends 13th Ed. 975QX429-1	Frosty Friends	1992	$10	$30
Frosty Friends 14th Ed. 975QX414-2	Frosty Friends	1993	$10	$29
Frosty Friends 15th Ed. 995QX529-3	Frosty Friends	1994	$10	$25
Frosty Friends 16th Ed. QX516-9	Frosty Friends	1995	$11	$22
Frosty Friends 17th Ed. QX568-1	Frosty Friends	1996	$11	$15
Frosty Friends 18th Ed. QX625-5	Frosty Friends	1997	$11	$13
Frosty Friends 19th Ed.QX622-6	Frosty Friends	1998	$11	$25
Frosty Friends 20th Ed. QX6297	Frosty Friends	1999	$13	$20
Frosty Friends Anniversary Ed. 2000QX568-2	Frosty Friends	1993	$20	$29
Frosty Friends QBG6067	Crown Reflections	1999	$35	$45

Chris Mouse Jelly, 1994, 10th in the Chris Mouse series, **$15.**

Gingerbread Fantasy, 1994, **$42.**

Neighborhood Drugstore, 1994, 11th in the Nostalgic Houses and Shops series, **$28.**

Fabulous Decade, 1994, **$10.**

Frosty Friends, 1994, 15th in the Frosty Friends series, **$25.**

Ornament Title	Series	Year	Issue Price	Current Value
Frosty Friends QBG690-7	Frosty Friends	1998	N/A	$65
Full Of Love 775QEO514-9	Easter Ornaments	1991	$8	$39
Fun On A Big Scale 1075QX513-4	General Line	1992	$11	$12
Furrball QXM4459	Miniature Ornaments	1995	$6	$8
Future Ballerina QX675-6	General Line	1998	$8	$12
Future Star QXM4232	Miniature Ornaments	1997	$6	$6
G.I. Joe, Action Soldier 35th Anniversary QX6537	General Line	1999	$14	$15
Galloping Into Christmas 1975QXC477-9	Collector's Club	1991	$20	$110
Garden Bouquet QX6752	Nature's Sketchbook	1997	$15	$18
Garden Bunnies QEO8702	Nature's Sketchbook	1997	$15	$21
Garden Capers	Tender Touches	1993	$20	$20
Garden Club 1st Ed. QEO820-9	Garden Club	1995	$8	$10
Garden Club 2nd Ed. QEO809-1	Garden Club	1996	$8	$6
Garden Club 3rd Ed. QEO8665	Garden Club	1997	$8	$9
Garden Club 4th Ed. QEO8426	Garden Club	1998	$8	$9
Garden Of Piglet & Pooh 1295QEO8403	Easter Ornaments	1998	$13	$14
Garfield 1295QX575-3	General Line	1994	$13	$18
Garfield 475QX230-3	General Line	1990	$5	$14
Garfield 775QX517-7	General Line	1991	$8	$12
Garfield 775QX537-4	General Line	1992	$8	$18
Garfield QX500-7	General Line	1995	$11	$23
Gay Parisienne Barbie 6th Ed. QXI5301	Barbie	1999	$16	$19
Genius At Work 1075QX537-1	General Line	1992	$11	$10
Gentle Dreamers 875QX475-6	Artists' Favorites	1990	$9	$24
Gentle Giraffes QXM1221	Miniature Ornaments-Noah's Ark	1997	$6	$14
Gentle Guardian QEO8732	Easter Ornaments	1997	$7	$4
Gentle Lamb 675QEO515-9	Easter Ornaments	1991	$7	$14
Gentle Lullaby QK115-7	All Is Bright	1995	$12	$12
Gentle Nurse 695QX597-3	Handcrafted Ornaments	1994	$7	$12
Gentle Tidings 2500QXC544-2	Collector's Club	1993	$25	$35
Georgetown Hoyas QSR2447	Collegiate Collection	1999	$10	$5
Gerbil Inc. 375QXM592-4	Miniature Ornaments	1992	$4	$5
Gift Bearers 1st Ed. QX6437	Gift Bearers	1999	$13	$18
Gift Car 395XPR973-1	Claus & Co. R.R. Ornaments	1991	$4	$10
Gift Exchange 7th Ed. 1475QX429-4	Mr. & Mrs. Claus	1992	$15	$20
Gift From Rodney, A QXC4129	Collector's Club	1995	$5	$8
Gift Of Friendship QXE6835	General Line	1997	N/A	$14
Gift Of Joy 875QX531-9	Commemoratives	1991	$9	$12
Gifted Gardener QX673-6	General Line	1998	$8	$9
Gingerbread Elf 575QX503-3	General Line	1990	$6	$11
Gingerbread Fantasy 4400QLX738-2	Magic Ornaments	1994	$44	$42
Girl Talk QXD4069	Mickey & Co.	1999	$13	$21
Glad Tidings QX623-1	Collector's Choice	1996	$15	$10
Glee Club Bears 875QX496-9	Tender Touches	1991	$9	$10

The Cowardly Lion, 1994, from the Wizard of Oz Collection, **$40.**

The Scarecrow, 1994, from the Wizard of Oz Collection, **$39.**

Dorothy and Toto, 1994, from the Wizard of Oz Collection, **$43.**

The Tin Man, 1994, from the Wizard of Oz Collection, **$39.**

Ornament Title	Series	Year	Issue Price	Current Value
Glinda & Wicked Witch Of The West QXM4233	Miniature Ornaments	1998	$15	$19
Glinda, Witch Of The North QX574-9	Wizard Of Oz Collection	1995	$14	$26
Glorious Angel 1st Ed. QX649-3	Madame Alexander Holiday Angels	1998	$15	$16
Glowing Angel QXL7435	Magic Ornaments	1997	$19	$30
Glowing Pewter Wreath 1875QX530-2	General Line	1993	$19	$12
Goal Line Glory QX600-1	General Line	1996	$13	$24
Godchild 675QX317-6	Commemoratives	1990	$7	$15
Godchild 675QX548-9	Commemoratives	1991	$7	$6
Godchild 675QX594-1	Commemoratives	1992	$7	$18
Godchild 875QX587-5	General Line	1993	$9	$9
Godchild 895QX445-3	Handcrafted Ornaments	1994	$9	$9
Godchild QX570-7	Handcrafted Ornaments	1995	$8	$14
Godchild QX584-1	General Line	1996	$9	$9
Godchild QX6662	General Line	1997	$8	$10
Godchild QX670-3	General Line	1998	$8	$12
Godchild QX6759	General Line	1999	$8	$12
Godparent 500QX242-3	General Line	1994	$5	$20
Godparent QX241-7	General Line	1995	$5	$12
God's Gift Of Love QX6792	General Line	1997	$17	$33
Goin' Fishin' 1495QP602-3	Personalized Ornaments	1994	$15	$10
Goin' Golfin' 1295QP601-2	Personalized Ornaments	1994	$13	$13
Going Golfin' 1275QP601-2	Personalized Ornaments	1993	$13	$11
Going Places 375QXM587-1	Miniature Ornaments	1992	$4	$6
Going Sledding 450QXM568-3	Miniature Ornaments	1990	$4	$11
Going To Town 1575QX116-6	Folk Art Americana	1994	$16	$24
Going Up? Charlie Brown 995QEO8433	Easter Ornaments	1998	$10	$12
Gold QBG6836	Crown Reflections	1998	$22	$28
Gold QBG6836	Crown Reflections	1999	$22	$19
Golf's A Ball 675QX598-4	General Line	1992	$7	$15
Golf's My Bag 775QX496-3	Handcrafted Ornaments	1990	$8	$15
Gone Wishin' 875QX517-1	General Line	1992	$9	$12
Gone With The Wind 3 Pc. Set QXM421-1	Miniature Ornaments	1996	$20	$40
Good Luck Dice QX681-3	General Line	1998	$10	$4
Good Sledding Ahead 2800QLX724-4	Magic Ornaments	1992	$28	$60
Goody Gumballs! QLX736-7	Magic Ornaments	1995	$12	$30
Goofy As Santa's Helper QXD4079	Mickey & Co.	1999	$13	$21
Goofy Soccer Star QXD4123	Disney Collection	1998	$11	$10
Goofy Soccer Star QXD412-3	General Line	1998	$11	$14
Goofy's Ski Adventure QXD4042	General Line	1997	$13	$12
Goose Cart 775QX523-6	General Line	1990	$8	$15
Gopher Fun QX588-7	Handcrafted Ornaments	1995	$10	$18
Gordie Howe 3rd Ed. QXI4047	Hockey Greats	1999	$16	$15
Graceful Carousel Horse 775QXM405-6	Miniature Ornaments	1994	$8	$8
Graceful Fawn 1175QK103-3	General Line	1994	$12	$20

Murray Fire Truck, 1995, from the Kiddie Car Classics series, **$16.**

A Gift From Rodney, 1995, **$8.**

1956 Ford Truck, 1995, 1st in the All-American Trucks series, **$25.**

Cozy Christmas, 1995, **$12.**

Collecting Memories, 1995, from the Hallmark Keepsake Ornament Collector's Club, **$10.**

Santa's Roadster, 1995, 17th in the Here Comes Santa series, **$28.**

Ornament Title	Series	Year	Issue Price	Current Value
Grandchild 675QEO517-7	Easter Ornaments	1991	$7	$14
Grandchild 675QEO835-2	Easter Ornaments	1993	$7	$9
Grandchild 675QEO927-4	Easter Ornaments	1992	$7	$10
Grandchild's 1st Christmas 450QXM569-7	Miniature Ornaments	1991	$4	$4
Grandchild's First Christmas 575QXM550-1	Miniature Ornaments	1992	$6	$7
Grandchild's First Christmas 795QX567-6	Handcrafted Ornaments	1994	$8	$12
Grandchild's First Christmas QX555-2	General Line	1993	$7	$8
Grandchild's First Christmas QX577-7	Handcrafted Ornaments	1995	$8	$14
Grandchild's First Christmas 600QXM572-3	Miniature Ornaments	1990	$6	$6
Granddaughter 475QX228-6	Commemoratives	1990	$5	$19
Granddaughter 475QX229-9	Commemoratives	1991	$5	$10
Granddaughter 675QX560-4	Commemoratives	1992	$7	$7
Granddaughter 675QX563-5	General Line	1993	$7	$5
Granddaughter 695QX552-3	Handcrafted Ornaments	1994	$7	$5
Granddaughter First Christmas BBY 280-2	Baby Celebrations	1993	$14	$20
Granddaughter QX569-7	General Line	1996	$8	$9
Granddaughter QX577-9	Handcrafted Ornaments	1995	$7	$10
Granddaughter QX6622	General Line	1997	$8	$20
Granddaughter QX668-3	General Line	1998	$8	$10
Granddaughter QX6739	General Line	1999	$9	$15
Granddaughter's 1st Christmas 675QX463-4	Commemoratives	1992	$7	$10
Granddaughter's 1st Christmas 675QX511-9	Commemoratives	1991	$7	$10
Granddaughter's First Xmas 675QX310-6	Commemoratives	1990	$7	$10
Grandma 450QXM516-2	Miniature Ornaments	1993	$4	$6
Grandma 450QXM551-4	Miniature Ornaments	1992	$4	$5
Grandma QX584-4	General Line	1996	$9	$8
Grandma QX6625	General Line	1997	$9	$12
Grandma's Memories QX668-6	General Line	1998	$9	$12
Grandmother 475QX201-1	Commemoratives	1992	$5	$12
Grandmother 475QX223-6	Commemoratives	1990	$5	$18
Grandmother 475QX230-7	Commemoratives	1991	$5	$13
Grandmother 675QX566-5	General Line	1993	$7	$10
Grandmother 795QX567-3	Handcrafted Ornaments	1994	$8	$16
Grandmother QX576-7	Handcrafted Ornaments	1995	$8	$6
Grandpa 795QX561-6	Handcrafted Ornaments	1994	$8	$5
Grandpa QX576-9	Handcrafted Ornaments	1995	$9	$8
Grandpa QX585-1	General Line	1996	$9	$8
Grandparents 475QX200-4	Commemoratives	1992	$5	$10
Grandparents 475QX208-5	General Line	1993	$5	$10
Grandparents 475QX225-3	Commemoratives	1990	$5	$10
Grandparents 475QX230-9	Commemoratives	1991	$5	$10
Grandparents 500QX242-6	General Line	1994	$5	$12
Grandparents QX241-9	General Line	1995	$5	$12
Grandpa's Gift QXM4829	Miniature Ornaments	1995	$6	$8
Grandson 475QX229-3	Commemoratives	1990	$5	$10
Grandson 475QX229-7	Commemoratives	1991	$5	$12

Happy Holidays photo holder, 1995, **$5.**

Rocking Horse, 1995, **$22.**

1969 Chevrolet Camaro, 1995, 5th in the Classic American Cars series, **$13.**

PEZ Santa, 1995, **$12.**

Tender Car, 1995, 2nd in the Yuletide Central series, **$15.**

Grandmother, 1995, **$6.**

Ornament Title	Series	Year	Issue Price	Current Value
Grandson 675QX561-1	Commemoratives	1992	$7	$10
Grandson 675QX563-2	General Line	1993	$7	$10
Grandson 695QX552-6	Handcrafted Ornaments	1994	$7	$11
Grandson QX569-9	General Line	1996	$8	$9
Grandson QX578-7	Handcrafted Ornaments	1995	$7	$12
Grandson QX6615	General Line	1997	$8	$15
Grandson QX667-6	General Line	1998	$8	$8
Grandson WX6737	General Line	1999	$9	$18
Grandson's First Christmas 675QX306-3	Commemoratives	1990	$7	$10
Grandson's First Christmas 675QX462-1	Commemoratives	1992	$7	$10
Grandson's First Christmas 675QX511-7	Commemoratives	1991	$7	$11
Grandson's First Christmas BBY 280-1	Baby Celebrations	1993	$14	$18
Grant Hill 4th Ed. QXI684-6	Hoop Stars	1998	$15	$15
Great Connections 1075QX540-2	General Line	1993	$11	$16
Greatest Story 1st Ed. 1275QX465-6	Greatest Story	1990	$13	$10
Greatest Story 2nd Ed. 1275QX412-9	Greatest Story	1991	$13	$10
Greatest Story 3rd Ed. 1275QX425-1	Greatest Story	1992	$13	$10
Green Bay Packers QSR5063	NFL Collection	1998	$10	$10
Green Bay Packers QSR5237	NFL Collection	1999	$11	$12
Green Bay Packers QSR5372	NFL Collection	1997	$10	$10
Green Bay Packers QSR642-1	NFL Collection	1996	$10	$10
Green Thumb Santa 775QX510-1	General Line	1992	$8	$8
Grey 10th & Final Ed. QXM4302	Rocking Horse Miniatures	1997	$5	$7
Grey Arabian 4th Ed. 450QXM563-7	Rocking Horse Miniatures	1991	$4	$19
Grinch, The QXI6466	General Line	1998	$14	$55
Grocery Store 15th Ed. QX6266	Nostalgic Houses & Shops	1990	$17	$20
Growth Of A Leader Boys Scouts Of America QX554-1	General Line	1996	$10	$10
Guardian Friend QX654-3	General Line	1998	$9	$14
Guiding Santa QK103-7	Folk Art Americana	1995	$19	$25
Gus & Jaq, Cinderella QXD4052	General Line	1997	$13	$12
Halls Station QX683-3	25th Anniversary Edition	1998	$25	$25
Ham 'N Eggs QEO827-7	Easter Ornaments	1995	$8	$8
Hamton 575QXM412-6	Tiny Toon Adventure	1994	$6	$6
Han Solo 3rd Ed. QXI4007	Star Wars	1999	$14	$20
Handled With Care QX6769	General Line	1999	$9	$9
Handwarming Present, A 9th Ed. 1495QX528-3	Mr. & Mrs. Claus	1994	$15	$20
Hang In There 675QX471-3	General Line	1990	$7	$10
Hank Aaron 2nd. Ed. QXI6152	At The Ballpark	1997	$15	$15
Happy Birthday, Jesus 1295QX542-3	Handcrafted Ornaments	1994	$13	$16
Happy Bubble Blower QEO8437	Easter Ornaments	1999	$8	$8
Happy Christmas To All! QXC5132	Collector's Club	1997	N/A	$18
Happy Diploma Day QEO8357	World Of Wishes	1999	$11	$11
Happy Diploma Day! 795QEO8476	World Of Wishes	1998	$8	$11
Happy Haul-idays 15th Ed. 1475QX410-2	Here Comes Santa	1993	$15	$35

Frosty Friends, 1995, 16th in the Frosty Friends series, **$22.**

Christmas Eve Kiss, 1995, 10th and final edition in the Mr. and Mrs. Claus series, **$15.**

Photo courtesy Hallmark

Barbie: Solo in the Spotlight, 1995, 1st in the Barbie series, **$15.**

Holiday Barbie, 1995, 3rd in the Holiday Barbie Collection, **$18.**

Ornament Title	Series	Year	Issue Price	Current Value
Happy Holidays: Photoholder QX630-7	Handcrafted Ornaments	1995	$3	$5
Happy Holi-Doze QX590-4	General Line	1996	$10	$8
Happy Voices 675QX464-5	General Line	1990	$7	$7
Happy Woodcutter 975QX476-3	Artists' Favorites	1990	$10	$9
Happy Wrappers QX603-7	Handcrafted Ornaments	1995	$11	$12
Hark! It's Herald 2nd Ed. 675QX446-3	Hark! It's Herald	1990	$7	$10
Hark! It's Herald 3rd Ed. 675QX437-9	Hark! It's Herald	1991	$7	$10
Hark! It's Herald 4th & Final Ed. 775QX446-4	Hark! It's Herald	1992	$8	$10
Harmony Trio 1175QXM547-1	Miniature Ornaments	1992	$12	$12
Harvest Joy 995QX599-3	Garden Elves Collection	1994	$10	$5
Harvest Of Grapes QBG6047	Crown Reflections	1999	$25	$35
Hat Shop 7th Ed. 700QXM514-3	Old English Village	1994	$7	$11
Hattie Chapeau QXM425-1	Miniature Ornaments	1996	$5	$5
Have A Cookie 575QXM516-6	Miniature Ornaments	1994	$6	$8
Hays Train Station, The 795XPR945-2	Sarah, Plain & Tall Collection	1994	$8	$15
He Is Born 975QX536-2	General Line	1993	$10	$12
He Is Born QXM4235	Miniature Ornaments	1997	$8	$10
Headin' Home QLX732-7	Magic Ornaments	1995	$22	$35
Heart Of Christmas 1st Ed. 1375QX472-6	Heart Of Christmas	1990	$14	$40
Heart Of Christmas 2nd Ed. 1375QX435-7	Heart Of Christmas	1991	$14	$14
Heart Of Christmas 3rd Ed. 1375QX441-1	Heart Of Christmas	1992	$14	$10
Heart Of Christmas 4th Ed. 1475QX448-2	Heart Of Christmas	1993	$15	$10
Heart Of Christmas 5th & Final Ed. 1495QX526-6	Heart Of Christmas	1994	$15	$15
Hearts A-Sail 575QXM400-6	Miniature Ornaments	1994	$6	$14
Hearts Full Of Love QXM81-4	General Line	1996	$10	$10
Hearts In Harmony 1095QX440-6	General Line	1994	$11	$9
Heather 12 Ed. QX6329	Mary's Angels	1999	$8	$12
Heavenly Angels 1st Ed. 775QX436-7	Heavenly Angels	1991	$8	$14
Heavenly Angels 2nd Ed. 775QX445-4	Heavenly Angels	1992	$8	$7
Heavenly Angels 3rd & Final Ed. 775QX494-5	Heavenly Angels	1993	$8	$5
Heavenly Melody QX657-6	General Line	1998	$19	$19
Heavenly Minstrel 975QXM568-7	Miniature Ornaments	1991	$10	$10
Heavenly Music QXM4292	Miniature Ornaments	1997	$6	$7
Heavenly Song QX6795	General Line	1997	$13	$20
Heaven's Gift QX605-7	Handcrafted Ornaments	1995	$20	$35
Hello, Hello QX6777	General Line	1999	$15	$14
Hello-Ho-Ho 975QX514-1	General Line	1992	$10	$10
Helpful Shepherd 895QX553-6	Handcrafted Ornaments	1994	$9	$20
Hercules QXI4005	General Line	1997	$13	$15
Here Comes Easter 1st Ed. QEO809-3	Here Comes Easter	1994	$8	$20
Here Comes Easter 2nd Ed. QEO821-7	Here Comes Easter	1995	$8	$10
Here Comes Easter 3rd Ed. QEO809-4	Here Comes Easter	1996	$8	$10
Here Comes Easter 4th & Final Ed. QEO8682	Here Comes Easter	1997	$8	$9

Snow Scene, 1995, from A Charlie Brown Christmas series, **$25.**

Charlie Brown, 1995, from A Charlie Brown Christmas series, **$24.**

The complete set of ornaments from A Charlie Brown Christmas series, **$91.** The series includes Charlie Brown, Snoopy, Lucy, and Linus ornaments, plus the Snow Scene display.

Snoopy, 1995, from A Charlie Brown Christmas series, **$22.**

Lucy, 1995, from A Charlie Brown Christmas series, **$10.**

Linus, 1995, from A Charlie Brown Christmas series, **$10.**

Ornament Title	Series	Year	Issue Price	Current Value
Here's Your Fortune 1075QP600-2	Personalized Ornaments	1993	$11	$9
Heritage Springer 1st Ed. QXI8007	Harley-Davidson Milestones	1999	$15	$26
Herr Drosselmeyer 2nd Ed. QXM4135	Nutcracker Ballet	1997	$6	$9
Hey Diddle, Diddle 2nd Ed. 1395QX521-3	Mother Goose	1994	$14	$24
Hickory, Dickory, Dock 375QXM586-1	Miniature Ornaments	1992	$4	$12
Hidden Treasure/Li'l Keeper 1500QXC476-9	Collector's Club	1991	$15	$20
High Hopes QEO825-9	Tender Touches	1995	$9	$12
High Style QX606-4	Handcrafted Ornaments	1996	$9	$5
High Top-Purr 875QX533-2	General Line	1993	$9	$8
Hillside Express QX613-4	Handcrafted Ornaments	1996	$13	$12
Hippity Hop Delivery QEO814-4	Easter Ornaments	1996	$8	$15
Hockey Pup QX591-7	Handcrafted Ornaments	1995	$10	$10
Holiday Barbie 1st In Ed. 1495QX572-5	Holiday Barbie Collection	1993	$15	$50
Holiday Barbie 2nd In Ed. 1495QX521-6	Holiday Barbie Collection	1994	$15	$25
Holiday Barbie 3rd In Ed. QXI505-7	Holiday Barbie Collection	1995	$15	$18
Holiday Barbie 4th In Ed. QXI537-1	Holiday Barbie Collection	1996	$15	$14
Holiday Barbie 5th In Ed. QXI6212	Holiday Barbie Collection	1997	$15	$13
Holiday Barbie 6th & Final Ed. QXI402-3	Holiday Barbie Collection	1998	$16	$25
Holiday Bunny QXC4191	Santa's Club Soda	1996	$9	$10
Holiday Cafe 875QX539-9	Matchbox Memories	1991	$9	$10
Holiday Camper QX678-3	General Line	1998	$13	$16
Holiday Cardinal 300QXM552-6	Miniature Ornaments	1990	$3	$9
Holiday Cardinals 775QX524-3	General Line	1990	$8	$13
Holiday Decorator QX656-6	General Line	1998	$14	$9
Holiday Express QXM545-2	Miniature Ornaments	1993	$50	$80
Holiday Flash 1800QLX733-3	Magic Ornaments	1990	$18	$40
Holiday Flurries 1st Ed. QXM4547	Holiday Flurries	1999	$7	$12
Holiday Glow 1400QLX717-7	Magic Ornaments	1991	$14	$12
Holiday Haul QX620-1	Handcrafted Ornaments	1996	$15	$28
Holiday Hello 2495QXR611-6	Personalized Ornaments	1994	$25	$40
Holiday Holly 975QXM536-4	Miniature Ornaments	1992	$10	$18
Holiday Home 7th Ed. 1475QX469-6	Nostalgic Houses & Shops	1990	$15	$58
Holiday Memo 775QX504-4	Commemoratives	1992	$8	$13
Holiday Memories Barbie Ornament QHB 602-0	General Line	1998	$15	$15
Holiday Patrol 895QX582-6	Handcrafted Ornaments	1994	$9	$9
Holiday Pursuit QXC482-3	Collector's Club	1994	$12	$10
Holiday Serenade QXL7485	Magic Ornaments	1997	$24	$35
Holiday Snowflake 300QXM599-7	Miniature Ornaments	1991	$3	$14
Holiday Splash 575QXM583-4	Miniature Ornaments	1992	$6	$9
Holiday Swim QLX731-9	Magic Ornaments	1995	$19	$30
Holiday Teatime 1475QX543-1	General Line	1992	$15	$15
Holiday Traditions Barbie QHB6002	Barbie	1997	N/A	$20
Holiday Voyage Barbie Ornament QHB 601-6	General Line	1998	$15	$15
Holiday Wishes 775QX513-1	General Line	1992	$8	$12
Holly Basket, The QK109-4	Nature's Sketchbook	1996	$19	$20

Glinda, Witch of the North, 1995, from the Wizard of Oz Collection, **$26.**

Holiday Barbie, 1996, 4th in the Holiday Barbie Collection, **$14.**

Cinderella-1995, 1996, Madame Alexander, **$20.**

Fabulous Decade, 1995, **$10.**

Native American Barbie, 1996, 1st in the Dolls of the World series, **$16.**

Barbie: Enchanted Evening, 1996, 3rd in the Barbie series, **$16.**

Ornament Title	Series	Year	Issue Price	Current Value
Holly-Jolly Jig QXM4266	Miniature Ornaments	1998	$7	$8
Holy Family QBG6127	Crown Reflections	1999	$30	$40
Holy Family QX6523	Blessed Nativity Collection	1998	$25	$29
Holy Family QX6523	Blessed Nativity Collection	1999	$25	$29
Home For Christmas 775QX556-2	General Line	1993	$8	$4
Home For The Holidays 1575QK112-3	Showcase Ornaments/ Christmas Lights	1994	$16	$16
Home For The Owlidays 675QX518-3	General Line	1990	$7	$9
Home From The Woods QXC105-9	Collector's Club	1995	$16	$24
Home On The Range 3200QLX739-5	Magic Ornaments	1993	$32	$70
Home Sweet Home QXM4222	Miniature Ornaments	1997	$6	$7
Honest George 775QX506-4	General Line	1992	$8	$8
Honey Of A Gift QXD4255	General Line	1997	$7	$10
Honey Time 2nd Ed. QXD4129	Winnie The Pooh Collection	1999	$14	$14
Honored Guests QX6745	Nature's Sketchbook	1997	$15	$21
Hooked On Santa 775QX410-9	Artists' Favorites	1991	$8	$18
Hoop It Up 450QXM583-1	Miniature Ornaments	1992	$4	$12
Hop 'N Pop Popper 2000QLX735-3	Magic Ornaments	1990	$20	$30
Hot Dogger 775QX497-6	General Line	1990	$8	$14
Hot Wheels 30th Anniversary QX643-6	General Line	1998	$14	$13
House On Holly Lane 16th Ed. QX6349	Nostalgic Houses & Shops	1999	$17	$22
Houston Oilers QSR5375	NFL Collection	1997	$10	$10
Houston Oilers QSR642-4	NFL Collection	1996	$10	$8
Houston Rockets QSR1029	NBA Collection	1999	$11	$4
Houston Rockets QSR1245	NBA Collection	1997	$10	$4
Howdy Doody Lunchbox QX6519	General Line	1999	$15	$15
Howdy Doody QX6272	General Line	1997	$13	$13
Howling Good Time 975QX525-5	General Line	1993	$10	$9
Humpty-Dumpty 1st Ed. 1375QX528-2	Mother Goose	1993	$14	$17
Hurrying Downstairs QX607-4	General Line	1996	$9	$12
I Dig Golf QX589-1	General Line	1996	$11	$8
I Dream Of Santa 375QXM405-5	Miniature Ornaments	1993	$4	$11
Iago, Abu & The Genie QXD407-6	Disney Collection	1998	$13	$12
Ice Cold Coca-Cola QXM4252	Miniature Ornaments	1997	$7	$8
Ice Show 795QX594-6	Handcrafted Ornaments	1994	$8	$10
Icicle Bicycle 975QX583-5	General Line	1993	$10	$20
Important Memo QX584-7	Handcrafted Ornaments	1995	$9	$9
In A Heartbeat QX581-7	Handcrafted Ornaments	1995	$9	$9
In The Pink 995QX576-3	Handcrafted Ornaments	1994	$10	$14
In The Workshop QX6979	General Line	1999	$10	$10
In Time With Christmas QX604-9	Handcrafted Ornaments	1995	$13	$12
Incredible Hulk QX547-1	General Line	1997	$13	$24
Indiana Pacers QSR1037	NBA Collection	1999	$11	$4
Indiana Pacers QSR1252	NBA Collection	1997	$10	$4
Indianapolis Colts QSR5411	NFL Collection	1997	$10	$10
Indianapolis ColtsQSR643-1	NFL Collection	1996	$10	$9

Santa, 1996, from the Hallmark Keepsake Ornament Collector's Club, **$14.**

Holiday Bunny, 1996, from the Santa's Club Soda series, **$10.**

Rudolph's Helper, 1996, from the Hallmark Keepsake Ornament Collector's Club, **$6.**

Santa, Rudolph's Helper, Rudolph the Red-Nosed Reindeer, and Holiday Bunny, 1996, from the Hallmark Keepsake Ornament Collector's Club.

Rudolph the Red-Nosed Reindeer, 1996, from the Hallmark Keepsake Ornament Collector's Club, **$10.**

Ornament Title	Series	Year	Issue Price	Current Value
Inn 4th Ed. 850QXM562-7	Old English Village	1991	$8	$14
Inside Santa's Workshop QLZ4239	Laser Creations	1999	$9	$10
Inside Story 725QXM588-1	Miniature Ornaments	1992	$7	$8
Inspirational Angel QEO8347	Easter Ornaments	1999	$13	$13
Into The Woods 375QXM404-5	Miniature Ornaments	1993	$4	$10
Invitation To The Games QXE551-1	Olympic Spirit Collection	1996	$15	$14
Iris 4th Ed. 675QX427-9	Mary's Angels	1991	$7	$55
Iris Angel 3rd Ed. QX615-6	Language Of Flowers	1998	$16	$15
Irish Nollaig Shona 6th Ed. 1075QX463-6	Windows Of The World	1990	$11	$10
Italy 1st Ed. 1175QX512-9	Peace On Earth	1991	$12	$10
It's A Strike 895QX585-6	Handcrafted Ornaments	1994	$9	$9
It's A Wonderful Life 2000QLX723-7	Magic Ornaments	1991	$20	$45
It's A Wonderful Life QXI653-1	It's A Wonderful Life	1996	$15	$36
It's In The Mail QXC527-2	Collector's Club	1993	$10	$10
Ivy 6th Ed. 675QX428-2	Mary's Angels	1993	$7	$32
Izzy The Mascot QXE572-4	Olympic Spirit Collection	1996	$10	$10
Jack & Jill 3rd Ed. QX509-9	Mother Goose	1995	$14	$15
Jackie Robinson 4th & Final Ed. QX620-2	Baseball Heroes	1997	$13	$13
Jackpot Jingle QX591-1	General Line	1996	$10	$14
Jacksonville Jaguars QSR5415	NFL Collection	1997	$10	$10
Jacksonville Jaguars QSR643-4	NFL Collection	1996	$10	$9
Jasmine & Aladdin, QXD4062	Aladdin & The King Of Thieves	1997	$15	$12
Jasmine 7th Ed. 695QX527-6	Mary's Angels	1994	$7	$25
Jazzy Jalopy QX6549	General Line	1999	$24	$30
Jeff Gordon 1st Ed. QXI616-5	Stock Car Champions	1997	$16	$17
Jemima Puddle-Duck 2nd Ed. QEO8645	Beatrix Potter	1997	$9	$16
Jesus Loves Me 675QX315-6	Commemoratives	1990	$7	$15
Jesus Loves Me 775QX302-4	General Line	1992	$8	$9
Jesus Loves Me 775QX314-7	Commemoratives	1991	$8	$18
Jet Threat Car With Case Hot Wheels QX6527	General Line	1999	$13	$14
Jetsons, The QLX741-1	Magic Ornaments	1996	$28	$50
Jingle Bears 2500QLX732-3	Magic Ornaments	1991	$25	$50
Jingle Bell Band 1095QX578-3	Handcrafted Ornaments	1994	$11	$14
Jingle Bell Jester QX6695	General Line	1997	$10	$10
Joe Cool 1st Ed. QX6453	Spotlight On Snoopy	1998	$10	$15
Joe Montana/Kansas City QXI620-7	Football Legends	1995	$15	$30
Joe Montana/San Francisco 1st Ed. QXI575-9	Football Legends	1995	$15	$20
Joe Montana: Notre Dame QXI6843	Football Legends	1998	$15	$12
Joe Namath 3rd Ed. QXI6182	Football Legends	1997	$15	$14
Jolly Dolphin 675QX468-3	General Line	1990	$7	$32
Jolly Holly Santa QXC483-3	Collector's Club	1994	$22	$29
Jolly Locomotive QX6859	General Line	1999	$15	$19
Jolly Old Santa QXC5145	Collector's Club	1997	N/A	$12

Winnie the Pooh and Piglet, 1996, **$12.**

Happy Holi-doze, 1996, **$8.**

Early American Soldier, 1996, 2nd in the Miniature Clothespin Soldier series, **$7.**

Santa's 4x4, 1996, 18th in the Here Comes Santa series, **$18.**

Ornament Title	Series	Year	Issue Price	Current Value
Jolly Postman 1575QK116-2	General Line	1993	$16	$18
Jolly Santa 1375QK104-6	General Line	1994	$14	$23
Jolly Santa QX108-7	Symbols Of Christmas	1995	$16	$22
Jolly Snowman QBG6059	Crown Reflections	1999	$20	$22
Jolly Visitor 575QXM405-3	Miniature Ornaments	1994	$6	$5
Jolly Wolly Ark QX622-1	Handcrafted Ornaments	1996	$13	$12
Jolly Wolly Santa 775QX541-9	General Line	1991	$8	$18
Jolly Wolly Snowman 375QXM409-3	Miniature Ornaments	1994	$4	$4
Jolly Wolly Snowman 775QX542-7	General Line	1991	$8	$15
Jolly Wolly Soldier 775QX542-9	General Line	1991	$8	$15
Journey To Bethlehem 575QXM403-6	Miniature Ornaments	1994	$6	$18
Journey To Bethlehem QX622-3	Collector's Choice	1998	$17	$9
Journey To The Forest 1375QK101-2	Holiday Enchantment	1993	$14	$10
Joy Bearer 875QEO933-4	Easter Ornaments	1992	$9	$15
Joy Is In The Air 775QX550-3	General Line	1990	$8	$13
Joy Of Sharing 1575QK114-2	Portraits In Bisque	1993	$16	$9
Joy QK113-7	Angel Bells	1995	$13	$13
Joy To The World QX586-7	Handcrafted Ornaments	1995	$9	$9
Joy To The World QXL7512	Magic Ornaments	1997	$15	$24
Joyful Angels 1st Ed. QEO818-4	Joyful Angels	1996	$10	$16
Joyful Angels 2nd Ed. QEO865-5	Joyful Angels	1997	$11	$10
Joyful Angels 3rd & Final Ed. QEO8386	Joyful Angels	1998	$11	$9
Joyful Lamb 1175QK103-6	General Line	1994	$12	$11
Joyful Lamb 575QEO820-6	Easter Ornaments	1994	$6	$10
Joyful Messenger QXI673 3	25th Anniversary Edition	1990	$19	$16
Joyful Santa 1st Ed. QX8949	Joyful Santa	1999	$15	$21
Joyful Santa QXM4089	Miniature Ornaments	1995	$5	$7
Joyous Angel QX6787	General Line	1999	$9	$15
Joyous Angel QXM423-1	Miniature Ornaments	1996	$5	$6
Joyous Christmas QX6827	General Line	1999	$6	$12
Joyous Memories Photoholder 675QX536-9	General Line	1991	$7	$7
Joyous Song 895QX447-3	Handcrafted Ornaments	1994	$9	$14
Juggling Stars QX6595	General Line	1997	$10	$18
Jukebox Party QLX733-9	Magic Ornaments	1996	$25	$52
Julianne & Teddy 2175QX529-5	General Line	1993	$22	$19
Jump-Along Jackalope 895QX575-6	Handcrafted Ornaments	1994	$9	$15
Jumping For Joy QLX734-7	Magic Ornaments	1995	$28	$50
Just My Size 375QXM408-6	Miniature Ornaments	1994	$4	$9
Kanga & Roo 975QX561-7	General Line	1991	$10	$20
Kanga & Roo 975QX567-2	General Line	1993	$10	$15
Kansas City Chiefs QSR6257	Football Helmet Collection	1995	$10	$28
Kansas City Chiefs QSR5013	NFL Collection	1998	$10	$10
Kansas City Chiefs QSR5197	NFL Collection	1999	$11	$8
Kansas City Chiefs QSR5302	NFL Collection	1997	$10	$10
Kansas City Chiefs QSR636-1	NFL Collection	1996	$10	$5
Keep On Mowin' 895QX541-3	Handcrafted Ornaments	1994	$9	$8

This Big!, 1996, **$10.**

Airmail for Santa, 1996, from the Hallmark Keepsake Ornament Collector's Club, **$18.**

1959 Cadillac DeVille, 1996, 6th in the Classic American Cars series, **$21.**

1955 Chevy Cameo, 1996, 2nd in the All-American Trucks series, **$18.**

Ornament Title	Series	Year	Issue Price	Current Value
Ken Griffey Jr. QXI4037	At The Ballpark	1999	$15	$18
Kentucky Wildcats QSR2449	Collegiate Collection	1999	$10	$5
Key Note QP614-9	Personalized Ornaments	1995	$13	$15
Key To Love 450QXM568-9	Miniature Ornaments	1991	$4	$8
Kickin' Roo 795QX591-6	Handcrafted Ornaments	1994	$8	$10
Kindly Shepherd QX627-4	General Line	1996	$13	$14
King Kharoof-Second King QX618-6	Legend Of Three Kings Collection	1998	$13	$24
King Klaus 775QX410-6	General Line	1990	$8	$14
King Malh-Third King QX6797	Legend Of Three Kings Collection	1999	$14	$23
King Noor-First King QX6552	Legend Of Three Kings Collection	1997	$13	$24
King Of The Forest Set Of 4 QXM4262	Wizard Of Oz Collection	1997	$24	$34
Kitty In A Mitty 450QXM587-9	Magic Ornaments	1991	$4	$10
Kitty's Best Pal 675QX471-6	General Line	1990	$7	$9
Kitty's Catamaran 1095QX541-6	Handcrafted Ornaments	1994	$11	$11
Klingon Bird Of Prey 2400QLX738-6	Star Trek	1994	$24	$25
Kolyada 3rd. & Final Ed. QX617-2	Christmas Visitors	1997	$15	$12
Kolyada 4th Ed. 500QX212-4	Gift Bringers	1992	$5	$10
Kringle Bells QXC4486	Collector's Club	1998	N/A	$6
Kringle Tours 14th Ed. 1475QX434-1	Here Comes Santa	1992	$15	$28
Kringle Trolley 2000QLX741-3	Magic Ornaments	1994	$20	$45
Kringle's Kayak 795QX588-6	Handcrafted Ornaments	1994	$8	$18
Kringle's Whirligig QX6847	General Line	1999	$13	$16
Kringles, The 2nd Ed. 600QXM575-3	Kringles, The	1990	$6	$15
Kringles, The 3rd Ed. 6000QXM564-7	Kringles, The	1991	$6	$18
Kringles, The 4th Ed. 600QXM530-1	Kringles, The	1992	$6	$10
Kringles, The 5th & Final Ed. 575QXM513-5	Kringles, The	1993	$6	$9
Kringles's Bumper Cars 2500QLX711-9	Magic Ornaments	1991	$25	$35
Lady Daphne QX5505	Dickens Caroler Bells	1993	$22	$30
Lamplighter, The 1800QLX719-2	Magic Ornaments	1993	$18	$20
Larry Bird 2nd Ed. QXI501-4	Hoop Stars	1996	$15	$15
Larry, Moe & Curly The Three Stooges QX650-3	General Line	1998	$27	$29
Larry, Moe & Curly, The Three Stooges QX6499	General Line	1999	$30	$36
Last Minute Shopping 2800QLX738-5	Magic Ornaments	1993	$28	$62
Laverne, Victor & Hugo QXI635-4	Hunchback Of Notre Dame	1996	$13	$16
Leading The Way QX6782	General Line	1997	$17	$30
Learning To Skate 300QXM412-2	Miniature Ornaments	1993	$3	$10
Learning To Skate QK104-7	Folk Art Americana	1995	$15	$21
Lego Fireplace With Santa QX476-9	Handcrafted Ornaments	1995	$11	$19
Let It Snow! QLX7427	General Line	1999	$19	$20
Let Us Adore Him QLX738-1	Magic Ornaments	1996	$16	$20
Letter To Santa 1400QLX722-6	Magic Ornaments	1990	$14	$32

Frosty Friends, 1996, 17th in the Frosty Friends series, **$15.**

Pansy Angel, 1996, 1st in the Language of Flowers series, **$44.**

Rocking Horse, 1996, 16th and final edition in the Rocking Horse series, **$15.**

Victorian Painted Lady, 1996, 13th in the Nostalgic Houses and Shops series, **$21.**

Over the Rooftops, 1996, **$28.**

Ornament Title	Series	Year	Issue Price	Current Value
Liberty Mouse QSM8475	Tender Touches	1993	$21	$18
Lieutenant Commander Worf QXI4139	Star Trek: Deep Space Nine	1999	$15	$16
Lighthouse Greetings 1st Ed. QLX7442	Lighthouse Greetings	1997	$24	$75
Lighthouse Greetings 2nd Ed. QLX753-6	Lighthouse Greetings	1998	$24	$45
Lighthouse Greetings 3rd Ed. QLX7379	Lighthouse Greetings	1999	$24	$32
Lighting A Path 300QXM411-5	Miniature Ornaments	1993	$3	$5
Lighting The Flame QXE744-4	Olympic Spirit Collection	1996	$28	$19
Lighting The Way 1800QLX723-1	Magic Ornaments	1992	$18	$40
Lighting The Way QX612-4	General Line	1996	$13	$10
Li'l Dipper 675QEO514-7	Easter Ornaments	1991	$7	$19
Li'l Peeper 775QEO831-2	Easter Ornaments	1993	$8	$11
Li'l Popper 450QXM589-7	Miniature Ornaments	1991	$4	$12
Lily 5th Ed. 675QX427-4	Mary's Angels	1992	$7	$80
Lily Egg 975QEO513-9	Easter Ornaments	1991	$10	$11
Lincoln Memorial QXL7522	Magic Ornaments	1997	$24	$40
Linus QRP421-7	A Charlie Brown Christmas	1995	$4	$10
Lion & Lamb 450QXM567-6	Miniature Ornaments	1990	$4	$7
Lion & Lamb QX6602	General Line	1997	$8	$10
Little Bear 620XPR972-3	Little Frosty Friends	1990	$3	$5
Little Beeper QXM4469	Miniature Ornaments	1995	$6	$7
Little Bo Peep 2nd Ed. QEO8373	Children's Collector Barbie	1998	$15	$8
Little Boy Blue 5th & Final Ed. QX621-5	Mother Goose	1997	$14	$14
Little Cloud Keeper QX6877	General Line	1999	$17	$27
Little Drummer Boy 775QX523-3	General Line	1990	$8	$10
Little Drummer Boy 875QX537-2	General Line	1993	$9	$8
Little Frosty 620XPR972-0	Little Frosty Friends	1990	$3	$28
Little Husky 620XPR972-2	Little Frosty Friends	1990	$3	$8
Little Red Riding Hood 2nd Ed. QX6155	Madame Alexander	1997	$15	$16
Little Seal 620XPR972-1	Little Frosty Friends	1990	$3	$5
Little Soldier 450QXM567-5	Miniature Ornaments	1990	$4	$9
Little Song & Dance, A QX621-1	Handcrafted Ornaments	1996	$10	$18
Little Spooners QX550-4	General Line	1996	$13	$13
Little Town Of Bethlehem 300QXM586-4	Miniature Ornaments	1992	$3	$16
Littlest Angel, The 5th & Final Ed. 1400QLX730-3	Christmas Classics	1990	$14	$28
Locomotive 1989-1998 Anniversary Pewter Ed. QXM4286	Noel Railroad	1998	$11	$10
Locomotive 1st Ed. 1895QX531-6	Yuletide Central	1994	$19	$16
Locomotive 1st Ed. QEO807-4	Cottontail Express	1996	$8	$40
Locomotive 975QX531-1	Christmas Sky Line Collection	1992	$10	$25
Locomotive & Tender 1st Ed. QXM4549	Lionel Norfolk & Western	1999	$11	$20
Locomotive XPR9730	Claus & Co. R.R. Ornaments	1991	$4	$20
Lollipop Guild QX8029	Wizard Of Oz Collection	1999	$20	$39
Lone Ranger Lunchbox QX626-5	General Line	1997	$13	$10
Long Winter's Nap 675QX470-3	General Line	1990	$7	$18
Long Winter's Nap QXM424-4	Miniature Ornaments	1996	$6	$9

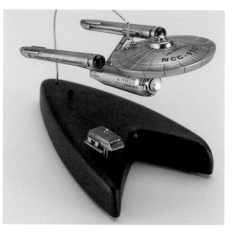

Star Trek 30 Years, 1996, from the Star Trek series, **$64.**

The Vehicles of Star Wars, 1996, Star Wars, **$29.**

Millennium Falcon, 1996, Star Wars, **$40.**

Ornament Title	Series	Year	Issue Price	Current Value
Look For The Wonder 1275QX568-5	General Line	1993	$13	$15
Look Out Below 875QX495-9	Tender Touches	1991	$9	$10
Look What I Found! QEO818-1	Easter Ornaments	1996	$8	$21
Look! It's Santa 1400QLX709-4	Magic Ornaments	1992	$14	$20
Lop-Eared Bunny 575QEO831-5	Easter Ornaments	1993	$6	$15
Lord Chadwick QX4554	Dickens Caroler Bells	1992	$22	$30
Los Angeles Lakers QSR1039	NBA Collection	1999	$11	$4
Los Angeles Lakers QSR1262	NBA Collection	1997	$10	$4
Lou Gehrig 2nd. Ed. QX502-9	Baseball Heroes	1995	$13	$15
Lou Rankin Bear QX406-9	General Line	1995	$10	$14
Lou Rankin Polar Bear QX574-5	General Line	1993	$10	$15
Lou Rankin Seal QX545-6	General Line	1994	$10	$14
Lovable Dears 875QX547-6	General Line	1990	$9	$10
Love Is Born 600QXM595-9	Miniature Ornaments	1991	$6	$9
Love To Sew QX6435	General Line	1997	$8	$12
Love To Share QXM4557	Miniature Ornaments	1999	$7	$11
Love To Skate 875QX484-1	Commemoratives	1992	$9	$10
Love Was Born 450QXM404-3	Miniature Ornaments	1994	$4	$9
Lovely Lamb 975QEO837-2	Easter Ornaments	1993	$10	$14
Loving Hearts 300QXM552-3	Miniature Ornaments	1990	$3	$7
Loving Shepherd 775QX515-1	General Line	1992	$8	$10
Loving Stitches 875QX498-7	Tender Touches	1991	$9	$10
Lucinda & Teddy 2175QX481-3	Handcrafted Ornaments	1994	$22	$20
Lucy Gets In Pictures/I Love Lucy QX654/	General Line	1999	$14	$22
Lucy QRP420-2	A Charlie Brown Christmas	1995	$4	$10
Ludwig The Musician 875QX528-1	North Pole Nutcrackers	1992	$9	$12
Luke Skywalker 1st Ed. QXI548-4	Star Wars	1997	$14	$24
Lulu & Family 600QXM567-7	Miniature Ornaments	1991	$6	$15
Lunar Rover Vehicle 4th & Final Ed. QXL7377	Journeys Into Space	1999	$24	$23
Mad Hatter 2nd Ed. QXM407-4	Alice In Wonderland	1996	$7	$10
Madonna & Child 600QXM564-3	Miniature Ornaments	1990	$6	$8
Madonna & Child QK114-4	Sacred Masterworks	1996	$16	$30
Madonna & Child QX632-4	General Line	1996	$13	$10
Madonna & Child QX651-6	General Line	1998	$13	$14
Madonna & Child QXL7425	Magic Ornaments	1997	$20	$34
Madonna Del Rosario QX6545	General Line	1997	$13	$9
Magi, The 1375QK102-5	Holiday Enchantment	1993	$14	$28
Magi, The 5th & Final Ed. 500QX206-5	Gift Bringers	1993	$5	$10
Magic Carpet Ride 795QX588-3	Handcrafted Ornaments	1994	$8	$9
Magic Johnson 3rd Ed. QXI6832	Hoop Stars	1997	$15	$15
Magic School Bus, The QX584-9	Handcrafted Ornaments	1995	$11	$16
Mail Car 3rd Ed. QX501-1	Yuletide Central	1996	$19	$19
Mailbox Delivery 1475QP601-5	Personalized Ornaments	1993	$15	$11
Mailbox Delivery 1495QP601-5	Personalized Ornaments	1994	$15	$15
Mailbox Delivery 1495QP601-5	Personalized Ornaments	1995	$15	$15
Majestic Deer 2500QXC483-6	Collector's Club	1994	$25	$29

Yogi Bear and Boo Boo, 1996, **$19.**

A Tree for Woodstock, 1996, Peanuts, **$14.**

Witch of the West, 1996, from the Wizard of Oz Collection, **$22.**

Mail Car, 1996, 3rd in the Yuletide Central series, **$19.**

Murray Airplane, 1996, 3rd in the Kiddie Car Classics series, **$35.**

Ornament Title	Series	Year	Issue Price	Current Value
Make-Believe Boat QXD411-3	General Line	1998	$13	$4
Makin' Music 975QX532-5	General Line	1993	$10	$12
Makin' Tractor Tracks 16th Ed. 1495QX529-6	Here Comes Santa	1994	$15	$50
Making His Rounds QX627-1	General Line	1996	$15	$15
Making His Way QXC4523A	Collector's Club	1998	$13	$12
Making It Bright 895QX540-3	Handcrafted Ornaments	1994	$9	$19
Making Waves 975QX577-5	General Line	1993	$10	$19
Mama Bearinger 495XPR974-5	Bearingers Of Victoria Circle	1993	$5	$5
Marbles Champion QX6342	General Line	1997	$11	$10
March Of The Teddy Bears 1st Ed. 450QXM400-5	March Of The Teddy Bears	1993	$4	$8
March Of The Teddy Bears 2nd Ed. 450QXM510-6	March Of The Teddy Bears	1994	$4	$8
March Of The Teddy Bears 3rd Ed. 475QXM4799	March Of The Teddy Bears	1995	$5	$6
March Of The Teddy Bears 4th & Final Ed. 475QXM409-4	March Of The Teddy Bears	1996	$5	$12
Marilyn Monroe 2nd Ed. QX633-3	Marilyn Monroe	1998	$15	$21
Marilyn Monroe 3rd & Final Ed. QX6389	Marilyn Monroe	1999	$15	$22
Marilyn Monroe, Pink Gown 1st Ed. QX570-4	Marilyn Monroe	1997	$15	$15
Mario Lemieux 2nd Ed. QXI647-6	Hockey Greats	1998	$16	$10
Marvin The Martian QX545-1	Looney Tunes	1996	$11	$25
Marvin The Martian QXM4657	Looney Tunes	1999	$9	$14
Mary Engelbreit 475QX223-7	General Line	1991	$5	$30
Mary Engelbreit 500QX207-5	General Line	1993	$5	$15
Mary Engelbreit 500QX241-6	Handcrafted Ornaments	1994	$5	$10
Mary Engelbreit QX240-9	General Line	1995	$5	$18
Mary Had A Little Lamb 4th Ed. QX564-4	Mother Goose	1996	$14	$14
Mary's Bears QX5569	General Line	1999	$13	$9
Matchless Memories QX606-1	General Line	1996	$10	$15
Max Rebo Band QXI4597	General Line	1999	$20	$8
Max The Tailor 875QX525-1	North Pole Nutcrackers	1992	$9	$12
Maxine 10th Ann. Of Shoebox Greetings QX622-4	Handcrafted Ornaments	1996	$10	$25
Maxine 2000QLX750-3	Magic Ornaments	1994	$20	$48
Maxine 875QX538-5	General Line	1993	$9	$19
Maxine QX644-6	General Line	1998	$10	$9
Maypole Stroll 2800QEO839-5 Set Of Three	Easter Ornaments	1993	$28	$15
Meadow Snowman QX6715	General Line	1997	$13	$18
Megara & Pegasus QXI4012	General Line	1997	$17	$14
Melchior-The Magi QX6819	Blessed Nativity Collection	1999	$13	$13
Melchoir (Gold) QK118-1	Magi Bells	1996	$14	$13
Melodic Cherub 375QXM406-6	Miniature Ornaments	1994	$4	$6
Memories Of Christmas QX240-6	General Line	1998	$6	$18
Memories To Cherish 1075QX516-1	General Line	1992	$11	$30
Memory Wreath 620XPR972-4	Little Frosty Friends	1990	$3	$8

700E Hudson Steam Locomotive, 1996, 1st in the Lionel Trains series, **$70.**

Joe Namath, 1997, 3rd in the Football Legends series, **$14.**

1935 Steelcraft Streamline Velocipede, 1997, 1st in the Sidewalk Cruisers series, **$20.**

Green Bay Packers blimp, 1997, from the NFL Collection, **$10.**

Ornament Title	Series	Year	Issue Price	Current Value
Meow Mart 775QX444-6	General Line	1990	$8	$14
Merry "Swiss" Mouse 775QX511-4	General Line	1992	$8	$10
Merry Carolers 2975QX479-9	Christmas Carol Collection, A	1991	$30	$44
Merry Carpoolers QX558-4	General Line	1996	$15	$26
Merry Chime QX6692	General Line	1998	$10	$22
Merry Fishmas 895QX591-3	Handcrafted Ornaments	1994	$9	$10
Merry Flight, A 575QX407-3	Miniature Ornaments	1994	$6	$8
Merry Grinch-Mas! QXI4627	Miniature Ornaments	1999	$20	$22
Merry Mascot 375QXM404-2	Miniature Ornaments	1993	$4	$8
Merry Motorcycle QX6637	General Line	1999	$9	$15
Merry Olde Santa 10th & Final Ed. QX6359	Merry Olde Santa	1999	$16	$18
Merry Olde Santa 1st Ed. QX473-6	Merry Olde Santa	1990	$15	$45
Merry Olde Santa 2nd Ed. QX435-9	Merry Olde Santa	1991	$15	$45
Merry Olde Santa 3rd Ed. QX441-4	Merry Olde Santa	1992	$15	$25
Merry Olde Santa 4th Ed. QX484-2	Merry Olde Santa	1993	$15	$30
Merry Olde Santa 5th Ed. QX525-6	Merry Olde Santa	1994	$15	$24
Merry Olde Santa 6th Series QX513-9	Merry Olde Santa	1995	$15	$17
Merry Olde Santa 7th Ed. QX565-4	Merry Olde Santa	1996	$15	$19
Merry Olde Santa 8th Ed. QX6225	Merry Olde Santa	1997	$15	$18
Merry Olde Santa 9th Ed. QX6386	Merry Olde Santa	1998	$16	$19
Merry RV QX602-7	Handcrafted Ornaments	1995	$13	$16
Merry Walruses QXM4057	Miniature Ornaments-Noah's Ark	1995	$6	$18
Message For Santa QXM425-4	Miniature Ornaments	1996	$7	$7
Messages Of Christmas QLX747-2	Handcrafted Ornaments	1993	$35	$23
Mexican Barbie 3rd Ed. QX6356	Dolls Of The World	1998	$15	$16
Miami Dolphins QSR5096	NFL Collection	1998	$10	$10
Miami Dolphins QSR5239	NFL Collection	1999	$11	$9
Miami Dolphins QSR5472	NFL Collection	1997	$10	$7
Miami Dolphins QSR645-1	NFL Collection	1996	$10	$5
Michigan J. Frog QX6332	General Line	1997	$10	$13
Michigan Wolverines QSR2457	Collegiate Collection	1999	$10	$5
Mickey & Minnie Handcar QXD4116	General Line	1998	$15	$10
Mickey & Minnie In Paradise 2nd Ed. QXD4049	Romantic Vacations	1999	$15	$26
Mickey's Comet QXD7586	General Line	1998	$24	$28
Mickey's Favorite Reindeer QXD4013	General Line	1998	$14	$13
Mickey's Long Shot QXD6412	General Line	1997	$11	$10
Mickey's Snow Angel QXD4035	General Line	1997	$10	$12
Midge 35th Anniversary 1495QEO8413	Easter Ornaments	1998	$15	$13
Military On Parade QX6639	General Line	1999	$11	$22
Milk 'N Cookies Express QX6839	General Line	1999	$9	$14
Milk Tank Car 7th QXM481-7	Noel Railroad	1995	$7	$14
Millennium Falcon QLX747-4	General Line	1996	$24	$40
Millennium Princess Barbie QXI4019	Barbie	1999	$16	$35
Millennium Snowman QX8059	General Line	1999	$9	$45

The Night Before Christmas, 1997, **$44.**

Waitin' on Santa, 1997, Winnie the Pooh, **$13.**

Little Red Riding Hood-1991, 1997, Madame Alexander, **$16.**

Frosty Friends, 1997, 18th in the Frosty Friends series, **$13.**

Ornament Title	Series	Year	Issue Price	Current Value
Minnesota Vikings QSR6267	Football Helmet Collection	1995	$10	$24
Minnesota Vikings QSR5126	NFL Collection	1998	$10	$10
Minnesota Vikings QSR5247	NFL Collection	1999	$11	$9
Minnesota Vikings QSR5475	NFL Collection	1997	$10	$10
Minnesota Vikings QSR6454	NFL Collection	1996	$10	$9
Minnie Plays The Flute 2nd Ed. QXD4106	Mickey's Holiday Parade	1998	$14	$9
Minnie Trims The Tree 3rd & Final Ed. QXD4059	Hallmark Archives	1999	$13	$14
Minted For Santa 375QXM585-4	Miniature Ornaments	1992	$4	$10
Miracle In Bethlehem QX6513	General Line	1998	$13	$34
Mischievous Kittens 1st Ed. QX6427	Mischievous Kittens	1999	$10	$39
Miss Gulch QX637-2	Wizard Of Oz Collection	1997	$14	$32
Mistletoe Fairy QX6216	General Line	1998	$13	$16
Mistletoe Kiss 1575QK114-5	Portraits In Bisque	1993	$16	$9
Mistletoe Surprise 1295QX599-6	Handcrafted Ornaments	1994	$13	$15
Mole Family Home 2000QLX714-9	Magic Ornaments	1991	$20	$20
Mom 450QXM401-3	Miniature Ornaments	1994	$4	$8
Mom 450QXM515-5	Miniature Ornaments	1993	$4	$8
Mom 450QXM550-4	Miniature Ornaments	1992	$4	$15
Mom 600QXM569-9	Miniature Ornaments	1991	$6	$10
Mom 775QX516-4	Commemoratives	1992	$8	$4
Mom 775QX585-2	General Line	1993	$8	$5
Mom 795QX546-6	Handcrafted Ornaments	1994	$8	$5
Mom & Dad 875QX459-3	Commemoratives	1990	$9	$19
Mom & Dad 975QX467-1	Commemoratives	1992	$10	$12
Mom & Dad 975QX546-7	Commemoratives	1991	$10	$13
Mom & Dad 975QX584-5	General Line	1993	$10	$5
Mom & Dad 995QX566-6	Handcrafted Ornaments	1994	$10	$28
Mom & Dad QX565-7	Handcrafted Ornaments	1995	$10	$12
Mom & Dad QX582-1	General Line	1996	$10	$8
Mom & Dad QX6522	General Line	1997	$10	$8
Mom & Dad QX6653	General Line	1998	$10	$9
Mom & Dad QX6709	General Line	1999	$10	$14
Mom QX564-7	Handcrafted Ornaments	1995	$8	$8
Mom QX582-4	General Line	1996	$8	$15
Mom QX6525	General Line	1997	$9	$8
Mom QX6656	General Line	1998	$9	$13
Mom QX6717	General Line	1999	$9	$10
Mom-To-Be 575QX487-7	Commemoratives	1991	$6	$18
Mom-To-Be 575QX491-6	Commemoratives	1990	$6	$19
Mom-To-Be 675QX461-4	Commemoratives	1992	$7	$13
Mom-To-Be 675QX553-5	General Line	1993	$7	$5
Mom-To-Be 795QX550-6	Handcrafted Ornaments	1994	$8	$16
Mom-To-Be QX565-9	Handcrafted Ornaments	1995	$8	$9
Mom-To-Be QX579-1	General Line	1996	$8	$8
Monkey Melody 575QXM409-2	Miniature Ornaments	1993	$6	$8

1950 Santa Fe F3 Diesel Locomotive, 1997, 2nd in the Lionel Train series, **$26.**

Miss Gulch, 1997, from the Wizard of Oz Collection, **$32.**

Snowdrop Angel, 1997, 2nd in the Language of Flowers series, **$16.**

King of the Forest, 1997, from the Wizard of Oz Collection, **$34.**

Ornament Title	Series	Year	Issue Price	Current Value
Moonbeams 1575QK111-6	Showcase Ornaments/ Christmas Lights	1994	$16	$18
Mooy Christmas 675QX493-3	General Line	1990	$7	$22
Mop Top Billy QEO8337	Madame Alexander	1999	$15	$15
Mop Top Wendy 3rd Ed. QX635-3	Madame Alexander	1998	$15	$20
Mother 450QXM571-6	Miniature Ornaments	1990	$4	$8
Mother 975QX545-7	Commemoratives	1991	$10	$35
Mother & Child 1575QK112 6	Showcase Ornaments/ Christmas Lights	1994	$16	$20
Mother & Daughter QX6696	General Line	1998	$9	$12
Mother & Daughter QX6757	General Line	1999	$9	$20
Mother Goose 1375QX498-4	Artists' Favorites	1992	$14	$15
Mother Is Love 875QX453-6	Commemoratives	1990	$9	$11
Motorcycle Chums QXL7495	Magic Ornaments	1997	$24	$30
Mouse King 4th Ed. QXM4407	Nutcracker Ballet	1999	$6	$8
Mouseboat 775QX475-3	Artists' Favorites	1990	$8	$9
Moustershire Christmas, A QXM4839	Miniature Ornaments	1995	$25	$23
Mr. Ashbourne QX5056	Dickens Caroler Bells	1990	$22	$20
Mr. Potato Head QX6335	General Line	1997	$11	$18
Mr. Spock QXI554-4	Star Trek	1996	$15	$19
Mrs. Beaumont QX5039	Dickens Caroler Bells	1991	$22	$30
Mrs. Claus' Cupboard QXC484-3	Hallmark Expo Ornaments	1994	$55	$150
Mrs. Claus QK120-4	Folk Art Americana	1996	$19	$17
Mrs. Claus's Story	Artists on Tour	1997	N/A	$24
Mrs. Cratchit 1375QX499-9	Christmas Carol Collection, A	1991	$14	$16
Mrs. Parkley's General Store 795YPR945 1	Sarah, Plain & Tall Collection	1994	$8	$12
Mrs. Potato Head QX6886	General Line	1998	$11	$19
Mrs. Santa's Kitchen 2500QLX726-3	Magic Ornaments	1990	$25	$45
Mufasa & Simba 1495QX540-6	Lion King	1994	$15	$15
Muhammad Ali QXI4147	Sports Collection	1999	$15	$25
Mulan, Mushu & Cri-Kee QXD415 6	General Line	1998	$15	$29
Muletide Greetings QX600-9	Handcrafted Ornaments	1995	$8	$8
Munchkinland Mayor & Coroner QX6463	Wizard Of Oz Collection	1998	$14	$14
Murray Airplane 3rd Ed. QX536-4	Kiddie Car Classics	1996	$14	$35
Murray Champion 1st Ed. 1395QX542-6	Kiddie Car Classics	1994	$14	$30
Murray Champion 1st Ed. QXM4079	Miniature Kiddie Car Classics	1995	N/A	$13
Murray Dump Truck 4th Ed. QX6195	Kiddie Car Classics	1997	$14	$14
Murray Dump Truck/Orange 4th Ed. QXM4183	Miniature Kiddie Car Classics	1998	N/A	$12
Murray Fire Truck 2nd Ed. QX502-7	Kiddie Car Classics	1995	$14	$16
Murray Fire Truck 2nd Ed. QXM403-1	Miniature Kiddie Car Classics	1996	$7	$12
Murray Pursuit Airplane 3rd Ed. QXM4132	Miniature Kiddie Car Classics	1997	N/A	$12
Musician Of Note, A QX6567	General Line	1999	$8	$13
My First Hot Wheels QLX727-9	Magic Ornaments	1995	$28	$30
My Sister, My Friend QX6749	General Line	1999	$10	$12
Myrrh QBG 689-3	Crown Reflections	1998	$22	$19

Luke Skywalker, 1997, 1st in the
Star Wars series, **$24.**

Darth Vader, 1997, Star Wars, **$19.**

Yoda, 1997, Star Wars, **$15.**

C-3PO and R2-D2, set of two, 1997, Star Wars, **$23.**

Ornament Title	Series	Year	Issue Price	Current Value
N. Pole Buddy 450QXM592-7	Miniature Ornaments	1991	$4	$8
Naboo Star Fighter QXI7613	General Line	1999	$19	$21
National Salute QX6293	General Line	1998	$9	$22
Native American Barbie 1st Ed. QX556-1	Dolls Of The World	1996	$15	$16
Nativity 450QXM570-6	Miniature Ornaments	1990	$4	$12
Nativity Tree QX6575	General Line	1997	$15	$32
Nativity, The 1st Ed. QXM4156	Nativity	1998	$10	$19
Nativity, The 2nd Ed. QXM4497	Nativity	1999	$10	$18
Nature's Angels 1st Ed. 450QXM573-3	Nature's Angels	1990	$4	$20
Nature's Angels 2nd Ed. 450QXM565-7	Nature's Angels	1991	$4	$13
Nature's Angels 3rd Ed. 450QXM545-1	Nature's Angels	1992	$4	$11
Nature's Angels 4th Ed. 450QXM512-2	Nature's Angels	1993	$4	$11
Nature's Angels 5th Ed. 450QXM512-6	Nature's Angels	1994	$4	$5
Nature's Angels 6th Ed. QXM4809	Nature's Angels	1995	$5	$8
Nature's Angels 7th & Final Ed. QXM411-1	Nature's Angels	1996	$5	$6
Nebraska Cornhuskers QSR2459	Collegiate Collection	1999	$10	$5
Neighborhood Drugstore 11th Ed. 1495QX528-6	Nostalgic Houses & Shops	1994	$15	$28
Nephew 675QX573-5	General Line	1993	$7	$6
Nephew 795QX554-6	Handcrafted Ornaments	1994	$8	$5
New Arrival QX6306	General Line	1998	$19	$15
New Christmas Friend QXC4516	Collector's Club	1998	$19	$12
New England Patriots QSR6228	Football Helmet Collection	1995	$10	$24
New England Patriots QSR5279	NFL Collection	1999	$11	$9
New England Patriots QSR5482	NFL Collection	1997	$10	$10
New England Patriots QSR646-1	NFL Collection	1996	$10	$9
New Home 675QX434-3	Commemoratives	1990	$7	$20
New Home 675QX544-9	Commemoratives	1991	$7	$12
New Home 775QX590-5	General Line	1993	$8	$18
New Home 875QX519-1	Commemoratives	1992	$9	$10
New Home 895QX566-3	Handcrafted Ornaments	1994	$9	$5
New Home QX583-9	Handcrafted Ornaments	1995	$9	$6
New Home QX588-1	General Line	1996	$9	$14
New Home QX6347	General Line	1999	$10	$12
New Home QX6652	General Line	1997	$9	$8
New Home QX6713	General Line	1998	$10	$28
New Orleans Saints QSR5485	NFL Collection	1997	$10	$10
New Orleans Saints QSR646-4	NFL Collection	1996	$10	$9
New Pair Of Skates QXD4032	Disney Collection	1997	$14	$13
New York Giants QSR5143	NFL Collection	1998	$10	$10
New York Giants QSR5249	NFL Collection	1999	$11	$8
New York Giants QSR5492	NFL Collection	1997	$10	$10
New York Giants QSR647-1	NFL Collection	1996	$10	$5
New York Jets QSR5495	NFL Collection	1997	$10	$10
New York Knickerbockers QSR1272	NBA Collection	1997	$10	$4
New York Knicks QSR1047	NBA Collection	1999	$11	$4

Little Boy Blue, 1997, 5th and final edition in the Mother Goose series, **$14.**

The Lone Ranger lunch box, 1997, **$10.**

Jeff Gordon, 1997, 1st in the Stock Car Champions series, **$17.**

1953 GMC, 1997, 3rd in the All-American Trucks series, **$23.**

Dad, 1997, **$8.**

1969 Hurst Olds 442, 1997, 7th in the Classic American Cars series, **$15.**

Ornament Title	Series	Year	Issue Price	Current Value
Nick's Wish List QX6863	General Line	1998	$9	$19
Niece 675QX573-2	General Line	1993	$7	$5
Niece 795QX554-3	Handcrafted Ornaments	1994	$8	$5
Night Before Christmas 1st Ed. 1375QXM5541	Night Before Christmas	1992	$14	$12
Night Before Christmas 2nd Ed. 450QXM5115	Night Before Christmas	1993	$4	$10
Night Before Christmas 3rd Ed. 450QXM5123	Night Before Christmas	1994	$4	$8
Night Before Christmas 4th Ed. 475QXM4807	Night Before Christmas	1995	$5	$8
Night Before Christmas 5th & Final Ed. 575QXM4104	Night Before Christmas	1996	$6	$8
Night Before Christmas 975QX530-7	General Line	1991	$10	$15
Night Before Christmas QX5721	General Line	1997	$24	$44
Night Watch QX6725	General Line	1998	$10	$12
Nikki QX6142	All God's Children	1997	$13	$13
Nine Ladies Dancing 675QX303-1	Twelve Days Of Christmas	1992	$7	$16
Noah's Ark 1375QX486-7	Artists' Favorites	1991	$14	$25
Noah's Ark 2450QXM410-6 Set Of Three	Miniature Ornaments	1994	$25	$58
Noah's Ark QX6809	General Line	1999	$13	$13
Noel 300QXM598-9	Miniature Ornaments	1991	$3	$5
Noelle QK113-9	Angel Bells	1995	$13	$28
Nolan Ryan 1st Ed. QXI571-1	At The Ballpark	1996	$15	$15
Norman Rockwell Art 475QX229-6	General Line	1990	$5	$19
Norman Rockwell Art 500QX222-4	General Line	1992	$5	$15
Norman Rockwell Art 500QX225-9	General Line	1991	$5	$10
Norman Rockwell Art 500QX241-3	General Line	1994	$5	$9
North Carolina Tar Heels QSR2467	Collegiate Collection	1999	$10	$5
North Pole 911 QX595-7	Handcrafted Ornaments	1995	$11	$22
North Pole Fire Fighter 975QX510-4	General Line	1992	$10	$18
North Pole Fire Truck 475QXM410-5	Miniature Ornaments	1993	$5	$9
North Pole Merrython QLX739-2	Magic Ornaments	1993	$25	$55
North Pole Mr. Potato Head QX8027	General Line	1999	$11	$20
North Pole Reserve QX6803	General Line	1998	$11	$14
North Pole Star QX6589	General Line	1999	$9	$9
North Pole Volunteers QLX747-1	Special Edition	1996	$42	$58
Notes Of Cheer 575QX535-7	General Line	1991	$6	$8
Notre Dame Fighting Irish QSR2427	Collegiate Collection	1999	$10	$5
Novel Idea 1295QP606-6	Personalized Ornaments	1994	$13	$13
Novel Idea QP606-6	Personalized Ornaments	1995	$13	$14
Number One Teacher QX594-9	Handcrafted Ornaments	1995	$8	$15
Nut Sweet Nut 1000QLX708-1	Magic Ornaments	1992	$10	$25
Nutcracker 3rd Ed. QXM4146	Nutcracker Ballet	1998	$6	$8
Nutcracker Ballet, The 1st Ed. QXM4064	Nutcracker Ballet	1996	$15	$18
Nutcracker Guild 1st Ed. 575QXM514-6	Nutcracker Guild	1994	$6	$18

Right: Away to the Window, 1997, from the Hallmark Keepsake Ornament Collector's Club, **$8.**

Far right: Ready for Santa, 1997, from the Hallmark Keepsake Ornament Collector's Club, **$8.**

Right: Happy Christmas to All!, 1997, from the Hallmark Keepsake Ornament Collector's Club, **$18.**

Far right: Jolly Old Santa, 1997, from the Hallmark Keepsake Ornament Collector's Club, **$12.**

Away to the Window, Ready for Santa, Jolly Old Santa, and Happy Christmas to All!, 1997, from the Hallmark Keepsake Ornament Collector's Club.

Ornament Title	Series	Year	Issue Price	Current Value
Nutcracker Guild 2nd Ed. QXM4787	Nutcracker Guild	1995	$6	$7
Nutcracker Guild 3rd Ed. QXM408-4	Nutcracker Guild	1996	$6	$14
Nutcracker Guild 4th Ed. QXM4165	Nutcracker Guild	1997	$7	$9
Nutcracker Guild 5th Ed. QXM4203	Nutcracker Guild	1998	$11	$9
Nutcracker Guild 6th Ed. QXM4587	Nutcracker Guild	1999	$7	$9
Nutshell Chat 675QX519-3	General Line	1990	$7	$10
Nutshell Holiday 575QX465-2	Handcrafted Ornaments	1990	$6	$25
Nutshell Nativity 675QX517-6	General Line	1991	$7	$25
Nutty Eggs 675QEO838-2	Easter Ornaments	1993	$7	$10
Nutty Squirrel 575QX483-3	General Line	1991	$6	$9
O Christmas Tree 1075QX541-1	Gold Crown Exclusives	1992	$11	$27
O Holy Night- 4 Pc QXM420-4	Special Edition	1996	$25	$18
Oakland Raiders QSR6249	Football Helmet Collection	1995	$10	$30
Oakland Raiders QSR5086	NFL Collection	1998	$10	$10
Oakland Raiders QSR5257	NFL Collection	1999	$11	$10
Oakland Raiders QSR5422	NFL Collection	1997	$10	$10
Oakland Raiders QSR644-1	NFL Collection	1996	$10	$10
Old-Fashioned Sled 875QX431-7	General Line	1991	$9	$10
Olive Oyl & Swee' Pea QX548-1	Handcrafted Ornaments	1996	$11	$12
Olympic Triumph QXE573-1	Olympic Spirit Collection	1996	$11	$9
On A Roll 675QX534-7	General Line	1991	$7	$9
On Cloud Nine 1200QXC485-3	Collector's Club	1994	$12	$15
On Her Toes 875QX526-5	General Line	1993	$9	$10
On My Way, Photoholder QX586-1	General Line	1996	$8	$15
On The Billboard 1275QP602-2	Personalized Ornaments	1993	$13	$11
On The Billboard 1295QP602-2	Personalized Ornaments	1994	$13	$11
On The Billboard QP602-2	Personalized Ornaments	1995	$13	$14
On The Ice QX604-7	Handcrafted Ornaments	1995	$8	$11
On The Road 1st Ed. 575QXM400-2	On The Road	1993	$6	$13
On The Road 2nd Ed. 575QXM510-3	On The Road	1994	$6	$10
On The Road 3rd Ed. QXM479-7	On The Road	1995	$6	$8
On The Road 4th Ed. QXM410-1	On The Road	1996	$6	$6
On The Road 5th Ed. QXM417-2	On The Road	1997	$6	$6
On The Road 6th & Final Ed. QXM4213	On The Road	1998	$6	$6
On Thin Ice Maxine QX6489	General Line	1999	$11	$8
One-Elf Marching Band 1275QX534-2	General Line	1993	$13	$11
Open-&-Shut Holiday 995QX569-6	Handcrafted Ornaments	1994	$10	$10
Orlando Magic QSR1059	NBA Collection	1999	$11	$5
Orlando Magic QSR1282	NBA Collection	1997	$10	$7
Otto The Carpenter 875QX525-4	North Pole Nutcrackers	1992	$9	$21
Our 1st Christmas Together Photo QX595-2	General Line	1993	$9	$10
Our 25th Anniversary	Collector's Club	1998	N/A	$N/A
Our Christmas Together 1075QX594-2	General Line	1993	$11	$6
Our Christmas Together 995QX481-6	Handcrafted Ornaments	1994	$10	$10
Our Christmas Together Photoholder QX580-4	General Line	1996	$9	$16

Murray Dump Truck, 1997, 4th in the Kiddie Car Classics series, **$14.**

Toy Freight Car, 1997, 4th in the Yuletide Central series, **$20.**

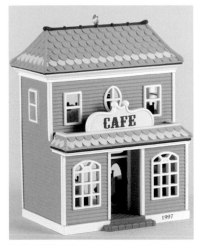

Snowshoe Rabbits in Winter, 1997, 1st in the Majestic Wilderness series, **$20.**

Café, 1997, 14th in the Nostalgic Houses and Shops series, **$19.**

The Flight at Kitty Hawk, 1997, 1st in the Sky's the Limit series, **$19.**

Victorian Christmas, 1997, 1st in the Thomas Kinkade, Painter of Light series, **$19.**

Ornament Title	Series	Year	Issue Price	Current Value
Our Christmas Together QX579-4	General Line	1996	$19	$28
Our Christmas Together QX579-9	Handcrafted Ornaments	1995	$10	$10
Our Christmas Together QX5809	Commemoratives	1995	$10	$10
Our Christmas Together QX6475	General Line	1997	$17	$14
Our Christmas Together QX6689	General Line	1999	$10	$13
Our Family Photoholder QX5576	General Line	1994	$8	$20
Our Family Photoholder 775QX589-2	General Line	1993	$8	$9
Our Family QX570-9	Handcrafted Ornaments	1995	$8	$9
Our Fifth Anniversary 1000AGA731-9	Anniversary Ornaments	1992	$10	$20
Our Fifth Anniversary 1000AGA786-6	Anniversary Ornaments	1993	$10	$20
Our First Anniversary 1000AGA731-8	Anniversary Ornaments	1992	$10	$20
Our First Anniversary 1000AGA786-5	Anniversary Ornaments	1993	$10	$20
Our First Christmas Photoholder QX565-3	General Line	1994	$9	$12
Our First Christmas Together 1875QX595-5	General Line	1993	$19	$25
Our First Christmas Together 1895QX570-6	General Line	1994	$19	$15
Our First Christmas Together 475QX213-6	Commemoratives	1990	$5	$20
Our First Christmas Together 675QX301-1	Commemoratives	1992	$7	$10
Our First Christmas Together 675QX301-5	General Line	1993	$7	$18
Our First Christmas Together 675QX314-6	Commemoratives	1990	$7	$20
Our First Christmas Together 695QX318-6	General Line	1994	$7	$18
Our First Christmas Together 975QX488-3	Commemoratives	1990	$10	$25
Our First Christmas Together 975QX506-1	Commemoratives	1992	$10	$15
Our First Christmas Together 975QX564-2	General Line	1993	$10	$8
Our First Christmas Together 995QX564-3	General Line	1994	$10	$9
Our First Christmas Together Photoholder QX590-7	Handcrafted Ornaments	1995	$9	$12
Our First Christmas Together QLX735-5	Magic Ornaments	1993	$20	$44
Our First Christmas Together QX305-1	General Line	1996	$7	$10
Our First Christmas Together QX317-7	General Line	1995	$7	$10
Our First Christmas Together QX3182	General Line	1997	$8	$8
Our First Christmas Together QX3193	General Line	1998	$8	$12
Our First Christmas Together QX3207	General Line	1999	$8	$15
Our First Christmas Together QX579-7	Handcrafted Ornaments	1995	$17	$15
Our First Christmas Together QX579-9	Handcrafted Ornaments	1995	$9	$10
Our First Christmas Together QX6465	General Line	1997	$11	$15
Our First Christmas Together QX6472	General Line	1997	$9	$10
Our First Christmas Together QX6636	General Line	1998	$9	$5
Our First Christmas Together QX6643	General Line	1998	$19	$12
Our First Christmas Together QX6697	General Line	1999	$9	$11
Our First Christmas Together QX6699	General Line	1999	$22	$20
Our First Christmas Together 2000QLX7221	Magic Ornaments	1992	$20	$33
Our First Xmas/Photoholder 775QX488-6	Commemoratives	1990	$8	$17
Our Lady Of Guadalupe QXM4275	Miniature Ornaments	1997	$9	$8
Our Little Blessings QX520-9	Handcrafted Ornaments	1995	$13	$12
Our Song QX6183	General Line	1998	$10	$3
Our Tenth Anniversary 1000AGA731-7	Anniversary Ornaments	1992	$10	$20

Wedding Day Barbie, 1997, from the Barbie series, **$18.**

Holiday Barbie, 1997, 5th in the Holiday Barbie Collection, **$13.**

Our 25th Anniversary, 1998, from the Hallmark Keepsake Ornament Collector's Club, no established value.

Chinese Barbie, 1997, 2nd in the Dolls of the World series, **$18.**

Canadian Mountie, 1997, 3rd in the Miniature Clothespin Soldier series, **$7.**

Ornament Title	Series	Year	Issue Price	Current Value
Our Tenth Anniversary 1000AGA786-7	Anniversary Ornaments	1993	$10	$20
Out Of This World Teacher 795QX576-6	Handcrafted Ornaments	1994	$8	$10
Outstanding Teacher QX6627	General Line	1999	$9	$6
Over The Rooftops QLX737-4	Magic Ornaments	1996	$14	$28
Owl 975QX561-4	General Line	1992	$10	$20
Owl 975QX569-5	General Line	1993	$10	$11
Owliver 1st Ed. 775QX454-4	Owliver	1992	$8	$11
Owliver 2nd Ed. 775QX542-5	Owliver	1993	$8	$5
Owliver 3rd & Final Ed. 795QX522-6	Owliver	1994	$8	$5
Packed With Memories Photoholder QX563-9	Handcrafted Ornaments	1995	$8	$9
Panda's Surprise 450QXM561-6	Miniature Ornaments	1990	$4	$8
Pansy Angel 1st Ed. QK117-1	Language Of Flowers	1996	$16	$44
Papa Bearinger 495XPR974-6	Bearingers Of Victoria Circle	1993	$5	$7
Parade Of Nations QXE574-1	Olympic Spirit Collection	1996	$11	$4
Parade Pals QEO815-1	Easter Ornaments	1996	$8	$22
Park Avenue Wendy & Alex The Bellhop QFM8499	Madame Alexander	1999	$13	$20
Partridge In A Pear Tree 975QX529-7	General Line	1991	$10	$10
Partridge In Pear Tree 875QX523-4	General Line	1992	$9	$9
Partridges In A Pear 1400QLX721-2	Magic Ornaments	1990	$14	$18
Passenger Car 395XPR973-2	Claus & Co. R.R. Ornaments	1991	$4	$10
Passenger Car 3rd Ed. 995QEO8376	Cottontail Express	1998	$10	$15
Passenger Car 3rd Ed. QXM564-9	Noel Railroad	1991	$8	$50
Peaceful Christmas QXM421-4	Miniature Ornaments	1996	$5	$6
Peaceful Dove 1175QK104-3	General Line	1994	$12	$6
Peaceful Kingdom 475QX210-6	Commemoratives	1990	$5	$20
Peaceful Pandas QXM4253	Miniature Ornaments-Noah's Ark	1998	$6	$10
Peaceful Village 1575QK110-6	Showcase Ornaments/ Christmas Lights	1994	$16	$16
Peanuts 1st Ed. 1800QLX722-9	Peanuts (Magic)	1991	$18	$80
Peanuts 2nd Ed. 1800QLX721-4	Peanuts (Magic)	1992	$18	$55
Peanuts 3rd Ed. 1800QLX715-5	Peanuts (Magic)	1993	$18	$48
Peanuts 475QX223-3	General Line	1990	$5	$19
Peanuts 4th Ed. 2000QLX740-6	Peanuts (Magic)	1994	$20	$30
Peanuts 5 & Final Ed. 2450QLX727-7	Peanuts (Magic)	1995	$25	$48
Peanuts 500QX224-4	General Line	1992	$5	$34
Peanuts 500QX225-7	General Line	1991	$5	$24
Peanuts 775QEO817-6	Easter Ornaments	1994	$8	$30
Peanuts 900QP604-5	Personalized Ornaments	1993	$9	$9
Peanuts Gang 1st Ed. 975QX531-5	Peanuts Gang	1993	$10	$30
Peanuts Gang 2nd Ed. QX520-3	Peanuts Gang	1994	$10	$15
Peanuts Gang 3rd Ed. QX505-9	Peanuts Gang	1995	$10	$16
Peanuts Gang 4th & Final Ed. QX538-1	Peanuts Gang	1996	$10	$12
Peanuts QEO825-7	Easter Ornaments	1995	$8	$20

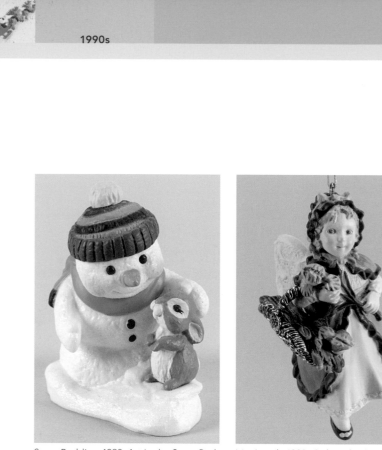

Snow Buddies, 1998, 1st in the Snow Buddies series, **$22.**

Iris Angel, 1998, 3rd in the Language of Flowers series, **$15.**

Frosty Friends, 1998, 19th in the Frosty Friends series, **$25.**

Victorian Christmas II, 1998, from the Thomas Kinkade, Painter of Light series, **$28.**

Ornament Title	Series	Year	Issue Price	Current Value
Pear-Shaped Tones 375QXM405-2	Miniature Ornaments	1993	$4	$8
Pebbles & Bamm-Bamm QXM4757	Miniature Ornaments	1995	$10	$9
Peekaboo Bears QX6563	General Line	1998	$13	$18
Peekaboo Pup 2000QLX742-3	Magic Ornaments	1994	$20	$20
Peek-A-Boo Tree QX524-4	General Line	1993	$11	$25
Peep Inside 1375QX532-2	General Line	1993	$14	$16
Peeping Out 675QEO820-3	Easter Ornaments	1994	$7	$12
Penguin Pal 3rd Ed. 450QXM574-6	Penguin Pals	1990	$4	$10
Penguin Pal 4th & Final Ed. 450QXM562-9	Penguin Pals	1991	$4	$8
Penn State Nittany Lions QSR2469	Collegiate Collection	1999	$10	$5
Pennsylvania GG-1 Locomotive 3rd Ed. QX634-6	Lionel Trains	1998	$19	$22
People Friendly 875QX593-2	General Line	1993	$9	$8
Pepe Lepew & Penelope QX6507	Looney Tunes	1999	$13	$32
Peppermint Painter QXM4312	Miniature Ornaments	1997	$5	$8
Peppermint Surprise QX623-4	Handcrafted Ornaments	1996	$8	$9
Pepperoni Mouse 675QX497-3	General Line	1990	$7	$14
Percy The Small Engine-No. 6 QX631-4	Thomas The Tank Engine & Friends	1996	$10	$15
Percy, Flit & Meeko QXI617-9	Pocahontas	1995	$10	$15
Perfect Balance 300QXM557-1	Miniature Ornaments	1992	$3	$16
Perfect Balance QX592-7	Handcrafted Ornaments	1995	$8	$6
Perfect Catch 775QX469-3	General Line	1990	$8	$19
Perfect Fit 450QXM551 6	Miniature Ornaments	1990	$4	$14
Perfect Match 875QX577-2	General Line	1993	$9	$8
Perfect Match, A QX6633	General Line	1998	$11	$19
Perfect Tree, Tender Touches QX6572	Premiere Exclusive	1997	$15	$15
Peter Rabbit 1st Ed. QEO807-1	Beatrix Potter	1996	$9	$50
Pewter Rocking Horse QX616-7	Anniversary Ornaments	1995	$20	$40
PEZ Santa QX526-7	Handcrafted Ornaments	1995	$8	$12
PEZ Snowman QX653-4	Handcrafted Ornaments	1996	$8	$11
Philadelphia Eagles QSR6259	Football Helmet Collection	1995	$10	$24
Philadelphia Eagles QSR5153	NFL Collection	1998	$10	$10
Philadelphia Eagles QSR5259	NFL Collection	1999	$11	$9
Philadelphia Eagles QSR5502	NFL Collection	1997	$10	$10
Philadelphia Eagles QSR648-1	NFL Collection	1996	$10	$5
Phoebus & Esmeralda QXD6344	Hunchback Of Notre Dame	1997	$15	$13
Phoenix Suns QSR1292	NBA Collection	1997	$10	$4
Piano Player Mickey QXD7389	Mickey & Co.	1999	$24	$45
Picture Perfect, Crayola Crayon QEO824-9	Easter Ornaments	1995	$8	$11
Piglet & Eeyore 975QX557-7	General Line	1991	$10	$25
Pinball Wonder QLX745-1	Handcrafted Ornaments	1996	$28	$50
Pink Panther, The 1275QX575-5	General Line	1993	$13	$18
Pink Poinsettias QBG6926	Crown Reflections/General Line	1998	$25	$35
Pinocchio & Geppetto QXD4107	Pinocchio	1999	$17	$24

New Christmas Friend, Making His Way, and Kringle Bells, 1998, from the Hallmark Keepsake Ornament Collector's Club.

Kringle Bells, 1998, from the Hallmark Keepsake Ornament Collector's Club, **$6.**

Making His Way, 1998, from the Hallmark Keepsake Ornament Collector's Club, **$12.**

New Christmas Friend, 1998, from the Hallmark Keepsake Ornament Collector's Club, **$12.**

Ornament Title	Series	Year	Issue Price	Current Value
Pinto 3rd Ed. 450QXM574-3	Rocking Horse Miniatures	1990	$4	$25
Pittsburgh Steelers QSR5163	NFL Collection	1998	$10	$10
Pittsburgh Steelers QSR5267	NFL Collection	1999	$11	$10
Pittsburgh Steelers QSR5512	NFL Collection	1997	$10	$10
Pittsburgh Steelers QSR649-1	NFL Collection	1996	$10	$8
Pixie Parachute QXM4256	Miniature Ornaments	1998	$5	$6
Playful Pals 1475QX574-2	Handcrafted Ornaments	1993	$15	$20
Playful Penguins QXM4059	Miniature Ornaments-Noah's Ark	1995	$6	$22
Playful Shepherd QX6592	General Line	1997	$10	$20
Playful Snowman QX6867	General Line	1999	$13	$22
Playing Ball 1275QP603-2	Personalized Ornaments	1993	$13	$11
Playing Ball 1295QP603-2	Personalized Ornaments	1994	$13	$11
Playing Ball 1295QP603-2	Personalized Ornaments	1995	$13	$14
Playing With Pooh 1st Ed. QXD4197	Winnie The Pooh & Christopher Robin Too	1999	$14	$14
Please Pause Here 1475QX529-1	General Line	1992	$15	$22
Plucky Duck 575QX412-3	Tiny Toon Adventure	1994	$6	$8
Plum Delightful 875QX497-7	Tender Touches	1991	$9	$10
Pocahontas & Capt. John Smith QXI619-7	Pocahontas	1995	$15	$17
Pocahontas QXI617-7	Pocahontas	1995	$13	$16
Pogo Stick 5th & Final Ed. 450QXM5391	Kittens In Toyland	1992	$4	$17
Poky Little Puppy QX6479	General Line	1999	$12	$19
Poland 3rd & Final Ed. 1175QX524-2	Peace On Earth	1993	$12	$13
Polar Bear Adventure 1500QK105-5	Folk Art Americana	1993	$15	$50
Polar Bowler QX6746	General Line	1990	$8	$4
Polar Buddies QXM4332	Miniature Ornaments	1997	$5	$9
Polar Circus Wagon 1375QX439-9	Artists' Favorites	1991	$14	$10
Polar Classic 675QX528-7	General Line	1991	$7	$22
Polar Coaster QX611-7	Handcrafted Ornaments	1995	$9	$19
Polar Cycle QX603-4	General Line	1996	$13	$13
Polar Jogger 575QX466-6	General Line	1990	$6	$7
Polar Pair 575QX462-6	General Line	1990	$6	$9
Polar Polka 450QXM553-4	Miniature Ornaments	1992	$4	$8
Polar Post 875QX491-4	Artists' Favorites	1992	$9	$10
Polar Sport 775QX515-6	General Line	1990	$8	$15
Polar Tv 775QX516-6	General Line	1990	$8	$8
Polar V.I.P. 575QX466-3	General Line	1990	$6	$10
Polar Video 575QX463-3	General Line	1990	$6	$9
Pony Express Rider 1st Ed. QX6323	Old West	1998	$14	$10
Pony For Christmas, A 1st Ed. QX6316	Pony For Christmas	1998	$11	$24
Pony For Christmas, A 2nd Ed. QX6299	Pony For Christmas	1999	$11	$17
Poolside Walrus 775QX498-6	General Line	1990	$8	$10
Popcorn Party 5th Ed. 1375QX439-3	Mr. & Mrs. Claus	1990	$14	$40
Popeye QX525-7	Handcrafted Ornaments	1995	$11	$10
Popping Good Times 1475QX539-2	General Line	1993	$15	$15

Green Bay Packers Helmet, 1998, from the NFL Collection, **$10.**

1937 Ford V-8, 1998, 4th in the All-American Trucks series, **$23.**

Richard Petty, 1998, 2nd in the Stock Car Champions series, **$13.**

1970 Plymouth Hemi 'Cuda, 1998, 8th in the Classic American Cars series, **$10.**

Hot Wheels 30th Anniversary, 1998, **$13.**

Ornament Title	Series	Year	Issue Price	Current Value
Porcelain Hinged Box QX6772	General Line	1997	$15	$18
Pork N' Beans QEO817-4	Easter Ornaments	1996	$8	$5
Porky Pig 875QX565-2	Looney Tunes	1993	$9	$15
Pour Some More 575QXM515-6	Miniature Ornaments	1994	$6	$7
Practice Makes Perfect 895QX586-3	Handcrafted Ornaments	1994	$9	$5
Practice Swing-Donald Duck 1095QEO8396	Easter Ornaments	1998	$11	$9
Praise Him QX6542	General Line	1997	$9	$18
Praise The Day QX6799	General Line	1999	$15	$12
Prancer & Vixen 495XPR973-6	Santa & His Reindeer Collection	1992	$5	$15
Prayer For Peace QX626-1	Collector's Choice	1996	$8	$8
Praying Madonna QK115-4	Sacred Masterworks	1996	$16	$12
Precious Baby 995QEO8463	World Of Wishes	1998	$10	$8
Precious Baby QEO8417	Easter Ornaments	1999	$10	$10
Precious Child QX624-1	Collector's Choice	1996	$9	$7
Precious Creations QXM4077	Miniature Ornaments	1995	$10	$10
Presents From Pooh QXD4093	General Line	1999	$15	$15
Princess Aurora QXD4126	Sleeping Beauty	1998	$13	$26
Princess Leia 2nd Ed. QXI4026	Star Wars	1998	$14	$13
Prize Topiary QX6675	General Line	1997	$15	$19
Promise Of Easter 875QEO931-4	Easter Ornaments	1992	$9	$10
Prospector 2nd Ed. QX6317	Old West	1999	$14	$20
Pull Out A Plum 575QXM409-5	Miniature Ornaments	1993	$6	$8
Puppet Show 300QXM557-4	Miniature Ornaments	1992	$3	$10
Puppy Love 1st Ed. 775QX537-9	Puppy Love	1991	$8	$77
Puppy Love 2nd Ed. 775QX440-4	Puppy Love	1992	$8	$57
Puppy Love 3rd Ed. 775QX504-5	Puppy Love	1993	$8	$24
Puppy Love 4th Ed. 795QX525-3	Puppy Love	1994	$8	$25
Puppy Love 5th Ed. QX513-7	Puppy Love	1995	$8	$26
Puppy Love 600QXM566-6	Miniature Ornaments	1990	$6	$14
Puppy Love 6th Ed. QX565-1	Puppy Love	1996	$8	$25
Puppy Love 7th Ed. QX622-2	Puppy Love	1997	$8	$24
Puppy Love 8th Ed. QX6163	Puppy Love	1998	$8	$15
Puppy Love 9th Ed. QX6327	Puppy Love	1999	$8	$15
Pup-Tenting QX601-1	General Line	1996	$8	$18
Purr-Fect Little Deer QX6526	General Line	1998	$8	$28
Purr-Fect Princess QEO8715	Easter Ornaments	1997	$8	$11
Puttin' Around QX6763	General Line	1998	$9	$8
Putt-Putt Penguin 975QX579-5	General Line	1993	$10	$12
Quasimodo QXI634-1	Hunchback Of Notre Dame	1996	$10	$5
Queen Amidala QXI4187	General Line	1999	$15	$15
Quick As A Fox 875QX579-2	General Line	1993	$9	$12
Rabbit 975QX560-7	General Line	1991	$10	$20
Rabbit 975QX570-2	General Line	1993	$10	$15
Racing Through The Snow 1575QK117-3	Folk Art Americana	1994	$16	$29
Radiant Window 775QEO836-5	Easter Ornaments	1993	$8	$8

Mexican Barbie, 1998, 3rd in the Dolls of the World series, **$16.**

Princess Leia, 1998, 2nd in the Star Wars series, **$13.**

Boba Fett, 1998, Star Wars, **$13.**

Ewoks, 1998, Star Wars, **$17.**

1955 Murray Tractor and Trailer, 1998, 5th in the Kiddie Car Classics series, **$16.**

Ornament Title	Series	Year	Issue Price	Current Value
Radio News Flash 2200QLX736-2	Magic Ornaments	1993	$22	$28
Raiding The Fridge 1600QLX718-5	Magic Ornaments	1993	$16	$35
Raising A Family QK106-7	Nature's Sketchbook	1995	$19	$20
Rapid Delivery 875QX509-4	General Line	1992	$9	$9
Rapunzel 1st Ed. QEO8635	Children's Collector Barbie	1997	$15	$10
Rarin' To Go 1575QK119-3	Folk Art Americana	1994	$16	$24
Ready For Christmas 2nd Ed. QXD400-6	Hallmark Archives	1998	$13	$28
Ready For Fun 775QX512-4	General Line	1993	$8	$15
Ready For Santa QXC5142	Collector's Club	1997	N/A	$8
Red Barn QX6947	General Line	1999	$16	$27
Red Hot Holiday 795QX584-3	Handcrafted Ornaments	1994	$8	$16
Red Poinsettias 1st Ed. QBG690-6	Crown Reflections/General Line	1998	$35	$25
Red Queen-Alice In Wonderland 4th Ed. QX6379	Madame Alexander	1999	$15	$15
Reel Fun QX6609	General Line	1999	$11	$15
Refreshing Flight 575QXM411-2	Miniature Ornaments	1993	$6	$9
Refreshing Gift QX406-7	Handcrafted Ornaments	1995	$15	$22
Regal Cardinal QX620-4	Handcrafted Ornaments	1996	$10	$28
Reindeer In The Sky 875QP605-5	Personalized Ornaments	1993	$9	$6
Reindeer Pro 795QX592-6	General Line	1994	$8	$10
Reindeer Rooters 1295QP605-6	Personalized Ornaments	1994	$13	$13
Reindeer Rooters QP605-6	Personalized Ornaments	1995	$13	$14
Rejoice! QX598-7	Handcrafted Ornaments	1995	$11	$11
Relaxing Moment 1495QX535-6	General Line	1994	$15	$21
Rhett Butler QX6467	Gone With The Wind	1999	$13	$24
Richard Petty 2nd Ed. QXI4143	Stock Car Champions	1998	$16	$13
Ricky QX6363	All God's Children	1998	$13	$20
Riding A Breeze 575QEO821-3	Easter Ornaments	1994	$6	$9
Riding In The Woods 1575QK106-5	Folk Art Americana	1993	$16	$48
Riding The Wind 1575QK104-5	Folk Art Americana	1993	$16	$39
Ring-A-Ding Elf 850QXM566-9	Miniature Ornaments	1991	$8	$9
Ringing In Christmas QLZ4277	Laser Creations	1999	$7	$6
Road Runner & Wile E. Coyote QLX741-5	Magic Ornaments	1993	$30	$70
Road Runner & Wile E. Coyote QX560-2	Looney Tunes	1994	$13	$18
Rock Candy Miner 2000QLX740-3	Magic Ornaments	1994	$20	$20
Rocket To Success QX6793	General Line	1998	$9	$4
Rocking Bunny 975QEO932-4	Easter Ornaments	1992	$10	$15
Rocking Horse 10th Ed. 1075QX464-6	Rocking Horse	1990	$11	$98
Rocking Horse 11th Ed. 1075QX414-7	Rocking Horse	1991	$11	$42
Rocking Horse 12th Ed. 1075QX426-1	Rocking Horse	1992	$11	$32
Rocking Horse 13th Ed. 1075QX416-2	Rocking Horse	1993	$11	$30
Rocking Horse 14th Ed. 1095QX501-6	Rocking Horse	1994	$11	$22
Rocking Horse 15th Ed. QX516-7	Rocking Horse	1995	$11	$20
Rocking Horse 16th & Final Ed. QX567-4	Rocking Horse	1996	$11	$15
Rodney Takes Flight QXC508-1	Collector's Club	1992	$10	$15

Pennsylvania GG-1 Locomotive, 1998, 3rd in the Lionel Trains series, **$22.**

1917 Curtiss JN-4D "Jenny, " 1998, 2nd in the Sky's the Limit series, **$39.**

Tonka 1956 Suburban Pumper No. 5, 1999, **$16.**

1957 Dodge Sweptside D100, 1999, 5th in the All-American Trucks series, **$19.**

Caboose, 1998, 5th and final edition in the Yuletide Central series, **$19.**

1939 Garton Ford Station Wagon, 1999, from the Hallmark Keepsake Ornament Collector's Club, **$19.**

Ornament Title	Series	Year	Issue Price	Current Value
Roll-A-Bear QXM4629	Miniature Ornaments	1999	$7	$4
Roller Whiz QX593-7	Handcrafted Ornaments	1995	$8	$8
Romulan Warbird QXI726-7	Star Trek	1995	$24	$25
Room For One More 875QX538-2	General Line	1993	$9	$28
Rose Angel 4th & Final Ed. QX6289	Language Of Flowers	1999	$16	$16
Rosebud 3rd Ed. 575QX442-3	Mary's Angels	1990	$6	$70
Round The Mountain QXM402-5	Miniature Ornaments	1993	$7	$10
Roundup Time 1675QK117-6	Folk Art Americana	1994	$17	$24
Ruby Reindeer 600QXM581-6	Miniature Ornaments	1990	$6	$6
Rudolph The Red-Nosed Reindeer QXC7341	Collector's Club	1996	N/A	$10
Rudolph's Helper QXC4171	Collector's Club	1996	N/A	$6
Runabout-U.S.S. Rio Grande QXI7593	Star Trek: Deep Space Nine	1999	$24	$29
Runaway Toboggan QXD4003	General Line	1998	$17	$18
Russian Barbie 4th Ed. QX6369	Dolls Of The World	1999	$15	$11
S. Claus Taxi 1175QX468-6	General Line	1990	$12	$15
Sailboat 3rd Ed. 450QXM573-6	Kittens In Toyland	1990	$4	$14
Sailor Bear QX6765	General Line	1997	$15	$11
Salvation Army Band 3000QLX727-3	Magic Ornaments	1991	$30	$45
San Diego Chargers QSR5515	NFL Collection	1997	$10	$10
San Diego Chargers QSR649-4	NFL Collection	1996	$10	$9
San Francisco 49ers QSR6239	Football Helmet Collection	1995	$10	$24
San Francisco 49ers QSR5173	NFL Collection	1998	$10	$10
San Francisco 49ers QSR5269	NFL Collection	1999	$11	$8
San Francisco 49ers QSR5522	NFL Collection	1997	$10	$7
San Francisco 49ers QSR650-1	NFL Collection	1996	$10	$10
Santa Claus 1675QK107-2	Folk Art Americana	1993	$17	$140
Santa Claus 3rd & Final Ed.QX1215	Turn Of The Century Parade	1997	$17	$15
Santa Claus 495XPR973-9	Santa & His Reindeer Collection	1992	$5	$9
Santa In Paris QX587-7	Handcrafted Ornaments	1995	$9	$25
Santa Jolly Wolly 775QX537-4	General Line	1992	$8	$7
Santa Mail QX6702	General Line	1997	$11	$20
Santa Maria 1275QX507-4	General Line	1992	$13	$9
Santa QXC4164	Collector's Club	1996	N/A	$14
Santa QXC4165	Collector's Club	1996	N/A	$10
Santa Sailor 975QX438-9	Artists' Favorites	1991	$10	$14
Santa Says 1475QP600-5	Personalized Ornaments	1993	$13	$13
Santa Says 1495QP600-5	Personalized Ornaments	1994	$15	$13
Santa Schnoz 675QX498-3	General Line	1990	$7	$19
Santa Special 4000QLX716-7	Magic Ornaments	1992	$40	$75
Santa Special 4000QLX716-7	Magic Ornaments	1991	$40	$40
Santa Sub 1800QLX732-1	Magic Ornaments	1992	$18	$25
Santa Time QXM4647	Miniature Ornaments	1999	$8	$10
Santa-Full 975QX599-1	General Line	1992	$10	$22
Santa's 4x4 18th Ed. QX568-4	Here Comes Santa	1996	$15	$18

Famous Flying Ace, 1999, 2nd in the Spotlight on Snoopy series, **$15.**

Snow Day, 1999, from the Hallmark Keepsake Ornament Collector's Club, **$39.**

Russian Barbie, 1999, 4th in the Dolls of the World series, **$11.**

Jet Threat Car With Case, 1999, Hot Wheels, **$14.**

1955 Chevrolet Nomad Wagon, 1999, 9th in the Classic American Cars, **$9.**

Ornament Title	Series	Year	Issue Price	Current Value
Santa's Answering Machine 2200QLX724-1	Magic Ornaments	1992	$22	$35
Santa's Antique Car 13th Ed. 1475QX434-9	Here Comes Santa	1991	$15	$40
Santa's Bumper Car 20th Ed. QX628-3	Here Comes Santa	1998	$15	$16
Santa's Club List 1500QXC729-1	Collector's Club	1992	$15	$15
Santa's Deer Friend QX6583	Artist's Studio Collection	1998	$24	$32
Santa's Diner QLX733-7	Magic Ornaments	1995	$25	$32
Santa's Flying Machine QX6573	General Line	1998	$17	$18
Santa's Friend 8th Ed. QX6685	Collectible Series	1997	$15	$15
Santa's Gifts QK112-4	Folk Art Americana	1996	$19	$28
Santa's Golf Cart 21st Ed. QX6337	Here Comes Santa	1999	$15	$23
Santa's Hidden Surprise QX6913	General Line	1998	$15	$15
Santa's Ho-Ho-Hoedown 2500QLX725-6	Magic Ornaments	1990	$25	$20
Santa's Hook Shot 1275QX543-4	General Line	1992	$13	$14
Santa's Hot Line 1800QLX715-9	Magic Ornaments	1991	$18	$28
Santa's Journey 850QXM582-6	Miniature Ornaments	1990	$8	$17
Santa's Lego Sleigh 1095QX545-3	Handcrafted Ornaments	1994	$11	$15
Santa's Little Big Top 1st Ed. QXM4779	Santa's Little Big Top	1995	$7	$16
Santa's Little Big Top 2nd Ed QXM408-1	Santa's Little Big Top	1996	$7	$9
Santa's Little Big Top 3rd & Final Ed. QXM4152	Santa's Little Big Top	1997	$7	$8
Santa's Magical Sleigh QX6672	General Line	1997	$24	$26
Santa's Merry Path QX6785	General Line	1997	$17	$20
Santa's Merry Workshop QX6816	Premiere Exclusive	1998	$32	$29
Santa's Polar Friend QX6755	General Line	1997	$17	$18
Santa's Premiere 1075QX523-7	Gold Crown Exclusives	1991	$11	$20
Santa's Roadster 17th Series QX(517-9	Here Comes Santa	1995	$15	$20
Santa's Roundup 875QX508-4	General Line	1992	$9	$24
Santa's Secret Gift QXL7455	Magic Ornaments	1997	$24	$36
Santa's Serenade QX601-7	Handcrafted Ornaments	1995	$9	$10
Santa's Show 'N Tell QXL7566	General Line	1998	$19	$18
Santa's Showboat QXL7465	Magic Ornaments	1997	$42	$75
Santa's Sing-Along 2400QLX747-3	Magic Ornaments	1994	$24	$30
Santa's Ski Adventure QX6422	General Line	1997	$13	$23
Santa's Snow-Getter 1800QLX735-2	Magic Ornaments	1993	$18	$24
Santa's Spin Top QXL7573	General Line	1998	$22	$30
Santa's Streetcar 850QXM576-6	Miniature Ornaments	1990	$8	$10
Santa's Studio 875QX539-7	Matchbox Memories	1991	$9	$9
Santa's Toy Shop QXC4201	Collector's Club	1996	$60	$95
Santa's Visit QXM4047	Miniature Ornaments	1995	$8	$10
Santa's Visitor: Norman Rockwell QX240-7	General Line	1995	$5	$18
Santa's Workshop 2800QLX737-5	Magic Ornaments	1993	$28	$60
Sarah's Maine Home 795XPR945-4	Sarah, Plain & Tall Collection	1994	$8	$10
Sarah's Prairie Home 795XPR945-3	Sarah, Plain & Tall Collection	1994	$8	$12
Satchel Paige 3rd Ed. QX530-4	Baseball Heroes	1996	$13	$12
Scarecrow 995QX543-6	Wizard Of Oz Collection	1994	$10	$39
Scarlett O'Hara 1st Ed. QX6125	Scarlett O'Hara	1997	$15	$14

Frosty Friends, 1999, 20th in the Frosty Friends series, **$20.**

Scarlett O'Hara, 1999, 3rd in the Scarlett O'Hara series, **$20.**

Rhett Butler, 1999, from the Gone With the Wind series, **$24.**

Han Solo, 1999, 3rd in the Star Wars series, **$20.**

Chewbacca, 1999, Star Wars, **$15.**

Ornament Title	Series	Year	Issue Price	Current Value
Scarlett O'Hara 2nd Ed. QX6336	Scarlett O'Hara	1998	$15	$18
Scarlett O'Hara 3rd Ed. QX6397	Scarlett O'Hara	1999	$15	$20
School 3rd Ed. 850QXM576-3	Old English Village	1990	$8	$20
Schroeder & Lucy QLX739-4	Peanuts Collection	1996	$19	$30
Scooby-Doo Lunch Box QX6997	General Line	1999	$15	$24
Scooting Along 675QXM517-3	Miniature Ornaments	1994	$7	$5
Scottie Pippen 5th Ed. QXI4177	Hoop Stars	1999	$15	$22
Scotttish Highlander 4th Ed. QXM4193	Miniature Clothespin Soldier	1998	$5	$7
Seaside Otter 450QXM590-9	Miniature Ornaments	1991	$4	$8
Seaside Scenes 1st Ed. QXM4649	Seaside Scenes	1999	$8	$12
Seattle Seahawks QSR5525	NFL Collection	1997	$10	$10
Seattle Seahawks QSR650-4	NFL Collection	1996	$10	$9
Seattle Supersonics QSR1067	NBA Collection	1999	$11	$4
Seattle Supersonics QSR1295	NBA Collection	1997	$10	$4
Secret Pal 375QXM517-2	Miniature Ornaments	1993	$4	$7
Secret Pal 775QX542-4	Commemoratives	1992	$8	$12
Secret Santa 795QX573-6	Handcrafted Ornaments	1994	$8	$10
Secrets For Santa 2375QXC479-7	Collector's Club	1991	$24	$50
Seeds Of Joy QXM4242	Miniature Ornaments	1997	$7	$7
Seven Swans-A-Swimming 675QX303-3	Twelve Days Of Christmas	1990	$7	$10
Sew Gifted QX6743	General Line	1998	$8	$8
Sew Handy QX6597	General Line	1999	$9	$14
Sew Sweet QX592-1	General Line	1996	$9	$9
Sew Talented QXM4195	Miniature Ornaments	1997	$6	$7
Sew, Sew Tiny 2900QXM579-4	Miniature Ornaments	1992	$29	$25
Shaquille O'Neal 1st Ed. QXI551-7	Hoop Stars	1995	$15	$40
Sharing A Soda QLX742-4	Magic Ornaments	1996	$25	$19
Sharing Christmas 2000QXC543-5	Collector's Club	1993	$20	$19
Sharing Joy QXM4273	Miniature Ornaments	1998	$5	$7
Sharp Flat, A 1095QX577-3	General Line	1994	$9	$18
Ships Of Star Trek, The, QXI4109	Star Trek	1995	$20	$20
Shopping With Santa QX567-5	Here Comes Santa	1993	$24	$28
Shutterbug QXM4212	Miniature Ornaments	1997	$6	$6
Shuttlecraft "Galileo" 2400QLX733-1	Magic Ornaments	1992	$21	$27
Silken Flame 5th Ed.QXI4043	Barbie	1998	$16	$18
Silver Bells 2475QK102-6	Old World Silver	1994	$25	$24
Silver Bows 2475QK102-3	Old World Silver	1994	$25	$20
Silver Dove Of Peace 2475QK107-5	Old World Silver	1993	$25	$20
Silver Poinsettia 2475QK100-6	Old World Silver	1994	$25	$30
Silver Santa 2475QK109-2	Old World Silver	1993	$25	$19
Silver Sleigh 2475QK108-2	Old World Silver	1993	$25	$36
Silver Snowflakes 2475QK101-6	Old World Silver	1994	$25	$23
Silver Star 2800QX532-4	General Line	1992	$28	$30
Silver Star & Holly 2475QK108-5	Old World Silver	1993	$25	$32
Silvery Noel 1275QX530-5	General Line	1993	$13	$30
Silvery Santa 975QXM567-9	Miniature Ornaments	1991	$10	$20

The Toymaker's Gift, 1999, from the Hallmark Keepsake Ornament Collector's Club, **$12.**

Arctic Artist, Snowy Surprise, and The Toymaker's Gift, 1999, from the Hallmark Keepsake Ornament Collector's Club.

Arctic Artist, 1999, from the Hallmark Keepsake Ornament Collector's Club, **$9.**

Snowy Surprise, 1999, from the Hallmark Keepsake Ornament Collector's Club, **$6.**

French Officer, 1999, 5th in the Miniature Clothespin Soldier series, **$8.**

746 Norfolk and Western Steam Locomotive, 1999, 4th in the Lionel Trains series, **$22.**

Ornament Title	Series	Year	Issue Price	Current Value
Simba & Nala QXD4073	Lion King	1998	$14	$14
Simba & Nala 1295QX530-3	Lion King	1994	$13	$20
Simba, Pumbaa & Timon QX615-9	Lion King	1995	$13	$9
Simba, Sarabi & Mufasa QLX751-3	Lion King	1994	$32	$30
Singin' In The Rain QXM4303	Miniature Ornaments	1998	$11	$12
Sister 475QX227-3	Commemoratives	1990	$5	$7
Sister 675QX468-1	Commemoratives	1992	$7	$9
Sister 675QX548-7	Commemoratives	1991	$7	$12
Sister 675QX554-5	General Line	1993	$7	$5
Sister 695QX551-3	Handcrafted Ornaments	1994	$7	$8
Sister QX568-7	Handcrafted Ornaments	1995	$7	$7
Sister To Sister 975QX588-5	General Line	1993	$10	$28
Sister To Sister 995QX553-3	Handcrafted Ornaments	1994	$10	$10
Sister To Sister QX568-9	Handcrafted Ornaments	1995	$8	$8
Sister To Sister QX583-4	General Line	1996	$10	$12
Sister To Sister QX6635	General Line	1997	$10	$10
Sister To Sister QX6693	General Line	1998	$9	$9
Skating With Pooh QXD4127	Miniature Ornaments	1999	$7	$9
Ski For Two 450QXM582-1	Miniature Ornaments	1992	$4	$12
Ski Hound QX590-9	Handcrafted Ornaments	1995	$9	$16
Ski Lift Bunny 675QX544-7	General Line	1991	$7	$9
Ski Trip 2800QLX726-6	Magic Ornaments	1991	$28	$60
Skiing 'Round 875QX521-4	General Line	1992	$9	$12
Sleddin' Buddies QX6849	General Line	1999	$10	$10
Slippery Day QLX741-4	General Line	1996	$25	$48
Smile! It's Christmas Photoholder QX533-5	General Line	1993	$10	$20
Snoopy & Woodstock 675QX472-3	General Line	1990	$7	$35
Snoopy & Woodstock 875QX595-4	General Line	1992	$9	$14
Snoopy & Woodstock 675QX519-7	General Line	1991	$7	$30
Snoopy Plays Santa QXL7475	Magic Ornaments	1997	$22	$38
Snoopy QRP421-9	A Charlie Brown Christmas	1995	$4	$22
Snow Angel 600QXM577-3	Miniature Ornaments	1990	$6	$9
Snow Bear Angel 775QX535-5	General Line	1993	$8	$9
Snow Bowling QX6395	General Line	1997	$7	$13
Snow Buddies 1st Ed. QX6853	Snow Buddies	1998	$8	$22
Snow Buddies 2nd Ed. QX6319	Snow Buddies	1999	$8	$22
Snow Day-Peanuts QXC4517	Collector's Club	1999	$19	$39
Snow Scene, Peanuts QRP4227	A Charlie Brown Christmas	1995	$4	$25
Snow Twins 875QX497-9	Tender Touches	1991	$9	$15
Snow White, Anniversary Ed. QXD4055	Disney Collection	1997	$17	$18
Snow White's Jealous Queen 2nd Ed. QXD4089	Unforgettable Villains	1999	$15	$15
Snowbird 775QX576-5	General Line	1993	$8	$8
Snowboard Bunny QXM4315	Miniature Ornaments	1997	$5	$6
Snowdrop Angel 2nd Ed. QX1095	Language Of Flowers	1997	$16	$16
Snowflake Ballet 1st Ed. QXM4192	Snowflake Ballet	1997	$6	$14

Snowmen of Mitford, 1999, set of three, **$30.**

1968 Murray Jolly Roger Flagship, 1999, 6th in the Kiddie Car Classics series, **$14.**

Mary's Bears, 1999, **$9.**

Victorian Christmas III, 1999, 3rd in the Thomas Kinkade, Painter of Light Series, **$15.**

Curtiss R3C-2 Seaplane, 1999, 3rd in the Sky's the Limit series, **$38.**

Ornament Title	Series	Year	Issue Price	Current Value
Snowflake Ballet 2nd Ed. QXM4173	Snowflake Ballet	1998	$6	$8
Snowflake Ballet 3rd Ed. QXM4569	Snowflake Ballet	1999	$6	$9
Snowgirl QX6562	General Line	1997	$8	$15
Snowmen Of Mitford QXI8587	Gold Crown Exclusives	1999	$16	$30
Snowshoe Bunny 375QXM556-4	Miniature Ornaments	1992	$4	$7
Snowshoe Rabbits In Winter 1st Ed. QX5694	Majestic Wilderness	1997	$13	$20
Snowy Hidewaway 975QX531-2	General Line	1993	$10	$9
Snowy Owl 775QX526-9	General Line	1991	$8	$14
Snowy Surprise QXC4529	Collector's Club	1999	N/A	$6
Snug Kitty 375QXM555-4	Miniature Ornaments	1992	$4	$7
Snuggle Birds 575QXM518-2	Miniature Ornaments	1993	$6	$10
Soaring With Angels QX6213	Folk Art Americana	1998	$17	$12
Somebunny Loves You 675QEO929-4	Easter Ornaments	1992	$7	$26
Son 575QEO518-7	Easter Ornaments	1991	$6	$26
Son 575QEO816-3	Easter Ornaments	1994	$6	$7
Son 575QEO833-5	Easter Ornaments	1993	$6	$6
Son 575QEO928-1	Easter Ornaments	1992	$6	$10
Son 575QX451-6	Commemoratives	1990	$6	$28
Son 575QX546-9	Commemoratives	1991	$6	$15
Son 675QX502-4	Commemoratives	1992	$7	$15
Son 675QX586-5	General Line	1993	$7	$10
Son 695QX562-6	General Line	1994	$7	$12
Son QEO824-7	Easter Ornaments	1995	$6	$6
Son QX566-9	Handcrafted Ornaments	1995	$7	$12
Son QX607-9	General Line	1996	$9	$13
Son QX6803	General Line	1997	$0	$15
Son QX6666	General Line	1998	$9	$10
Son QX6727	General Line	1999	$9	$15
Song & Dance 2000QLX725-3	Magic Ornaments	1990	$20	$45
Song Of The Chimes 2500QLX740-5	Magic Ornaments	1993	$25	$55
Space Shuttle Columbia QLX739-6	Magic Ornaments	1995	$24	$30
Space Shuttle QLX7396	Handcrafted Ornaments	1995	$25	$49
Spain 2nd Ed. 1175QX517-4	Peace On Earth	1992	$12	$10
Sparkling Angel 1800QLX715-7	Magic Ornaments	1991	$18	$38
Sparkling Crystal Angel QXM426-4	Precious Edition	1996	$10	$14
Special Cat Photoholder QX523-5	General Line	1993	$8	$7
Special Cat Photoholder QX541-4	Commemoratives	1992	$8	$7
Special Cat QX571-7	Handcrafted Ornaments	1995	$8	$15
Special Cat, Photoholder 795QX560-6	Handcrafted Ornaments	1994	$8	$5
Special Dog Photoholder QX586-4	General Line	1996	$8	$22
Special Dog Photoholder QX542-1	Commemoratives	1992	$8	$19
Special Dog Photoholder QX596-2	General Line	1993	$8	$10
Special Dog QX571-9	Handcrafted Ornaments	1995	$8	$4
Special Dog QX6632	General Line	1997	$8	$15
Special Dog QX6706	General Line	1998	$8	$16
Special Dog QX6767	General Line	1999	$8	$15

Ornament Title	Series	Year	Issue Price	Current Value
Special Dog, Photoholder 795QX560-3	Handcrafted Ornaments	1994	$8	$9
Special Friends 1295QEO8523	Easter Ornaments	1998	$13	$9
Special Friends 450QXM516-5	Miniature Ornaments	1993	$4	$6
Special Friends 600QXM572-6	Miniature Ornaments	1990	$6	$12
Special Friends 850QXM579-7	Miniature Ornaments	1991	$8	$12
Speedy Gonzales 895QX534-3	Looney Tunes	1994	$9	$12
Spellin' Santa QX6857	General Line	1999	$10	$10
Spencer Sparrow, Esq. 675QX431-2	Handcrafted Ornaments	1990	$7	$14
Spiderman QX575-7	Handcrafted Ornaments	1996	$13	$29
Spirit Of Christmas QX6585	General Line	1997	$10	$22
Spirit Of Christmas Stress 875QX523-1	General Line	1992	$9	$9
Spirit Of Easter 775QEO516-9	Easter Ornaments	1991	$8	$18
Spoon Rider 975QX549-6	General Line	1990	$10	$9
Spoonful Of Love QX6796	General Line	1998	$9	$8
Spotted 9th Ed. QXM412-1	Rocking Horse Miniatures	1996	$5	$10
Spring Chick QEO8469	Easter Ornaments	1999	$22	$22
Springtime Barbie 1st Ed. QEO806-9	Springtime Barbie	1995	$13	$10
Springtime Barbie 2nd Ed. QEO8081	Springtime Barbie	1996	$13	$10
Springtime Barbie 3rd & Final Ed. QEO8642	Springtime Barbie	1997	$13	$15
Springtime Bonnets 1st Ed. QEO832-2	Springtime Bonnets	1993	$8	$14
Springtime Bonnets 2nd Ed. QEO809-6	Springtime Bonnets	1994	$8	$22
Springtime Bonnets 3rd Ed. QEO822-7	Springtime Bonnets	1995	$8	$12
Springtime Bonnets 4th Ed. QEO8134	Springtime Bonnets	1996	$8	$9
Springtime Bonnets 5th & Final Ed. QEO8672	Springtime Bonnets	1997	$8	$8
Springtime Egg 875QEO932-1	Easter Ornaments	1992	$9	$14
Springtime Harvest QEO8429	Easter Ornaments	1999	$8	$8
Springtime Stroll 675QEO516-7	Easter Ornaments	1991	$7	$14
Sprinkling Stars QX6599	General Line	1999	$10	$8
Spunky Monkey 300QXM592-1	Miniature Ornaments	1992	$3	$14
St. Louis Rams QSR5093	NFL Collection	1998	$10	$10
St. Louis Rams QSR5425	NFL Collection	1997	$10	$10
St. Louis Rams QSR644-4	NFL Collection	1996	$10	$9
St. Lucia 2nd Ed. 500QX280-3	Gift Bringers	1990	$5	$10
St. Nicholas 1st Ed. QX508-7	Christmas Visitors	1995	$15	$12
St. Nicholas Circle QXI7556	Thomas Kinkade General Line	1998	$19	$19
Stamp Collector 450QXM562-3	Miniature Ornaments	1990	$4	$6
Stamp Of Approval 795QX570-3	Handcrafted Ornaments	1994	$8	$8
Star Of The Show QX600-4	General Line	1996	$9	$9
Star Of Wonder 675QX598-2	General Line	1993	$7	$15
Star Teacher Photoholder QX564-5	General Line	1993	$6	$6
Star Trek 30 Years QXI753-4	Star Trek	1996	$45	$64
Star Wars Lunchbox 1259QEO8406	Easter Ornaments	1998	$13	$17
Starlight Angel 1400QLX730-6	Magic Ornaments	1990	$14	$35
Starlit Nativity QXM4039	Miniature Ornaments	1995	$8	$19

Ornament Title	Series	Year	Issue Price	Current Value
Starship Christmas 1800QLX733-6	Magic Ornaments	1990	$18	$30
Starship Enterprise 2000QLX719-9	Star Trek	1991	$20	$285
Statue Of Liberty, The QLX742-1	Miniature Ornaments	1996	$25	$38
Stealing A Kiss QX6555	General Line	1997	$15	$12
Stitches Of Joy 775QX518-6	General Line	1990	$8	$8
Stock Car 6th Ed. QXM511-3	Noel Railroad	1994	$7	$15
Stock Car 975QX531-4	Christmas Sky Line Collection	1992	$10	$13
Stocked With Joy 775QX593-4	Artists' Favorites	1992	$8	$17
Stocking Kitten 675QX456-5	General Line	1990	$7	$20
Stocking Pals 1075QX549 3	General Line	1990	$11	$10
Stone Church 1st Ed. QLX7636	Candlelight Services	1998	$19	$25
Strange & Wonderful Love QX596-5	General Line	1993	$9	$11
Strawberry 1st Ed. QEO8369	Fairy Berry Bears	1999	$10	$10
Strawberry Patch QEO817-1	Easter Ornaments	1996	$7	$13
Strike Up The Band! QEO814-1	Easter Ornaments	1996	$15	$16
Stringing Along 850QXM560-6	Miniature Ornaments	1990	$8	$9
Sugar Plum Fairy 2775QXC447-3	Collector's Club	1990	$28	$38
Sugarplum Cottage QGB 6917	General Line	1998	$35	$50
Sugarplum Dreams QXM4099	Miniature Ornaments	1995	$5	$7
Sundae Golfer QX6617	General Line	1999	$13	$14
Sunny Bunny Garden 1500QEO814-6 Set Of 3	Easter Ornaments	1994	$15	$15
Sunny Wisher 575QEO934-4	Easter Ornaments	1992	$6	$12
Superman 1275QX575-2	General Line	1993	$13	$25
Superman Lunchbox QX6423	General Line	1998	$13	$8
Superman QLX730 9	Magic Ornaments	1995	$20	$30
Surfin' Santa QX801-9	Handcrafted Ornaments	1995	$10	$20
Surfin' The Net QX6607	General Line	1999	$10	$19
Surprise Catch QX6753	General Line	1998	$8	$8
Swat Team, The 1275QX539-5	General Line	1993	$13	$14
Sweet As Sugar 875QEO808-6	Easter Ornaments	1994	$9	$10
Sweet Birthday 795QEO8473	World Of Wishes	1998	$8	$15
Sweet Bouquet QXC480-6	Santa's Club Soda	1994	N/A	$10
Sweet Discovery QX6325	General Line	1997	$12	$22
Sweet Dreamer QX6732	General Line	1997	$7	$8
Sweet Dreams 300QXM409-6	Miniature Ornaments	1994	$3	$6
Sweet Easter Wishes 875QEO819-6	Easter Ornaments	1994	$9	$18
Sweet Friendship QX6709	General Line	1999	$10	$6
Sweet Greeting 1095QX580-3	Handcrafted Ornaments	1994	$11	$10
Sweet Memories Qgb 6933	General Line	1998	$45	$45
Sweet Rememberings QX6876	General Line	1998	$9	$10
Sweet Skater QX6579	General Line	1999	$8	$9
Sweet Slumber 450QXM566-3	Miniature Ornaments	1990	$4	$7
Sweet Song QX108-9	Symbols Of Christmas	1995	$16	$5
Sweet Talk 875QX536-7	General Line	1991	$9	$9
Sweet Treat QX643-3	Hershey's	1998	$11	$25

Ornament Title	Series	Year	Issue Price	Current Value
Sweetheart 1175QX489-3	Commemoratives	1990	$12	$15
Sweetheart 975QX495-7	Commemoratives	1991	$10	$24
Swinging In The Snow QX6775	General Line	1997	$13	$20
Swing-Time QEO8705	Easter Ornaments	1997	$8	$5
Sylvester & Tweety 975QX540-5	Looney Tunes	1993	$10	$22
Sylvester & Tweety QX501-7	Looney Tunes	1995	$14	$15
Takin' A Hike QX602-9	Handcrafted Ornaments	1995	$8	$10
Taking A Break QX6305	General Line	1997	$15	$17
Tale Of Peter Rabbit, The QEO8397	Easter Ornaments	1999	$20	$20
Tale Of Peter Rabbit-Beatrix Potter 500QX244-3	General Line	1994	$5	$10
Tamika QX630-1	General Line	1996	$8	$9
Tampa Bay Buccaneers QSR5532	NFL Collection	1997	$10	$10
Tampa Bay Buccaneers QSR651-1	NFL Collection	1996	$10	$10
Tannenbaum's Dept. Store 2600QX561-2	Nostalgic Houses & Shops	1993	$26	$45
Tasmanian Devil 895QX560-5	Looney Tunes	1994	$9	$28
Tasty Christmas 975QX599-4	General Line	1992	$10	$15
Tasty Surprise QXM4276	Miniature Ornaments	1998	$7	$7
Taz & The She-Devil QXM4619	Looney Tunes	1999	$9	$14
Tea W/Teddy 725QXM404-6	Miniature Ornaments	1994	$7	$4
Teacher 450QXM565-3	Miniature Ornaments	1990	$4	$6
Teacher 475QX226-4	Commemoratives	1992	$5	$11
Teacher 475QX228-9	Commemoratives	1991	$5	$15
Teacher 775QX448-3	Commemoratives	1990	$8	$5
Teapot Party QXL7482	Magic Ornaments	1997	$19	$22
Teddy-Bear Style 1st Ed. QXM4215	Teddy-Bear Style	1997	$12	$7
Teddy-Bear Style 2nd Ed. QXM4176	Teddy-Bear Style	1998	$10	$6
Teddy-Bear Style 3rd Ed. QXM4499	Teddy-Bear Style	1999	$6	$9
Ten Lords A Leaping QX301-2	Twelve Days of Christmas	1993	N/A	$12
Ten Years Together 475QX215-3	Commemoratives	1990	$5	$16
Ten Years Together 775QX492-9	Commemoratives	1991	$8	$2
Tender Car 2nd Ed. QX507-9	Yuletide Central	1995	$19	$15
Tender Lovin' Care QX611-4	General Line	1996	$8	$8
Tender-Lionel 746 Norfolk & Western QX6497	General Line	1999	$15	$18
Tennis, Anyone? QX590-7	Handcrafted Ornaments	1995	$8	$9
Terrific Teacher 675QX530-9	Commemoratives	1991	$7	$4
Thank You, Santa Photoholder QX585-4	General Line	1996	$8	$15
That's Entertainment 875QX534-5	General Line	1993	$9	$12
Thick 'N Thin 1095QX569-3	Handcrafted Ornaments	1994	$11	$12
Thimble Bells 1st Ed. 600QXM554-3	Thimble Bells	1990	$6	$14
Thimble Bells 2nd Ed. 600QXM565-9	Thimble Bells	1991	$6	$10
Thimble Bells 3rd Ed. 600QXM546-1	Thimble Bells	1992	$6	$12
Thimble Bells 4th & Final Ed. 575QXM514-2	Thimble Bells	1993	$6	$8
This Big! QX591-4	General Line	1996	$10	$10
Thomas The Tank Engine No. 1 QX585-7	Handcrafted Ornaments	1995	$10	$29

Ornament Title	Series	Year	Issue Price	Current Value
Three Little Piggies 775QX499-6	General Line	1990	$8	$12
Three Wishes QX597-9	Handcrafted Ornaments	1995	$8	$18
Thrill A Minute 895QX586-6	Handcrafted Ornaments	1994	$9	$8
Tigger 975QX560-9	General Line	1991	$10	$50
Tigger & Piglet 975QX570-5	General Line	1993	$10	$28
Tigger In The Garden 995QEO8436	Easter Ornaments	1998	$10	$10
Tigger Plays Soccer QXD4119	General Line	1999	$11	$15
Tiggerific Easter Delivery QEO8359	Easter Ornaments	1999	$11	$11
Timber Wolves At Play-Mark Newman 2nd Ed. QX627-3	Majestic Wilderness	1998	$13	$19
Time For A Treat QX546-4	Hershey's	1996	$12	$13
Time For Easter 875QEO838-5	Easter Ornaments	1993	$9	$15
Time For Love 475QX213-3	General Line	1990	$5	$12
Time Of Peace 795QX581-3	Handcrafted Ornaments	1994	$8	$8
Time Of Peace, A QX6807	Collector's Choice	1999	$9	$9
Timon & Pumbaa 895QX536-6	Lion King	1994	$9	$10
Timon, Pumbaa QXD406-5	Lion King	1997	$13	$10
Tin Airplane 775QX562-2	Holiday Fliers	1993	$8	$18
Tin Blimp 775QX562-5	Holiday Fliers	1993	$8	$12
Tin Hot Air Balloon 775QX561-5	Holiday Fliers	1993	$8	$15
Tin Locomotive QX6826	25th Anniversary Edition	1998	$25	$40
Tin Man 995QX544-3	Wizard Of Oz Collection	1994	$10	$39
Tiny Christmas Helpers Set Of 6 QXM426-1	Miniature Ornaments	1996	$29	$30
Tiny Green Thumbs QXM403-2 Set Of Six	Miniature Ornaments	1993	$29	$25
Tiny Home Improvers Set Of 6 QXM4282	Miniature Ornaments	1997	$29	$34
Tiny Tea Party 2900QXM502-7	Miniature Ornaments	1991	$29	$120
Tiny Tim 1075QX503-7	Christmas Carol Collection, A	1991	$11	$18
Tiny Treasures, Set Of 6, QXM4009	Miniature Ornaments	1995	$29	$30
To My Grandma 775QX555-5	General Line	1993	$8	$5
Tobin Fraley Carousel 1st Ed. 2800QX489-1	Tobin Fraley Carousel	1992	$28	$25
Tobin Fraley Carousel 2nd Ed. 2800QX550-2	Tobin Fraley Carousel	1993	$28	$28
Tobin Fraley Carousel 3rd Ed. 2800QX522-3	Tobin Fraley Carousel	1994	$28	$25
Tobin Fraley Carousel 4th & Final QX506-9	Tobin Fraley Carousel	1995	$28	$28
Tobin Fraley Holiday Carousel 1st Ed. 3200QLX749-6	Tobin Fraley Holiday Carousel	1994	$32	$39
Tobin Fraley Holiday Carousel 2nd Ed. QLX726-9	Tobin Fraley Holiday Carousel	1995	$32	$29
Tobin Fraley Holiday Carousel 3rd & Final Ed. QLC746-1	Tobin Fraley Holiday Carousel	1996	$32	$52
Toboggan Tail 775QX545-9	General Line	1992	$8	$9
Tom Kitten 4th Ed. QEO8329	Beatrix Potter	1999	$9	$10
Tomorrow's Leader QX6452	General Line	1997	$10	$20
Tonka 1956 Suburban Pumper No. 5 QX6459	General Line	1999	$14	$16
Tonka Mighty Dump Truck QX632-1	Tonka	1996	$14	$30
Tonka Mighty Front Loader 636-2	Tonka	1997	$14	$20
Tonka Road Grader QX6483	Tonka	1998	$14	$18

Ornament Title	Series	Year	Issue Price	Current Value
Top Banana 775QX592-5	General Line	1993	$8	$5
Top Hatter 600QXM588-9	Miniature Ornaments	1991	$6	$9
Tou Can Love 895QX564-6	Handcrafted Ornaments	1994	$9	$10
Town Church 12th Ed. QX515-9	Nostalgic Houses & Shops	1995	$15	$25
Toy Freight Car 4th Ed. QX5812	Yuletide Central	1997	$19	$20
Toy Shop 6th Ed. 700QXM513-2	Old English Village	1993	$7	$12
Toy Shop Santa QXC420-1	Keepsake Ornament Signature Collection	1996	$60	$35
Toyland Tower 2000QLX712-9	Magic Ornaments	1991	$20	$25
Toymaker's Gift QXC4519	Collector's Club	1999	N/A	$12
Tramp & Laddie 775QX439-7	Artists' Favorites	1991	$8	$18
Travel Case & Barbie Ornament QXI6129	Barbie	1999	$13	$15
Tread Bear 875QX509-1	General Line	1992	$9	$18
Treasured Memories QLX738-4	Magic Ornaments	1996	$19	$24
Tree For Snoopy, A QX550-7	Peanuts Collection	1996	$9	$18
Tree For Woodstock, A QXM476-7	Miniature Ornaments	1996	$6	$14
Tree Top Choir QX6506	General Line	1998	$10	$19
Tree Trimmin' Time QXD4236	Disney Collection	1998	$20	$21
Treeland Trio 850QXM589-9	Miniature Ornaments	1991	$8	$10
Treetop Cottage 975QEO818-6	Easter Ornaments	1994	$10	$8
Trestle Track For Train 295XPR973-4	Claus & Co. R.R. Ornaments	1991	$3	$10
Trimmed W/Memories 1200QXC543-2	Collector's Club	1993	$12	$20
Trimming Santa's Tree Set Of 2 QXC5175	Artists on Tour	1997	N/A	$85
Troy Aikman 2nd Ed. QXI502-1	Football Legends	1996	$15	$20
Trusty Reindeer QXM4617	Miniature Ornaments	1999	$6	$10
Tudor House 87th Ed. QXM481-9	Old English Village	1995	$7	$9
Tulip Time 995QX598-3	Garden Elves Collection	1994	$10	$5
Tunnel Of Love QXM4029	Miniature Ornaments	1995	$5	$8
Turtle Dreams 875QX499-1	Artists' Favorites	1992	$9	$18
Twelve Drummers Drumming QX300-9	Twelve Days Of Christmas	1995	$7	$8
Twenty-Five Years Together 975QX489-6	Commemoratives	1990	$10	$20
Two For Tea QX582-9	Handcrafted Ornaments	1995	$10	$10
Two Peas In A Pod 475QX492-6	General Line	1990	$5	$27
Two-Tone, 101 Dalmatians QXD4015	General Line	1997	$10	$16
Type Of Joy 450QXM564-6	Miniature Ornaments	1990	$4	$6
U.S. Christmas Stamps 1075QX529-2	U.S. Christmas Stamps	1993	$11	$12
U.S. Christmas Stamps 1095QX506-7	U.S. Christmas Stamps	1995	$11	$10
U.S. Christmas Stamps 1095QX520-6	U.S. Christmas Stamps	1994	$11	$12
U.S.S. Defiant QXI7481	Star Trek	1997	$24	$24
U.S.S. Enterprise Ncc-1701 QBG6117	Crown Reflections	1999	$25	$90
U.S.S. Enterprise QLX741-2	Magic Ornaments	1993	$24	$30
U.S.S. Voyager QXI7544	Star Trek	1996	$24	$28
Uncle Art's Ice Cream 875QX500-1	Artists' Favorites	1992	$9	$15
Uncle Sam 2nd Ed. QK108-4	Turn Of The Century Parade	1996	$17	$16
Under Construction 1800QLX732-4	Magic Ornaments	1992	$18	$37
Under The Mistletoe 875QX494-9	Commemoratives	1991	$9	$5

Ornament Title	Series	Year	Issue Price	Current Value
Up 'N' Down Journey 975QX504-7	General Line	1991	$10	$15
Upbeat Bear 600QXM590-7	Miniature Ornaments	1991	$6	$9
USS Enterprise NCC-1701 QXI8557	Star Trek	1999	$25	$15
Utah Jazz QSR1069	NBA Collection	1999	$11	$4
V.P. Of Important Stuff 675QX505-1	Commemoratives	1992	$7	$7
Vehicles Of Star Wars, The Set Of 3 QXM402-4	General Line	1996	$20	$29
Vera The Mouse QX553-7	General Line	1995	$9	$9
Very Merry Minutes 2400QLX744-3	Magic Ornaments	1994	$24	$45
Victorian Angel Miniature Tree Topper QXM4293	Tree Topper	1999	$13	$19
Victorian Christmas 1st Ed. QXM1613-5	Thomas Kinkade, Painter Of Light	1997	$11	$19
Victorian Christmas II 2nd Ed. QX6343	Thomas Kinkade, Painter Of Light	1998	$11	$28
Victorian Christmas III 3rd & Final Ed. QX6407	Thomas Kinkade, Painter Of Light	1999	$11	$15
Victorian Cross 895QEO8453	Easter Ornaments	1998	$9	$12
Victorian Cross QEO8725	Easter Ornaments	1997	$9	$12
Victorian Elegance Barbie QHB6004	Barbie	1997	N/A	$20
Victorian Home Teapot QX111-9	Invitation To Tea	1995	$16	$28
Victorian Painted Lady 13th Ed. QX567-1	Nostalgic Houses & Shops	1996	$15	$21
Victorian Skater 2500QXC406-7	Collector's Club	1992	$25	$25
Victorian Skater QXM4305	Miniature Ornaments	1997	$6	$6
Victorian Toy Box QLX735-7	Special Edition	1995	$42	$35
Video Party QLX743-1	Magic Ornaments	1996	$28	$21
Village Church QBG6057	Crown Reflections	1999	$30	$30
Village Depot 10th & Final Ed. QXM418-2	Old English Village	1997	$7	$8
Village Mill 9th Ed. QXM412-4	Old English Village	1996	$7	$7
Violet 9th Ed. QX566-4	Mary's Angels	1996	$7	$16
Violets & Butterflies QK107-9	Nature's Sketchbook	1995	$17	$34
Vision Of Santa 450QXM593-7	Miniature Ornaments	1991	$4	$9
Visions Of Acorns 450QXM585-1	Miniature Ornaments	1992	$4	$15
Visions Of Sugarplums 1375QK100-5	Holiday Enchantment	1993	$14	$12
Visions Of Sugarplums 725QXM402-2	Miniature Ornaments	1993	$7	$9
Visit From Piglet 1st Ed. QXD4086	Winnie The Pooh Collection	1998	$14	$14
Visit From St. Nicholas QLZ4229	Laser Creations	1999	$6	$12
Waitin' On Santa QXD6365	General Line	1997	$13	$13
Waiting For A Hug QXC4537	Collector's Club	1999	N/A	$10
Waiting Up For Santa QX610-6	Handcrafted Ornaments	1995	$9	$9
Wake-Up Call 875QX526-2	General Line	1993	$9	$10
Walt Disney's Sleeping Beauty 3rd Ed. QXD4097	Enchanted Memories Collection	1999	$15	$26
Walt Disney's Snow White 2nd Ed. QXD4056	Enchanted Memories Collection	1998	$15	$18
Warm & Cozy QX6866	General Line	1998	$9	$18

Ornament Title	Series	Year	Issue Price	Current Value
Warm & Special Friends QX589-5	General Line	1993	$11	$19
Warm Memories 450QXM571-3	Miniature Ornaments	1990	$4	$7
Warm Memories 775QEO931-1	Easter Ornaments	1992	$8	$8
Warm Welcome QXL7417	General Line	1999	$17	$24
Warmth Of Home QXI1754-5	Thomas Kinkade General Line	1997	$19	$16
Washington Monument QXL 7553	General Line	1998	$24	$19
Washington Redskins QSR6247	Football Helmet Collection	1995	$10	$28
Washington Redskins QSR5186	NFL Collection	1998	$10	$10
Washington Redskins QSR5277	NFL Collection	1999	$11	$8
Washington Redskins QSR5535	NFL Collection	1997	$10	$10
Washington Redskins QSR651-4	NFL Collection	1996	$10	$9
Watch Owls 1200QLX708-4	Magic Ornaments	1992	$12	$25
Watchful Shepherd QX6496	General Line	1998	$9	$15
Water Bed Snooze 975QX537-5	General Line	1993	$10	$10
Water Sports QX603-9	Handcrafted Ornaments	1995	$15	$22
Wayne Gretzky 1st Ed. QXI1627-5	Hockey Greats	1997	$16	$18
Wedding Day 4th Ed. 1959-1962 QXI6812	Barbie	1997	$16	$18
Wedding Memories 995QEO8466	World Of Wishes	1998	$10	$7
Wedding Memories QEO8407	World Of Wishes	1999	$10	$10
Wee Little Christmas QLX732-9	Magic Ornaments	1995	$22	$22
Wee Nutcracker 850QXM584-3	Miniature Ornaments	1990	$8	$10
Wee Three Kings 575QXM553-1	Miniature Ornaments	1992	$6	$9
Wee Toymaker 850QXM596-7	Miniature Ornaments	1991	$8	$5
Welcome Friends 1st Ed. QXM4205	Welcome Friends	1997	$7	$10
Welcome Friends 2nd Ed. QXM4153	Welcome Friends	1998	$7	$9
Welcome Friends 3rd & Final Ed. QXM4577	Welcome Friends	1999	$7	$9
Welcome Guest QX539-4	Coca-Cola Santa	1996	$15	$18
Welcome Him QX626-4	Collector's Choice	1996	$9	$12
Welcome Sign Tender Touches QX6331	Premiere Exclusive	1996	$15	$15
Welcome To 2000 QX6829	General Line	1999	$11	$29
Welcome, Santa 1175QX477-3	Artists' Favorites	1990	$12	$10
What A Deal! QX6442	General Line	1997	$9	$15
What's Your Name? 795QEO8443	Easter Ornaments	1998	$8	$9
Wheel Of Fortune QX6187	Anniversary Ornaments	1995	$13	$13
White Christmas 2800QLX746-3	Magic Ornaments	1994	$28	$40
White Poinsettias QGB6923	Crown Reflections/General Line	1998	$25	$25
White Rabbit 3rd Ed. QXM4142	Alice In Wonderland	1997	$7	$9
White/Tan Rocker 7th Ed. 450QXM511-6	Rocking Horse Miniatures	1994	$4	$11
Winnie The Pooh & Tigger QXM404-4	Miniature Ornaments	1996	$10	$14
Winnie The Pooh 2400QLX742-2	Magic Ornaments	1993	$24	$24
Winnie The Pooh 975QX556-9	General Line	1991	$10	$25

Ornament Title	Series	Year	Issue Price	Current Value
Winnie The Pooh 975QX571-5	General Line	1993	$10	$25
Winnie The Pooh & Piglet QX5454	General Line	1996	$13	$12
Winnie The Pooh & Tigger 1295QX574-6	General Line	1994	$13	$24
Winnie The Pooh & Tigger QX500-9	Handcrafted Ornaments	1995	$13	$25
Winnie The Pooh Parade 3200QLX749-3	Magic Ornaments	1994	$32	$32
Winnie The Pooh -Too Much Hunny QLX729-7	Magic Ornaments	1995	$25	$35
Winning Play, The QX588-9	Handcrafted Ornaments	1995	$8	$12
Winter Fun With Snoopy 1st Ed. QXM4243	Winter Fun With Snoopy	1998	$14	$18
Winter Fun With Snoopy 2nd Ed. QXM4559	Winter Fun With Snoopy	1999	$7	$26
Winter Surprise 2nd Ed. 1075QX444-3	Winter Surprise	1990	$11	$12
Winter Surprise 3rd Ed. 1075QX427-7	Winter Surprise	1991	$11	$11
Winter Surprise 4th & Final Ed. 1175QX427-1	Winter Surprise	1992	$12	$10
Wintertime Treat QX6989	General Line	1999	$13	$15
Wish For Peace QLZ4249	Laser Creations	1999	$7	$12
Wish List QX585-9	Premiere Exclusive	1995	$15	$13
Witch Of The West QX555-4	Wizard Of Oz Collection	1996	$14	$22
Wizard Of Oz, The QXC4161	Collector's Club	1996	$13	$64
Wonder Woman QX594-1	General Line	1996	$13	$15
Woodland Babies 1st Ed. 600QXM566-7	Woodland Babies	1991	$6	$13
Woodland Babies 2nd Ed. 600QXM544-4	Woodland Babies	1992	$6	$9
Woodland Babies 3rd & Final Ed. 575QXM510-2	Woodland Babies	1993	$6	$7
Woodland Santa QX613 1	General Line	1996	$13	$14
Woody The Sheriff QXD4163	Toy Story	1998	$15	$18
Woody's Roundup QXI4207	Toy Story 2	1999	$14	$19
World-Class Teacher 775QX505 4	Commemoratives	1992	$8	$3
Writing To Santa QX6533	General Line	1998	$8	$9
X-Wing Starfighter QXI7596	General Line	1998	$24	$29
Yoda QXI6355	General Line	1997	$10	$15
Yogi Bear & Boo Boo QX552-1	Handcrafted Ornaments	1996	$13	$19
Yosemite Sam 895QX534-6	Looney Tunes	1994	$9	$25
You'Re Always Welcome QXC569-2	Handcrafted Ornaments	1993	$10	$25
Yule Logger 875QX496-7	General Line	1991	$9	$8
Yuletide Charm QLZ4269	Laser Creations	1999	$6	$13
Yuletide Cheer 995QX597-6	Garden Elves Collection	1994	$10	$5
Yuletide Cheer QX605-4	General Line	1996	$8	$8
Yuletide Rider 2800QLX731-4	Magic Ornaments	1992	$28	$60
Yummy Memories QBG6049	Crown Reflections	1999	$45	$34
Yummy Recipe 775QEO814-3	Easter Ornaments	1994	$8	$8
Zebra Fantasy QX6559	Premiere Exclusive	1999	$15	$20
Ziggy QX652-4	General Line	1996	$10	$20

2000s

Hallmark continued to ride the crest of the wave of popular contemporary collectibles as it entered the new millennium with special commemorative ornaments: Millennium Time Capsule, New Millennium Baby, and Millennium Express.

With the new millennium came more new series—Toymaker Santa, Cool Decade, Fashion Afoot, and Robot Parade from 2000; Birthday Wishes Barbie and Kris and the Kringles from 2001; and Fire Brigade from 2003, among many others. Ornaments featuring Hot Wheels debuted in 2001.

Each year Hallmark delights collectors with new, innovative, and creative ornaments. We eagerly anticipate all the fun yet to come.

2000s Pricing

Ornament Title	Series	Year	Issue Price	Current Value
"All In" For Fun QXG2283	General Line	2006	$10	$10
"Suited" For The Season QXI6246	General Line	2006	$13	$13
100 Acre Express QXD5034	General Line	2004	$20	$20
100 Years Of Fun Crayola Crayons QXI8769	General Line	2003	$20	$20
102 Dalmatians QXI5231	Disney Collection	2000	$13	$28
1300 Old Oak Road QFO6037	Halloween	2003	$13	$13
1764-Kaya QAC6414	American Girls Collection	2003	$15	$15
1774-Felicity QAC6413	American Girls Collection	2003	$15	$15
1824-Josefina QAC6415	American Girls Collection	2003	$15	$15
1854-Kirsten QAC6416	American Girls Collection	2003	$15	$15
1864-Addy QAC6412	American Girls Collection	2003	$15	$15
1904-Samantha QAC6419	American Girls Collection	2003	$15	$15
1917 Curtiss JN-4D "Jenny" 2nd Ed. QXM4363	Sky's The Limit Miniature Series	2002	$7	$7
1924 Toledo Fire Engine #6 7th Ed. QX6691	Kiddie Car Classics	2000	$14	$20
1924 Toledo Fire Engine 7th Ed. QXM5192	Miniature Kiddie Car Classics	2001	$7	$12
1926 Murray Steelcraft Speedster 12th Ed. QX2295	Kiddie Car Classics	2005	$14	$14
1928 Jingle Bell Express 9th Ed. QX8076	Kiddie Car Classics	2002	$14	$11
1929 Chevrolet Fire Engine 1st Ed. QX8449	Fire Brigade	2003	$19	$24
1929 Chevrolet Fire Engine 1st Ed. QXM5164	Miniature Fire Brigade	2004	$10	$10
1930 Cadillac 4th Ed. QEO8555	Vintage Roadsters	2001	N/A	$23
1930 Custom Biplane 8th Ed. QX6975	Kiddie Car Classics	2001	$14	$20
1930 Custom Biplane 8th Ed. QXM4333	Miniature Kiddie Car Classics	2002	$7	$12
1931 Laird Super Solution 9th Ed. QX2045	Sky's The Limit	2005	$15	$17
1933 Flathead Model VLD 6th Ed. QXM5191	Mini Harley-Davidson Motorcycles	2004	$8	$8
1934 Kit QAC6417	American Girls Collection	2003	$15	$15
1934 Mickey Mouse Velocipede 5th Ed. QEO8552	Sidewalk Cruisers	2001	N/A	$30
1935 Auburn Speedster 3rd Ed. QEO8401	Vintage Roadsters	2000	$15	$30
1935 Steelcraft By Murray 3rd Ed. QXM5951	Miniature Kiddie Car Luxury Edition	2000	$7	$9
1935 Timmy Racer 11th & Final Ed. QXM8985	Miniature Kiddie Car Classics	2005	$7	$10
1935 Timmy Racer 11th Ed. QX8444	Kiddie Car Classics	2004	$14	$20
1936 Stinson Reliant 7th Ed. QX8147	Sky's The Limit	2003	$15	$21
1937 Garton Ford 4th & Final Ed. QXM5195	Miniature Kiddie Car Luxury Edition	2001	$7	$9
1937 Mickey Mouse Streamline Express Coaster Wagon 6th & Final Ed. QEO8516	Sidewalk Cruisers	2002	N/A	$25
1938 Chevrolet Fire Engine 3rd Ed. QX2035	Fire Brigade	2005	$19	$19
1938 Garton Lincoln Zephyr QXC4501	Collector's Club	2000	$16	$39
1939 Hiawatha Steam Locomotive 9th Ed. QX8454	Lionel Trains	2004	$19	$19

World-Famous Christmas Decorator, 2003, from the Peanuts Collection, **$50.**

Ornament Title	Series	Year	Issue Price	Current Value
1940 Garton Red Hot Roadster 2nd Ed. QEO8404	Winner's Circle	2000	$14	$11
1941 Garton Speed Demon 4th & Final Ed. QEO8503	Winner's Circle	2002	N/A	$18
1944 Molly QAC6418	American Girls Collection	2003	$15	$15
1947 Servi-Car 3rd Ed. QXI5282	Mini Harley-Davidson Motorcycles	2001	$8	$8
1948 Ford F-1 12th Ed. QX2376	All-American Trucks	2006	$15	$15
1948 Panhead 5th Ed. QXM4879	Mini Harley-Davidson Motorcycles	2003	$8	$8
1949 Gillham Sport 10th Ed. QX8139	Kiddie Car Classics	2003	$14	$16
1949 Gillham Sport Miniature 10th Ed. QXM5161	Miniature Kiddie Car Classics	2004	$7	$5
1950s Barbie Ornament QXI8882	Barbie	2001	$15	$20
1953 Buick Roadmaster Skylark QX6872 11th Ed.	Classic American Cars	2001	$14	$21
1954 Buick Wildcat II 5th & Final Ed. QEO8526	Vintage Roadsters	2002	N/A	$23
1955 Murray Dump Truck QBG4081	Kiddie Car Classics	2000	$35	$57
1957 Ford Ranchero 8th Ed. QX8066	All-American Trucks	2002	$15	$23
1957 XI Sportster 3rd Ed. QXI8125	Harley-Davidson Milestones	2001	$15	$23
1958 FI Duo-Glide 4th Ed. QXI4346	Mini Harley-Davidson Motorcycles	2002	$8	$8
1959 Chevrolet El Camino 7th Ed. QX6072	All-American Trucks	2001	$14	$23
1960 Eight Ball Racer 3rd Ed. QEO8562	Winner's Circle	2001	N/A	$13
1961 Barbie Hatbox Case QX6922	Barbie	2001	$10	$12
1961 Barbie Travel Pal Case & Accessories QX8293	Barbie	2002	$15	$15
1961 Chevrolet Impala QX2356 16th Ed.	Classic American Cars	2006	$15	$15
1961 GMC 4th Ed. QX2326	Fire Brigade	2006	$19	$19
1962 Barbie Hatbox Doll Case QX6791	Barbie	2000	$10	$17
1962 Duo-Glide 2nd Ed. QXI6001	Mini Harley-Davidson Motorcycles	2000	$8	$7
1963 Corvette Sting Ray Coupe QX8129 13th Ed.	Classic American Cars	2003	$15	$15
1964-1/2 Ford Mustang 13th & Final Ed. QX2343	Kiddie Car Classics	2006	$14	$14
1966 Oldsmobile Toronado Coupe QX8151 14th Ed.	Classic American Cars	2004	$15	$15
1968 Murray Jolly Roger Flagship 6th Ed. QXM5944	Miniature Kiddie Car Classics	2000	$7	$12
1968 Pontiac Firebird QX2025 15th Ed.	Classic American Cars	2005	$15	$15
1968 Silhouette & Case QX6605	Hot Wheels	2001	$15	$15
1969 Pontiac GTO-The Judge QX6584 10th Ed.	Classic American Cars	2000	$14	$30
1970 Ford Mach 1 Mustang QX8073 12th Ed.	Classic American Cars	2002	$15	$15
1971 FX-1200 Super Glide 4th Ed. QXI8123	Harley-Davidson Milestones	2002	$15	$15

Race Down Main Street, 2000, from the Snowmen of Mitford series, **$16.**

Frosty Friends, 2000, 21st in the Frosty Friends series, **$12.**

The Newborn Prince, 2000, Disney, **$14.**

Ringing Reindeer, 2000, from the Hallmark Keepsake Ornament Collector's Club, **$15.**

A Friend Chimes in, 2000, from the Hallmark Keepsake Ornament Collector's Club, **$12.**

Husky-Little Frosty Friends, 2000, from the Hallmark Keepsake Ornament Collector's Club, no established value.

Ornament Title	Series	Year	Issue Price	Current Value
1972 Chevrolet Cheyenne Super 9th Ed. QX8117	All-American Trucks	2003	$15	$18
1978 Dodge Li'l Red Express Truck 6th Ed. QX6581	All-American Trucks	2000	$14	$13
1986 Heritage Softail 8th Ed. QXM2093	Mini Harley-Davidson Motorcycles	2006	$8	$8
1990s Batmobile, The QXI8297	Batman	2003	$15	$15
1992 Happy Holidays Barbie Doll Ornament 5th & Final Ed. QXC4494	Happy Holidays Barbie	2000	$16	$23
1994 FLHR Road King 7th Ed. QXM2065	Mini Harley-Davidson Motorcycles	2005	$8	$8
1994 FLHR Road King 8th Ed. QX2333	Harley-Davidson Milestones	2006	$15	$15
2000 Ford F-150 10th Ed. QX8154	All-American Trucks	2004	$15	$15
2000 Oscar Meyer Weinermobile QX6935	General Line	2001	$13	$20
2000 Softail Deuce Motorcycle 7th Ed. QX2042	Harley-Davidson Milestones	2005	$15	$15
2001 Jeep Sport Wrangler QXI6362	General Line	2001	$15	$24
2001 Membership Ornaments/Twas The Night Before Christmas QXC2001	Collector's Club	2001	N/A	$24
2001 Time Capsule QX2802	General Line	2001	$10	$10
2001 Vacation QX2822	General Line	2001	$10	$8
2002 Vrsca V-Rod 6th Ed. QX8184	Harley-Davidson Milestones	2004	$15	$15
2003 100th Anniversary Ultra Classic Electra Glide 5th Ed. QX8169	Harley-Davidson Milestones	2003	$15	$20
2003 Chevrolet Silverado SS 11th Ed. QX2032	All-American Trucks	2005	$15	$15
2004 Token QEP2005	Heart Of Motherhood Collection	2004	$6	$6
29-C Fire Pumper QXI8846	Matchbox	2002	$15	$15
4449 Daylight Steam Locomotive 8th Ed. QX8087	Lionel Trains	2003	$19	$20
50 Years Of Music & Fun QXD4075	Disney Collection	2005	$20	$20
9620 Tractor QXI6263	John Deere	2006	$15	$15
A+ Teacher QXG2603	General Line	2006	$10	$10
Academics QXG4795	General Line	2005	$10	$10
Acrobats, The QFO6029	Halloween	2003	$5	$7
Adding The Right Touch QXM5214, Set Of 9	Miniature Ornaments	2004	$15	$10
Addy With Coin QAC6421	American Girls Collection	2004	$15	$15
Adobe Church 3rd Ed. QXL7334	Candlelight Services	2000	$19	$18
Adoption 2003 QXG2497	General Line	2003	$13	$13
Adoption 2004 QXG5641	General Line	2004	$13	$9
Adventures Of A Book Lover QXG8589	General Line	2003	$10	$10
Afternoon Tea 1st Ed. QXM4937	Afternoon Tea	2003	$7	$9
Afternoon Tea 2nd Ed. QXM5171	Afternoon Tea	2004	$7	$7
Afternoon Tea 3rd & Final Ed. QXM8955	Afternoon Tea	2005	$7	$7
Al Mundo Paz! QXG5471	General Line	2004	$15	$10
Alabama Crimson Tide QSR2132	Collegiate Collection	2001	$10	$3
Alabama Crimson Tide QSR2344	Collegiate Collection	2000	$10	$3

Green Eggs and Ham, 2000, Dr. Seuss, **$15.**

Charlie Brown, 2000, from A Snoopy Christmas series, **$5.**

Linus, 2000, from A Snoopy Christmas series, **$5.**

Lucy, 2000, from A Snoopy Christmas series, **$5.**

Snoopy, 2000, from A Snoopy Christmas series, **$5.**

Ornament Title	Series	Year	Issue Price	Current Value
Albert Pujols QX2282	At The Ballpark	2005	$15	$15
Alex Rodriguez QX2336	At The Ballpark	2006	$15	$15
Alice In Wonderland QEO8421	Easter Ornaments	2000	$15	$15
Alice Meets The Cheshire Cat 5th & Final Ed. QXD4011	General Line	2000	$15	$13
All Decked Out QXC5006	Collector's Club Exclusive	2005	$15	$15
All Is Calm QXG2683	General Line	2006	$14	$14
All Things Beautiful QX8351	General Line	2000	$14	$11
All-Sport Santa QX8332	General Line	2001	$10	$10
All-Star Kid Memory Keeper Ornament QX2805	General Line	2001	$10	$8
Always A Princess QMP4018	Gold Crown Exclusives	2006	$15	$15
Always Near QP1503	General Line	2002	$10	$10
Always Remembered QXG2673	General Line	2006	$13	$13
Amazing Little Tree, The QXI7517	Peanuts Collection	2003	$24	$24
Amazing No. 53 QXM8175	Disney Collection	2005	$7	$7
Amazing Number 53 QXD5071	Disney Collection	2004	$15	$15
America For Me! QX2882	General Line	2001	$10	$23
American Goldfinch 2nd Ed. QEO8535	Spring Is In The Air	2001	N/A	$9
American LaFrance 700 Series Pumper 2nd Ed. QX8424	Fire Brigade	2004	$19	$19
American LaFrance 700 Series Pumper 2nd Ed. QXM2062	Miniature Fire Brigade	2005	$10	$10
American Patriot Santa QXG2499	General Line	2003	$15	$15
American Robin 3rd & Final Ed. QEO8506	Spring Is In The Air	2002	N/A	$19
Amigo Por Siempre QXG2529	General Line	2003	$15	$10
Amigos De Verdad QXG4655	General Line	2005	$13	$13
Amigos Por Siempre QXG5754	General Line	2004	$13	$13
Amy March 4th & Final Ed. QX8404	Madame Alexander Little Women	2004	$16	$16
Anakin Skywalker & Obi-Wan Kenobi QXI6186	General Line	2006	$28	$28
Anakin Skywalker QX6942	General Line	2001	$15	$16
Anakin Skywalker QXI4071	General Line	2004	$15	$15
Anakin Skywalker's Jedi Starfighter QXI6192	General Line	2005	$28	$28
And The Winner Is QXI6195	Hot Wheels	2005	$15	$15
Angel At My Side QXG8659	General Line	2003	$10	$10
Angel In Disguise QX8983	General Line	2002	$10	$10
Angel In Training QXM4403	Miniature Ornaments	2002	$7	$7
Angel Light QLZ4311	Laser Gallery	2000	$8	$8
Angel Of Comfort QXI6363	General Line	2002	$15	$15
Angel Of Compassion QXG5381	Gold Crown Exclusives	2004	$15	$15
Angel Of Faith QXI5375	General Line	2001	$15	$15
Angel Of Grace QXG4375	General Line	2005	$15	$15
Angel Of Life QXG2686	Gold Crown Exclusives	2006	$15	$15
Angel Of Promise QXI4144	Gold Crown Exclusives	2000	$15	$24
Angel Of Serenity QXG8999	General Line	2003	$15	$15

Schoolhouse, 2000, 17th in the Nostalgic Houses and Shops series, **$26.**

Obi-Wan Kenobi, 2000, 4th in the Star Wars series, **$15.**

Snow Buddies, 2000, 3rd in the Snow Buddies series, **$15.**

Max, 2000, **$8.**

Ornament Title	Series	Year	Issue Price	Current Value
Angel On Earth QXG4372	General Line	2005	$10	$10
Angel-Blessed Tree QX8241	General Line	2000	$9	$8
Angelic Bell QXC4504	Collector's Club	2000	$17	$19
Angelic Trio QX8234	General Line	2000	$11	$18
Angelic Trio QXM8162	Miniature Ornaments	2005	$13	$13
Angelic Visitation QX2853	General Line	2002	$15	$15
Angelica Colorway QXE4466	Mary's Angels	2006	N/A	$21
Angels Of Virtue QXG8839	General Line	2003	$16	$16
Angels Over Bethlehem QLX7563	General Line	2000	$19	$28
Angel's Touch, An QXG5634	General Line	2004	$13	$9
Angels We Have Heard QLX7527	Magic Ornaments	2003	$24	$24
Angel's Whisper QX8852	General Line	2001	$10	$10
Antique Tractors 10th & Final Ed. QXM2143	Antique Tractors	2006	$7	$7
Antique Tractors 4th Ed. QXM5994	Antique Tractors	2000	$7	$16
Antique Tractors 5th Ed. QXM5252	Antique Tractors	2001	$7	$14
Antique Tractors 6th Ed. QXM4336	Antique Tractors	2002	$7	$14
Antique Tractors 7th Ed. QXM4889	Antique Tractors	2003	$7	$9
Antique Tractors 8th Ed. QXM5154	Antique Tractors	2004	$7	$7
Antique Tractors 9th Ed. QXM8992	Antique Tractors	2005	$7	$7
Anything For A Friend QXG5511	General Line	2004	$15	$15
Arctic Adventurers QXG4452	General Line	2005	$13	$13
Arianne QP1822	Joyful Tidings	2005	$13	$7
Ariel QXD5061	Disney Collection	2004	$13	$15
Arnold Palmer QXI4324	Sports Collection	2000	$15	$9
Around The Home QEO8017	Nature's Sketchbook-Bastin	2003	N/A	$18
Around The World-Harley Davidson QXI4894	General Line	2003	$44	$44
Arthur & D.W. A Perfect Christmas QX8843	Arthur	2002	$13	$13
Arthur & Pal A Perfect Christmas! QXI8359	General Line	2003	$10	$10
Arts & Crafts QXG3336	Kid Speak	2006	$13	$13
Asajj Ventress, Anakin Skywalker & Yoda QXM2113	General Line	2006	$15	$15
Away To The Manger QXG8669	General Line	2003	$10	$10
Azura QP1825	Joyful Tidings	2005	$13	$13
Baby Brilliana QP1683	Frostlight Faeries Collection	2002	$15	$15
Baby Candessa QP1676	Frostlight Faeries Collection	2002	$15	$15
Baby Delandra QP1666	Frostlight Faeries Collection	2002	$15	$15
Baby Estrella QP1663	Frostlight Faeries Collection	2002	$15	$15
Baby Floriella QP1673	Frostlight Faeries Collection	2002	$15	$15
Baby's First Christmas Photoholder QX8355	General Line	2001	$9	$14
Baby's First Christmas Photoholder QX8031	General Line	2000	$9	$14
Baby's First Christmas QX6914	Child's Age Collection	2000	$8	$18
Baby's First Christmas QX8034	General Line	2000	$11	$10
Baby's First Christmas QX8041	General Line	2000	$19	$19
Baby's First Christmas QX8326	Child's Age Collection	2002	$8	$12
Baby's First Christmas QX8362	General Line	2001	$9	$10
Baby's First Christmas QX8375	Child's Age Collection	2001	$8	$15

1978 Dodge Li'l Red Express Truck, 2000, 6th in the All-American Trucks series, **$13.**

Jingle Bell Kringle, 2000, from the Hallmark Keepsake Ornament Collector's Club, **$20.**

A Holiday Gathering, 2000, from the Thomas Kinkade general line, **$19.**

Spirit of St. Louis, 2000, 4th in the Sky's the Limit series, **$55.**

1969 Pontiac GTO-The Judge, 2000, 10th in the Classic American Cars series, **$30.**

Ornament Title	Series	Year	Issue Price	Current Value
Baby's First Christmas QX8482	Baby Looney Tunes	2001	$10	$14
Baby's First Christmas QX8596	General Line	2002	$10	$14
Baby's First Christmas QX8616	General Line	2002	$17	$20
Baby's First Christmas QX8806	General Line	2002	$10	$14
Baby's First Christmas QX8913	Baby Looney Tunes	2002	$10	$14
Baby's First Christmas QXG2433	Winnie The Pooh Collection	2006	$15	$15
Baby's First Christmas QXG2823	General Line	2006	$13	$13
Baby's First Christmas QXG2826	General Line	2006	$13	$13
Baby's First Christmas QXG2833	General Line	2006	$13	$13
Baby's First Christmas QXG2836	General Line	2006	$17	$17
Baby's First Christmas QXG4592	General Line	2005	$13	$16
Baby's First Christmas QXG4602	General Line	2005	$10	$10
Baby's First Christmas QXG4615	General Line	2005	$15	$13
Baby's First Christmas QXG4622	General Line	2005	$13	$13
Baby's First Christmas QXG4625	General Line	2005	$19	$19
Baby's First Christmas QXG5711	General Line	2004	$10	$14
Baby's First Christmas QXG5714	General Line	2004	$13	$20
Baby's First Christmas QXG5721	General Line	2004	$15	$15
Baby's First Christmas QXG5724	General Line	2004	$13	$13
Baby's First Christmas QXG5731	General Line	2004	$15	$12
Baby's First Christmas QXG8719	General Line	2003	$13	$13
Baby's First Christmas QXG8729	General Line	2003	$15	$15
Baby's First Christmas QXG8737	General Line	2003	$10	$10
Baby's First Christmas-Boy QX8365	General Line	2001	$9	$12
Baby's First Christmas-Girl QX8372	General Line	2001	$9	$12
Baby's Second Christmas QX6921	Child's Age Collection	2000	$8	$20
Baby's Second Christmas QX8333	Child's Age Collection	2002	$8	$15
Baby's Second Christmas QX8382	Child's Age Collection	2001	$8	$15
Baby's Second Christmas QXG8699	Child's Age Collection	2003	$9	$15
Back To School QX8696	General Line	2002	$10	$10
Backpack Bear QBG4071	General Line	2000	$30	$19
Bait Shop With Boat 2nd Ed. QX6631	Town & Country	2000	$16	$14
Baking Memories QX6956	General Line	2002	$13	$13
Ballerina Barbie QEO8471	Easter Ornaments	2000	$13	$13
Ballet Photoholder QX2873	General Line	2002	$10	$10
Ballet QXG4782	General Line	2005	$10	$10
Ballet, The QXI5311	I Love Lucy	2004	$17	$10
Bambi & Friends QXD5044	Disney Collection	2004	$17	$17
Bambi Discovers Winter QXD7541	Disney Collection	2001	$24	$26
Bananas For You QXG3253	General Line	2006	$10	$10
Bar & Shield QEO8544	Easter Ornaments	2000	$14	$14
Barber Shop & Beauty Shop 21st Ed. QX8181	Nostalgic Houses & Shops	2004	$15	$15
Barbie 2002 Ornament QXC4653	Collector's Club	2002	$24	$24
Barbie 45th Anniversary Ornament QHB6601	Barbie	2004	$25	$25

The Tender, 2000, Lionel, **$18.**

Lionel General Steam Locomotive, 2000, 5th in the Lionel Trains series, **$25.**

Tender-Lionel Chessie Steam Special, 2001, **$14.**

Lionel Chessie Steam Special Locomotive, 2001, 6th in the Lionel Trains series, **$19.**

Ornament Title	Series	Year	Issue Price	Current Value
Barbie & Kelly On The Ice Ornament QXI6915	Barbie	2001	$16	$9
Barbie & The Magic Of Pegasus QXI6415	Barbie	2005	$16	$16
Barbie Angel Of Joy QXI6861	Barbie	2000	$15	$14
Barbie Angel Ornament QXI6925	Barbie	2001	$16	$16
Barbie As Genevieve In The 12 Dancing Princesses QXI6213	Barbie	2006	$16	$16
Barbie As Rapunzel QXI5326	Barbie	2002	$15	$15
Barbie As Snowflake Ornament QXI8383	Barbie	2002	$15	$15
Barbie As The Princess & The Pauper QXI8614	Barbie	2004	$19	$12
Barbie As The Sugar Plum Princess Ornament QXI6132	Barbie	2001	$16	$16
Barbie As Titania Ornament QXI6412	Midsummer Night's Dream, A	2005	$15	$15
Barbie Fairytopia Ornament QXI6512	Barbie	2005	$19	$19
Barbie Fairytopia QXI6206	Barbie	2006	$15	$15
Barbie Fashion Minis QXM3156	Barbie	2006	$20	$20
Barbie In Busy Gal Fashion 8th Ed. QX6965	Barbie	2001	$16	$16
Barbie In The 12 Dancing Princesses QXI6346	Barbie	2006	$20	$20
Barbie In The Pink QXI8439	Barbie Fashion Model Collection	2003	$25	$25
Barbie Ornament In Sophisticated Lady Fashion 9th Ed. QX8203	Barbie	2002	$16	$16
Barbie Ornament Photoholder QXI4269	Barbie	2003	$15	$15
Barbie QXC6008	Barbie	2006	N/A	N/A
Barbie Shoe Tree Ornament QHB6601	Barbie	2004	$20	$20
Barbie Shoe Tree QXI6343	Barbie	2006	$19	$19
Barbie Swan Lake QXI8447	Barbie	2003	$15	$20
Barry Bonds QX8551	At The Ballpark	2004	$15	$10
Bartholomew Hauntswell QFO6322	Hauntington U.S.A. Collection	2005	$13	$8
Baseball/Softball QXG4762	General Line	2005	$10	$10
Bashful Bunny QEO8502	Easter Ornaments	2001	N/A	$8
Basket Of Joy QXG8599	General Line	2003	$10	$8
Basketball QXG4752	General Line	2005	$10	$10
Batcycle, The QXI8902	General Line	2005	$15	$15
Bateson The Butler QFO6054	Halloween	2004	$8	$8
Bathtime Dumbo QXD8353	General Line	2006	$15	$15
Baton Twirler Daisy 4th Ed. QXD4034	Mickey's Holiday Parade	2000	$14	$18
Bat-Signal, The QXI6153	Batman	2006	$17	$17
Battle Of Naboo Set Of 3 QXM5212	General Line	2001	$15	$20
Beaded Snowflakes Blue QP1712	Gold Crown Exclusives	2001	$10	$16
Beaded Snowflakes Blue QP1712	General Line	2002	$10	$10
Beaded Snowflakes Periwinkle QP1725	Gold Crown Exclusives	2001	$10	$16
Beaded Snowflakes Periwinkle QP1725	General Line	2002	$10	$10
Beaded Snowflakes Violet QP1732	Gold Crown Exclusives	2001	$10	$16

Gee Bee R-1 Super Sportster, 2001, 5th in the Sky's the Limit series, **$76.**

1959 Chevrolet El Camino, 2001, 7th in the All-American Trucks series, **$23.**

1953 Buick Roadmaster Skylark, 2001, 11th in the Classic American Cars series, **$21.**

1968 Silhouette and Case, 2001, Hot Wheels, **$15.**

Service Station, 2001, 18th in the Nostalgic Houses and Shops series, **$22.**

Ornament Title	Series	Year	Issue Price	Current Value
Beaded Snowflakes Violet QP1732	General Line	2002	$10	$10
Beaglescout 4th Ed. QX6085	Spotlight On Snoopy	2001	$10	$10
Beak To Beak QXG5331	General Line	2004	$10	$10
Bearing The Colors QXG2499	General Line	2003	$10	$10
Beatles, The, Yellow Submarine Lunchbox Set QXI5313	General Line	2002	$15	$10
Beautiful Angel Treetopper QXM4987	Miniature Ornaments	2003	$13	$13
Beautiful Cross QX8825	General Line	2001	$10	$10
Beginning Ballet QX2875	General Line	2001	$13	$15
Believe 2nd Ed. QXM4919	Paintbox Pixies	2003	$7	$7
Bell-Bearing Elf QXC4514	Collector's Club	2000	$18	$12
Belle QXD4946	Disney Collection	2002	$13	$13
Belle's Grand Entrance QXD8363	Disney Collection	2006	$17	$17
Bell-Ringing Santa-Mickey QXD4125	Disney Collection	2001	$10	$15
Best In Show QXG4705	General Line	2005	$10	$10
Best Night Of The Week QXD4085	Wonderful World Of Disney	2005	$24	$24
Big Twin Evolution Engine-Harley Davidson QXI7571	General Line	2000	$24	$19
Biggest Fan, The QX8733	General Line	2002	$10	$10
Billions Of Dreams Barbie QXC4009	Collector's Club Exclusive	2004	$20	$20
Birdhouse Row QEO8529	Tweedle Dee Deet	2003	N/A	$9
Birthday Wishes Barbie 1st Ed. QEO8575	Birthday Wishes Barbie	2001	N/A	$23
Birthday Wishes Barbie 2nd Ed. QEO8513	Birthday Wishes Barbie	2002	N/A	$23
Birthday Wishes Barbie 3rd & Final Ed. QEO8549	Birthday Wishes Barbie	2003	N/A	$24
Birthstones	Heart Of Motherhood Collection	2003	$6	$6
Black-Capped Chickadee QX2506	Beauty Of The Birds	2006	$15	$15
Blessed Family, The QLX7564	General Line	2000	$19	$15
Blessings & Family QP1306	General Line	2002	$15	$15
Blue & Periwinkle Blue's Clues QXI6142	Blue's Clues	2001	$10	$13
Blue Glass Angel QX8381	General Line	2000	$8	$10
Blueberry 2nd Ed. QEO8454	Fairy Berry Bears	2000	$10	$12
Blushing Bride Barbie QXI5323	Barbie	2002	$20	$20
Bluster B. Toboggan 2nd Ed. QX2583	Snowtop Lodge	2006	$19	$19
Blustery Day 3rd Ed. QXD4021	Winnie The Pooh Collection	2000	$14	$18
Bob The Tomato & Larry The Cucumber QXI4334	Veggie Tales	2000	$10	$9
Bonnie & Bones QFO6342	Hauntington U.S.A. Collection	2005	$15	$20
Boost For Piglet, A QXD5069	General Line	2003	$15	$15
Borg Cube Star Trek: Voyager QLX7354	Star Trek Voyager	2000	$24	$35
Born To Shop QXG5414	General Line	2004	$10	$10
Bounce Practice QXD4092	General Line	2005	$13	$13
Bouncin' Buddies QXD8326	General Line	2006	$13	$13
Bouncy Kangaroos QXM5332	Miniature Ornaments	2001	$6	$6

Mitford Snowman Jubilee, 2001, set of four, **$20.**

Snow Buddies, 2001, 4th in the Snow Buddies series, **$10.**

Frosty Friends, 2001, 22nd in the Frosty Friends series, **$12.**

Ornament Title	Series	Year	Issue Price	Current Value
Boy Token QEP2097	Heart Of Motherhood Collection	2004	$6	$6
Boy Token QEP2097	Heart Of Motherhood Collection	2003	$6	$6
Brand New Wheels QEO8245	Easter Ornaments	2005	N/A	$10
Brett Favre 7th Ed. QXI5232	Football Legends	2001	$15	$16
Bright Memories QXG3083	General Line	2006	$10	$10
Bringing Her Gift QX8334	General Line	2000	$11	$10
Bringing Home The Tree 1st Ed. QX8186	Winter Wonderland	2002	$13	$13
Bubble Bath Sylvester & Tweety QXI8277	Looney Tunes	2003	$15	$15
Bugs Bunny & Daffy Duck QXI4329	Looney Tunes	2003	$15	$15
Bugs Bunny & Elmer Fudd QXM5934	Looney Tunes	2000	$10	$16
Bugs Bunny & Gossamer QX6574	Looney Tunes	2000	$13	$21
Bugs Bunny QEO8524	Easter Ornaments	2000	$11	$11
Bugs The Barnstormer QXI8279	Looney Tunes	2003	$17	$17
Building A Snowman 3rd Ed. QX8251	Winter Wonderland	2004	$13	$13
Bunny Buggy QEO8232	Easter Ornaments	2005	N/A	$10
Bunny Business QEO8546	Peekaboo	2002	N/A	$15
Bunny Found A Carrot QEO8574	Easter Ornaments	2004	N/A	$13
Bunny Hug QXE3223	Premiere Exclusive	2006	N/A	$20
Bunny Skates — Maxine QXM4957	Miniature Ornaments	2003	$6	$6
Bunny's Dancing Egg QEO8394	Easter Ornaments	2004	N/A	$8
Burton, Coldwell & Windfield QXG2557	General Line	2003	$15	$15
Busy Bee Shopper QX6964	General Line	2000	$8	$8
Buzz A Dee Bugs QEO8537	Tweedle Dee Dept	2003	N/A	$12
Buzz Lightyear & RC Racer QXD4225	Toy Story	2005	$15	$15
Buzz Lightyear & The Claw QXD8671	Toy Story	2004	$15	$10
Buzz Lightyear QXD4606	Toy Story 2	2002	$15	$15
Buzz Lightyear QXI5234	Toy Story 2	2000	$15	$15
Buzz Lightyear, Space Ranger QXD8376	Toy Story	2006	$15	$15
By Heart QP1303	General Line	2002	$15	$15
C-3PO 7th Ed. QX8177	Star Wars	2003	$15	$14
Caboose 5th & Final Ed. QEO8464	Cottontail Express	2000	$10	$13
Calling All Firefighters! QX8746	General Line	2002	$10	$12
Calling The Caped Crusader QXI8856	Batman	2002	$15	$15
Calvin Carver QRP4646	Snow Cub Club	2002	N/A	$18
Camping QXG4775	General Line	2005	$10	$10
Candlelight Services 4th Ed. QX7552	Candlelight Services	2001	$19	$25
Candy Cane Treat QXM8752	Looney Tunes	2005	$7	$7
Candy Cane Trio QXM5114	General Line	2004	$13	$8
Caped Crusader, The QXI4041	Batman	2004	$15	$15
Captain Benjamin Sisko QX6865	Star Trek: Deep Space Nine	2001	$15	$15
Captain Jonathan Archer QXI8349	Enterprise	2003	$15	$15
Car Carrier & Caboose 3rd & Final Ed. QXM5265	Lionel Norfolk & Western	2001	$13	$13
Caregivers QXG2643	General Line	2006	$10	$10

Anakin Skywalker, 2001, Star Wars, **$16.**

JarJar Binks, 2001, Star Wars, **$15.**

R2-D2, 2001, 5th in the Star Wars series, **$39.**

Portrait of Scarlett, 2001, from the Gone With the Wind series, **$29.**

Scarlett O'Hara, 2002, from the Gone With the Wind series, **$16.**

Ornament Title	Series	Year	Issue Price	Current Value
Carmelo Anthony 11th & Final Ed. QX2345	Hoop Stars	2005	$15	$15
Caroler's Best Friend QX8354	General Line	2000	$13	$12
Caroling At The Door QXG8819	General Line	2003	$15	$15
Carousel Ride QX8481	Carousel Ride	2005	$45	$45
Carving Santa QX8265	General Line	2001	$13	$13
Cass Taspell QFO6302	Hauntington U.S.A. Collection	2005	$8	$10
Castle In The Forest QXD4953	Disney Collection	2002	$18	$18
Cat Arrives!, The QXI8379	Dr. Seuss' The Cat In The Hat	2003	$10	$10
Catch Of The Day QXG5541	General Line	2004	$10	$10
Catching Snowflakes QXE3256	General Line	2006	N/A	$24
Catwoman QXM6021	Miniature Ornaments	2000	$10	$9
Celebrate His Birth! QX2464	General Line	2000	$7	$17
Celebrate, Decorate, Enjoy! QXG8779	General Line	2003	$7	$7
Celebration Barbie 1st Ed. QXI6821	Celebration Barbie	2000	$16	$20
Celebration Barbie 2nd Ed. QXI5202	Celebration Barbie	2001	$16	$15
Celebration Barbie 3rd Ed. QXI8163	Celebration Barbie	2002	$16	$16
Celebration Barbie 4th Ed. QX2459	Celebration Barbie	2003	$16	$14
Celebration Barbie 5rd Ed. QX8604	Celebration Barbie	2004	$16	$10
Celebration Barbie 6th Ed. African American QXI6422	Celebration Barbie	2005	$16	$16
Celebration Barbie 6th Ed. QX2202	Celebration Barbie	2005	$16	$16
Celebration Barbie 7th Ed. QX2393	Celebration Barbie	2006	$16	$16
Celebration Barbie QXI8664	Celebration Barbie	2004	$16	$10
Celebrity Style QXG3173	General Line	2006	$13	$13
Celestial Bunny QXM6641	Miniature Ornaments	2000	$7	$6
Central Tower Church 8th Ed. QX2262	Candlelight Services	2005	$19	$19
Change Of Heart QXI5273	Dr. Seuss' How The Grinch Stole Christmas	2002	$15	$10
Charlie Brown Christmas Tree, A QXC6004	Collector's Club	2006	$20	$20
Charlie Brown QFO6066	It's The Great Pumpkin	2006	$9	$9
Charlie Brown QRP4191	A Snoopy Christmas	2000	$5	$5
Charmed Life, A QXG2733	General Line	2006	$19	$19
Charming Chick QEO8515	Easter Ornaments	2001	N/A	$6
Charming Hearts 1st Ed. QXM4939	Charming Hearts	2003	$10	$10
Charming Hearts 2nd Ed. QXM5194	Charming Hearts	2004	$10	$10
Charming Hearts 3rd & Final Ed. QXM8962	Charming Hearts	2005	$10	$10
Chatty Chickadees QEO8311	Nature's Sketchbook-Bastin	2004	N/A	$13
Checking The List QX8493	General Line	2002	$15	$15
Cheer For Fun! Barbie Ornament QXI8306	Barbie	2002	$15	$15
Cheerleading QXG4785	General Line	2005	$10	$10
Cheery Cargo QXI3186	Thomas The Tank Engine & Friends	2006	$13	$13
Chewbacca & C-3PO 8th Ed. QXI8431	Star Wars	2004	$15	$15
Chicken Little QXD4815	Disney Collection	2005	$13	$13
Chicky's Bouncing Daisies QEO8384	Easter Ornaments	2004	N/A	$9

The Invisibility Cloak, 2002, from Harry Potter & The Sorcerer's Stone, **$28.**

Frosty Friends, 2002, 23rd in the Frosty Friends series, **$11.**

Scooby-Doo and Shaggy, 2002, **$17.**

Calling the Caped Crusader, 2002, Batman, **$15.**

29-C Fire Pumper Set, 2002, from the Matchbox series, **$15.**

Ornament Title	Series	Year	Issue Price	Current Value
Child's Fifth Christmas QX6934	Child's Age Collection	2000	$8	$10
Child's Fifth Christmas QX8346	Child's Age Collection	2002	$8	$8
Child's Fifth Christmas QX8395	Child's Age Collection	2001	$8	$12
Child's Fifth Christmas QXG2906	Child's Age Collection	2006	$9	$9
Child's Fifth Christmas QXG4535	Child's Age Collection	2005	$9	$9
Child's Fifth Christmas QXG5774	Child's Age Collection	2004	$9	$6
Child's Fifth Christmas QXG8717	Child's Age Collection	2003	$9	$9
Child's Fourth Christmas QX6931	Child's Age Collection	2000	$8	$9
Child's Fourth Christmas QX8343	Child's Age Collection	2002	$8	$5
Child's Fourth Christmas QX8392	Child's Age Collection	2001	$8	$12
Child's Fourth Christmas QXG4532	Child's Age Collection	2005	$9	$9
Child's Fourth Christmas QXG5771	Child's Age Collection	2004	$9	$6
Child's Fourth Christmas QXG8709	Child's Age Collection	2003	$9	$9
Child's Third Christmas QX6924	Child's Age Collection	2000	$8	$15
Child's Third Christmas QX8336	Child's Age Collection	2002	$8	$8
Child's Third Christmas QX8385	Child's Age Collection	2001	$8	$12
Child's Third Christmas QXG5764	Child's Age Collection	2004	$9	$6
Child's Third Christmas QXG8707	Child's Age Collection	2003	$9	$8
Chocolate Treasures QXG2286	General Line	2006	$13	$13
Christmas Angel-Display QXM4573	Miniature Ornaments	2002	$17	$17
Christmas Around The World QX8436	General Line	2002	$7	$7
Christmas Belle QXG3023	General Line	2006	$13	$13
Christmas Belle, The QX8311	General Line	2000	$11	$9
Christmas Bells 10th Ed. QXM5134	Christmas Bells	2004	$5	$5
Christmas Bells 11th Ed. QXM8975	Christmas Bells	2005	$5	$5
Christmas Bells 6th Ed. QXM5984	Christmas Bells	2000	$5	$6
Christmas Bells 7th Ed. QXM5245	Christmas Bells	2001	$5	$6
Christmas Bells 8th Ed. QXM4326	Christmas Bells	2002	$5	$5
Christmas Bells 9th Ed. QXM4927	Christmas Bells	2003	$5	$5
Christmas Broadcast, A QLX7596	Magic Ornaments	2006	$24	$24
Christmas Cone QX8875	General Line	2001	$9	$6
Christmas Cookies! QLX7611	Magic Ornaments	2004	$25	$25
Christmas Countdown QXG4455	General Line	2005	$15	$15
Christmas Crossing QXI8661	Thomas The Tank Engine	2004	$13	$13
Christmas Eve Snack QXI4001	Looney Tunes	2004	$13	$13
Christmas Fairy QX8396	General Line	2002	$15	$15
Christmas Floral QX2963	General Line	2002	$7	$7
Christmas Greeting, A QXG2243	General Line	2006	$17	$17
Christmas Growth Chart QX8896	General Line	2002	$13	$13
Christmas Habitat Tweety QX2913	Looney Tunes	2002	$10	$10
Christmas Holly 5th Ed. QX6611	Madame Alexander	2000	$15	$30
Christmas In The Kitchen QX8956	General Line	2002	$13	$13
Christmas Joy QP1413	General Line	2002	$13	$13
Christmas Pageant, The QXM4406	Miniature Ornaments	2003	$10	$10
Christmas Parrot QX8175	General Line	2001	$9	$9

Lionel Blue Comet 400E Steam Locomotive, 2002, 7th in the Lionel Trains series, **$19.**

Sooo Fast Custom Car Set, 2002, from the Hot Wheels series, **$17.**

Lionel Blue Comet Passenger Car, 2002, **$13.**

Lionel Blue Comet 400T Oil Tender, 2002, **$19.**

Staggerwing, 2002, 6th in the Sky's the Limit series, **$57.**

1970 Ford Mach I Mustang, 2002, 12th in the Classic American Cars series, **$15.**

Ornament Title	Series	Year	Issue Price	Current Value
Christmas Rose 3rd & Final Ed. QBG4054	Crown Reflections/General Line	2000	$35	$57
Christmas Story, A QP1429	General Line	2003	$10	$10
Christmas Tea 11th Ed. QX2346	Madame Alexander	2006	$15	$15
Christmas To Remember, A QXI6316	Polar Express	2006	$15	$15
Christmas Tree Dreams QLX7477	Magic Ornaments	2003	$24	$24
Christmas Tree Gift Clip QX2896	General Line	2002	$10	$10
Christmas Tree Gift Clip QXG8637	General Line	2003	$10	$10
Christmas Tree Surprise QX8321	General Line	2000	$17	$23
Christmas Window 1 QXC3003	Christmas Windows	2003	N/A	$35
Christmas Window 2 QXC4003	Christmas Windows	2004	N/A	$30
Christmas Window 3 QXC5003	Christmas Windows	2005	$20	$20
Christmas Window 4 QXC6003	Christmas Windows	2006	$20	$20
Christmas With The Family QXD4235	Disney Collection	2005	$17	$17
Christmastime In The City QXG8817	General Line	2003	$13	$13
Chrysantha 14th Ed. QX6985	Mary's Angels	2001	$8	$9
Church Choir, The QXG2429	General Line	2003	$17	$17
Cinderella & Prince Charming QXD5139	Cinderella	2003	$17	$17
Cinderella QXD4956	Disney Collection	2002	$10	$10
Cinderella's Castle QXD4172	Disney Collection	2001	$18	$19
Cinderella's Slipper QMP4017	Cinderella	2006	$13	$13
Circle Of Love QEP1377	Family Tree	2004	$13	$13
Circus Mountain Railroad QLX7686	Magic Ornaments	2002	$42	$42
City On The Edge Of Forever QXI4094	Star Trek	2004	$28	$40
City Sidewalks QLX7635	Magic Ornaments	2005	$44	$35
Clara's Hallmark Shop QXC4583	Collector's Club	2002	$20	$20
Class Act QX8074	General Line	2000	$8	$13
Classic Red Riding Hood QXM5201	Miniature Ornaments	2004	$8	$8
Cleveland Browns QSR5161	NFL Collection	2000	$10	$8
Cleveland Browns QSR5572	NFL Collection	2001	$10	$8
Clever Cardinal QXM5019	Miniature Ornaments	2003	$7	$9
Click Your Heels QXI7487	Wizard Of Oz Collection	2003	$32	$32
Clone Trooper Lieutenant QXI6175	General Line	2005	$15	$15
Clone Troopers QXM5127	General Line	2003	$10	$14
Close In Heart QEP1353	Family Tree	2003	$13	$13
Close In Heart QP1353	Family Tree	2002	$13	$13
Close-Knit Friends QX8204	General Line	2000	$15	$15
Coach Of The Year QXG8639	General Line	2003	$10	$8
Coach QXG2236	General Line	2006	$10	$10
Cocoa For Two: Piglet & Pooh QXD8333	General Line	2006	$15	$15
Collection Of Memories, A QEP1371, Set Of 4	Family Tree	2004	$25	$25
Colonial Church 7th Ed. QX8451	Candlelight Services	2004	$19	$19
Color Crew Chief Crayola Crayon QX6185	General Line	2001	$11	$18
Color Me Curious QXI6222	Curious George	2005	$10	$10
Commander Trip Tucker QXI4091	Star Trek	2004	$15	$10
Commuter Set 7th Ed. QX6814	Barbie	2000	$16	$15

Barbie as Rapunzel, 2002, **$15.**

Topping the Tree, 2002, **$15.**

Woodland Friends, 2002, **$15.**

Scarlett O'Hara, 2003, from the Gone With the Wind series, **$16.**

Ornament Title	Series	Year	Issue Price	Current Value
Conductor's Watch-The Polar Express QXM6472	Polar Express	2005	$8	$8
Cookie Doe QXG5441	General Line	2004	$10	$10
Cool Character QX8271	General Line	2000	$13	$21
Cool Decade Colorway QXC6764C	Collector's Club	2000	N/A	$50
Cool Decade QX2195	Cool Decade	2005	$8	$8
Cool Decade QX2463	Cool Decade	2006	$9	$9
Cool Decade QX6764	Cool Decade	2000	$8	$8
Cool Decade QX6992	Cool Decade	2001	$8	$8
Cool Decade QX8016	Cool Decade	2002	$8	$8
Cool Decade QX8079	Cool Decade	2003	$8	$8
Cool Decade QX8134	Cool Decade	2004	$8	$8
Cool Friends QX8706	General Line	2002	$10	$10
Cool Holiday!, A QLX7621	Magic Ornaments	2004	$32	$32
Cool Sport Coca-Cola Polar Bear QHB9002	Special Issues	2001	N/A	$11
Cordelia QP1805	Joyful Tidings	2005	$13	$13
Cordelia QP1832	Joyful Tidings	2005	$13	$13
Corner Bank 23rd Ed. QX2576	Nostalgic Houses & Shops	2006	$15	$15
Countdown To Christmas QKK3001, Set Of 25 Plus Tree	Keepsake Kids	2004	$40	$40
Countdown To Christmas QLX7529	Magic Ornaments	2003	$20	$20
Country Church 5th Ed. QLX7653	Candlelight Services	2002	$19	$19
Cowardly Lion QXM4219	Wizard Of Oz Collection	2003	$7	$8
Cozy Home QX8965	General Line	2001	$10	$10
Crabby Caroler, The QLX7592	Magic Ornaments	2005	$20	$20
Crack The Whip! QXI6292	Peanuts Collection	2005	$24	$20
Creative Cutter QX8865	Cooking For Christmas	2001	$10	$10
Creeping Along The Corridors QXI6156	Harry Potter	2006	$15	$15
Cross Of Glory QXG8977	General Line	2003	$10	$10
Cuando El Nacio QXG5361	General Line	2004	$13	$9
Cup Of Friendship QX8472	General Line	2001	$9	$9
Curtiss R3C-2 Racer 3rd Ed. QXM4877	Sky's The Limit Miniature Series	2003	$7	$8
Cutest Kitty QXG4712	General Line	2005	$10	$10
Dad QX8071	General Line	2000	$9	$10
Dad QX8422	General Line	2001	$9	$15
Dad QX8936	General Line	2002	$10	$10
Dad QXG2916	General Line	2006	$10	$10
Dad QXG4672	General Line	2005	$10	$10
Dad QXG5551	General Line	2004	$10	$7
Dad QXG8889	General Line	2003	$10	$10
Dale Earnhardt QXI6754	NASCAR	2000	$15	$44
Dale Jarrett QXI5205	Sports Collection	2001	$15	$12
Dallas Cowboys QSR5121	NFL Collection	2000	$10	$9
Dallas Cowboys QSR5622	NFL Collection	2001	$10	$9
Dancer En Pointe QXG5394	General Line	2004	$13	$13

TIE Fighter, 2003, Star Wars, **$26.**

Clone Troopers, 2003, Star Wars, **$14.**

Jedi Master Yoda, 2003, Star Wars, **$15.**

1936 Stinson Reliant, 2003, 7th in the Sky's the Limit series, **$21.**

C-3PO, 2003, 7th in the Star Wars series, **$14.**

1972 Chevy Cheyenne Super, 2003, 9th in the All-American Trucks series, **$18.**

Ornament Title	Series	Year	Issue Price	Current Value
Dancer In Flight QXG8619	General Line	2003	$13	$18
Dancin' In Christmas QX6971	General Line	2000	$8	$6
Dancing Clara 9th Ed. QX8111	Madame Alexander	2004	$15	$15
Dancing Santa QXM8132	Miniature Ornaments	2005	$6	$6
Daniel In The Lion's Den 3rd Ed. QX8122	Favorite Bible Stories	2001	$14	$17
Darth Maul QXI6885	General Line	2000	$15	$15
Darth Vader 6th Ed. QX8136	Star Wars	2002	$15	$36
Darth Vader QXI6185	General Line	2005	$19	$19
Dash Away All QP1762	Santa's Midnight Ride	2005	$30	$30
Dashing Through The Snow QXM5335	Miniature Ornaments	2001	$7	$7
Daughter QX8081	General Line	2000	$9	$12
Daughter QX8425	General Line	2001	$9	$20
Daughter QX8946	General Line	2002	$10	$10
Daughter QXG2926	General Line	2006	$10	$10
Daughter QXG4682	General Line	2005	$10	$10
Daughter QXG5561	General Line	2004	$10	$10
Daughter QXG8899	General Line	2003	$10	$10
Dear Santa-Crayola QXG2306	General Line	2006	$13	$13
Death Star QLX7656	General Line	2002	$24	$17
Decision, The QXG8569	General Line	2003	$10	$10
Deck The Halls! QXI4004	Looney Tunes	2004	$15	$10
Deck The Halls, Charlie Brown QXI6166	Peanuts Collection	2006	$24	$24
Decorating Scooby-Doo Style QX8256	Scooby-Doo	2002	$13	$13
Decorating Scooby-Style QXI6146	Scooby-Doo	2006	$13	$13
Deer Creek Cottage QXI5276	Thomas Kinkade General Line	2002	$15	$10
Deer Friend QXG2773	Winter Garden	2006	$13	$13
Defending The Flag QXG8577	General Line	2003	$13	$13
Delicious Christmas QXG8657	General Line	2003	$15	$15
Delphine Barbie QXI6432	Barbie Fashion Model Collection	2005	$25	$25
Delta Flyer QLX7663	Star Trek Voyager	2002	$24	$35
Denver Broncos QSR5111	NFL Collection	2000	$10	$9
Denver Broncos QSR5545	NFL Collection	2001	$10	$9
Derek Jeter QXI5242	At The Ballpark	2002	$15	$15
Designer Spotlight Barbie Ornament QXC5008	Collector's Club Exclusive	2005	$20	$20
Detective 3rd Ed. QX6564	Spotlight On Snoopy	2000	$10	$10
Devoted Donkey QXM6044	Miniature Ornaments	2000	$7	$15
Disney Snowflake Miniatures QXM3153	Miniature Ornaments	2006	$20	$20
Disney's School Bus QXD4115	Disney Collection	2001	$15	$29
Display Base QP1553	General Line	2002	$10	$10
Display Wreath QP1139	Snowman's Land	2003	$20	$20
Doctor, The QX8226	Star Trek Voyager	2002	$15	$11
Dog Dish Dilemma QXD4044	Mickey & Co.	2000	$13	$13
Dollop QP1763	Merry Bakers	2006	$15	$15

Town Hall and Mayor's Christmas Tree, 2003, from the Nostalgic Houses and Shops series, **$29.**

The Amazing Little Tree, 2003, **$24.**

Christmas Window 1, 2003, 1st in the Christmas Windows series, **$35.**

Frosty Friends, 2003, 24th in the Frosty Friends series, **$18.**

Ornament Title	Series	Year	Issue Price	Current Value
Donald & Daisy At Lovers' Lodge 3rd Ed. QXD4031	Romantic Vacations	2000	$15	$14
Donald Goes Motoring QXD4122	Disney Collection	2001	$13	$13
Donovan McNabb 12th Ed. QX2386	Football Legends	2006	$15	$15
Don't Get Into Mischief, Beatrix Potter QX2906	General Line	2002	$10	$10
Dorothy & Cowardly Lion QXI4021	Wizard Of Oz Collection	2004	$16	$16
Dorothy & Scarecrow QX8246	Wizard Of Oz Collection	2002	$16	$16
Dorothy & The Munchkins QXI6106	Wizard Of Oz Collection	2006	$32	$32
Dorothy & Tin Man QXI8299	Wizard Of Oz Collection	2003	$16	$14
Dorothy QXM8922	Wizard Of Oz Collection	2005	$7	$7
Dousin' Dalmatian QX8024	General Line	2000	$10	$19
Downhill Delivery 1st Ed. QX2834	Nick & Christopher	2004	$13	$10
Dream 1st Ed. QXM4543	Paintbox Pixies	2002	$7	$7
Dreaming Big QXG4325	General Line	2005	$10	$8
Dreaming Of Christmas QXD8306	Disney Collection	2006	$15	$15
Dreams Have Wings QP1536	General Line	2002	$10	$10
Dressing Cinderella QXD4109	Cinderella	2000	$13	$15
Drummer Boy QXG4454	Veggie Tales	2004	$9	$9
Duck Dodgers & Marvin The Martian QXI8765	Looney Tunes	2005	$15	$15
Dusty & Smidgen QP1746	Merry Bakers	2006	$15	$15
E.T. The Extra Terrestrial QXI5333	General Line	2002	$15	$15
Easter Egg Surprise 3rd Ed. QEO8532	Easter Egg Surprise	2001	N/A	$19
Easter Eggspress QEO8536	Peekaboo	2002	N/A	$8
Eastern Bluebird 1st Ed. QEO8451	Spring Is In The Air	2000	$10	$17
Eeyore Helps Out QXD4145	General Line	2001	$13	$13
Eeyore Loses A Tail 9th Ed. QXD8336	Winnie The Pooh Collection	2006	$15	$15
Egg Hunt Hoppers QEO8039	Peekaboo	2003	N/A	$15
Electrical Spectacle! QLX7624	Magic Ornaments	2004	$42	$42
Elizabeth "Beth" March 3rd Ed. QX8187	Madame Alexander Little Women	2003	$16	$16
Empire Strikes Back Lunchbox QEO8585	Easter Ornaments	2001	N/A	$22
Enchanted Evening Case & Barbie Ornament QXM4383	Barbie	2002	$13	$10
Engravable Tag QEP2107	Heart Of Motherhood Collection	2004	$6	$6
Engravable Tag QP2109	Heart Of Motherhood Collection	2003	$6	$6
Eric Lindros 4th Ed. QXI6801	Hockey Greats	2000	$16	$24
Esmeralda QP1812	Joyful Tidings	2005	$13	$10
ESPN QXI6313	Magic Ornaments	2006	$15	$15
Evening Splendor Barbie 13th Ed. QX2373	Barbie	2006	$16	$16
Evening Splendor Barbie-Brunette 13th Ed. QXE4463	Barbie	2006	N/A	N/A
Eye Of God-Feliz Navidad QX8185	General Line	2001	$10	$10
Faerie Brilliana QP1672	Frostlight Faeries Collection	2001	$15	$19

4449 Daylight Steam Loco-
motive, 2003, 8th in the Lionel Trains series, **$20.**

1963 Corvette Sting Ray Coupe, 2003, 13th
in the Classic American Cars series, **$15.**

Lionel Daylight Oil Tender, 2003, **$15.**

Scarlett O'Hara and Rhett Butler, 2003,
from the Gone With the Wind series, **$19.**

Scarlett O'Hara, 2004, from the Gone With
the Wind series, **$16.**

Ornament Title	Series	Year	Issue Price	Current Value
Faerie Candessa QP1665	Frostlight Faeries Collection	2001	$15	$19
Faerie Delandra QP1685	Frostlight Faeries Collection	2001	$15	$19
Faerie Dust QP1752	Gold Crown Exclusives	2001	$6	$6
Faerie Estrella QP1695	Frostlight Faeries Collection	2001	$15	$10
Faerie Floriella QP1692	Frostlight Faeries Collection	2001	$15	$19
Faerie Gabriella & Faerie Castle Ornament Stand QXC4656	Collector's Club	2002	$35	$35
Familiar Face QXD4152	General Line	2001	$13	$13
Family Is A Bridge, A QEP1317	Family Tree	2003	$13	$13
Family Photoholder QX8693	General Line	2002	$13	$13
Family Stories QP1336	General Line	2002	$13	$13
Family Ties QXG4742	General Line	2005	$13	$13
Family Tree, The QP1366	General Line	2002	$40	$40
Fancy Footwork 4th Ed. QX8414	Snowball & Tuxedo	2004	$8	$8
Farewell Scene QLX/562	Gone With The Wind	2001	$24	$29
Fashion Afoot 1st Ed. QX8341	Fashion Afoot	2000	$15	$15
Fashion Afoot 2nd Ed. QX8105	Fashion Afoot	2001	$15	$15
Fashion Afoot 3rd & Final Ed. QX8116	Fashion Afoot	2002	$15	$15
Fashion Luncheon Barbie 12th Ed. QX2305	Barbie	2005	$16	$15
Fashion Pup Barbie Ornament Set QXM6336	Barbie	2006	$15	$15
Fashion QXG3353	Kid Speak	2006	$13	$13
Fat Boy 2nd Ed. QXI6774	Harley-Davidson Milestones	2000	$15	$26
Father Christmas 1st Ed. QX8471	Father Christmas	2004	$19	$19
Father Christmas 2nd Ed. QX2155	Father Christmas	2005	$19	$19
Father Christmas 3rd Ed. QX2566	Father Christmas	2006	$19	$19
Felicity With Horse Brush QAC6431	American Girls Collection	2004	$15	$15
Feliz Navidad QX8214	General Line	2000	$9	$9
Feliz Navidad QXG4492	General Line	2005	$13	$13
Feliz Navidad QXG5504	General Line	2004	$13	$13
Feliz Navidad QXG8689	General Line	2003	$13	$13
Fieldstone Church 6th Ed. QX7429	Candlelight Services	2003	$19	$22
Fill 'Er Up! Daffy Duck QX8266	Looney Tunes	2002	$10	$10
Find Yourself In A Garden	Nature's Sketchbook-Bastin	2006	N/A	$14
Fire Station No. 1 3rd Ed. QX8052	Town & Country	2001	$16	$15
Firefighters QXG2656	General Line	2006	$10	$10
Firehouse No. 2006 3rd Ed. QXM3096	Miniature Fire Brigade	2006	$10	$10
First Bouquet QEO8282	Nature's Sketchbook-Bastin	2005	N/A	$17
First Christmas Together QXG2716	General Line	2006	$15	$15
First Christmas Together QXG3257	General Line	2003	$9	$9
First Christmas Together QXG4392	General Line	2005	$9	$9
First Christmas Together QXG5334	General Line	2004	$13	$15
First Gift Of Christmas QSR5811	Polar Express	2004	$15	$15
First Snow, The QXI5266	Blue's Clues	2002	$10	$10
First Spring Songs	Nature's Sketchbook-Bastin	2006	N/A	$11
Fishin' Mission QX8736	General Line	2002	$10	$10

Frosty Friends, 2004, 25th in the Frosty Friends series, **$14.**

So Much to Do!, 2004, **$13.**

Winterfest, 2004, Frosty Friends special anniversary edition, **$17.**

Barber Shop & Beauty Shop, 2004, 21st in the Nostalgic Houses and Shops series, **$15.**

1966 Oldsmobile Toronado Coupe, 2004, 14th in the Classic American Cars series, **$15.**

2000 Ford F-150, 2004, 10th in the All-American Trucks series, **$15.**

Ornament Title	Series	Year	Issue Price	Current Value
Fishing Hole, The QX6984	General Line	2000	$13	$8
Flight At Kitty Hawk 1st Ed. QXM5215	Sky's The Limit Miniature Series	2001	$7	$9
Florida Gators QSR2165	Collegiate Collection	2001	$10	$3
Florida Gators QSR2324	Collegiate Collection	2000	$8	$3
Florida State Seminoles QSR2162	Collegiate Collection	2001	$10	$3
Florida State Seminoles QSR2341	Collegiate Collection	2000	$10	$3
Fluffy On Guard QXE4415	Harry Potter	2001	$13	$13
Flying Over London QXD5137	Peter Pan	2003	$15	$12
Flying School Airplane Hangar QX8172	General Line	2001	$16	$22
Football QXG4772	General Line	2005	$10	$10
Footprint Token QEP2001	Heart Of Motherhood Collection	2004	$6	$6
For A Friend QXG5604	General Line	2004	$10	$7
For Grandma QXG4695	General Line	2005	$10	$10
For Grandma QXG5574	General Line	2004	$10	$7
For Grandpa QXG4702	General Line	2005	$10	$10
For Grandpa QXG5581	General Line	2004	$10	$7
For You, Teacher! QXG4315	General Line	2005	$10	$10
Ford Thunderbird-50th Anniversary QXI6172	General Line	2005	$24	$24
Forever Friend QXG8967	General Line	2003	$15	$15
Forever In Her Heart QEP2003	Heart Of Motherhood Collection	2004	$17	$17
Forsythia 18th Ed. QX2315	Mary's Angels	2005	$8	$8
Four-Alarm Friends QX8325	General Line	2001	$10	$10
Fox In Socks 8th & Final Ed. QX2353	Dr. Seuss Books	2006	$15	$15
Foxes In The Forest 4th & Final Ed. QX6794	Majestic Wilderness	2000	$13	$19
Frederick O'Ghastly QFO6061, Set Of 3	Halloween	2004	$13	$13
Friend Chimes In, A QXC4491	Collector's Club	2000	N/A	$12
Friendly Elves QX8805	General Line	2001	$15	$15
Friendly Greeting QX8174	General Line	2000	$10	$7
Friends At Large QXI6495	Madagascar	2005	$13	$13
Friends Forever QXG5024	General Line	2004	$13	$13
Friends In Harmony QX8001	General Line	2000	$10	$10
Friends Of A Feather QEO8517	Tweedle Dee Deet	2003	N/A	$9
Friends We Keep Forever QEP1385	Family Tree	2004	$10	$10
Friendship Ornaments QX8713	General Line	2002	$15	$15
Friendship QXG8879	General Line	2003	$7	$7
Frodo Baggins QXI8624	Lord Of The Rings	2004	$15	$15
Frolicking Friends Bambi, Thumper & Flower QEO8434	Easter Ornaments	2000	$15	$15
From A Stable So Small Storybook Set QKK3014	Keepsake Kids	2004	$25	$25
Frostlight Faerie Sisters QXG2479	General Line	2003	$25	$25
Frostlight Faeries, Too Collection QXG5531, Set Of 3	Gold Crown Exclusives	2004	$20	$20

Father Christmas 1, 2004, **$19.**

Chewbaca and C-3PO, 2004, 8th in the Star Wars series, **$15.**

Anakin Skywalker, 2004, Star Wars, **$15.**

Jolly Old Kris Jingle, 2004, **$9.**

Star Destroyer and Blockade Runner, 2004, Star Wars, **$28.**

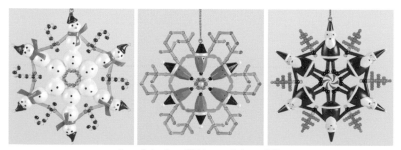

Snowflake Fun, 2004, set of three, **$10.**

Ornament Title	Series	Year	Issue Price	Current Value
Frostlight Fir Tree QP1762	Gold Crown Exclusives	2001	$45	$45
Frostlight Flowers QP1705	Gold Crown Exclusives	2001	$16	$22
Frosty Friends (Recolored Remake Of A Cool Yule)	Frosty Friends	2006	N/A	$15
Frosty Friends 21st Ed. QX6601	Frosty Friends	2000	$11	$12
Frosty Friends 22nd Ed. QX8012	Frosty Friends	2001	$11	$12
Frosty Friends 23rd Ed. QX8053	Frosty Friends	2002	$11	$11
Frosty Friends 24th Ed. QX8089	Frosty Friends	2003	$13	$18
Frosty Friends 25th Ed.QX8331	Frosty Friends	2004	$13	$14
Frosty Friends 26th Ed.QX2325	Frosty Friends	2005	$13	$13
Frosty Friends 27th Ed. QX2513	Frosty Friends	2006	$13	$13
Frosty Friends Porcelain Box	Collector's Club	2002	$19	$19
Frosty Friends Premiere Exclusive QX8524	Frosty Friends	2000	$19	$25
Frosty Friends QBG4094	General Line	2000	$40	$30
Fun-Stuffed Stocking QLZ4291	Laser Gallery	2000	$6	$6
G.I. Joe Action Pilot QX6734	General Line	2000	$14	$18
G.I. Joe Fighter Pilot QX6045	General Line	2001	$14	$23
G.I. Joe Lunchbox Set QX8286	General Line	2002	$15	$15
G.I. Joe QXI6262	General Line	2005	$15	$15
G.I. Joe QXI8601	General Line	2004	$15	$12
Gandalf The Grey QXI6232	Lord Of The Rings	2005	$15	$15
Garage Ramp Race QXI8631	Hot Wheels	2004	$10	$10
Garden Awakens QEO8285	Nature's Sketchbook-Bastin	2005	N/A	$19
Garden Greetings QXG3013	Winter Garden	2006	$13	$13
Garden Grows Happiness	Nature's Sketchbook-Bastin	2006	N/A	$11
Garden Is Calling QEO0263	Nature's Sketchbook-Bastin	2006	N/A	$14
Gardener's Christmas Corner QX2866	General Line	2002	$10	$10
Gardener's Paradise QXG4285	General Line	2005	$13	$13
Gearing Up For Christmas QXM5352	Miniature Ornaments	2001	$7	$7
Gee Bee R-1 Super Sportster 5th Ed. QX8005	Sky's The Limit	2001	$15	$76
Gee Bee R-1 Super Sportster 5th Ed. QXM2072	Sky's The Limit Miniature Series	2005	$7	$7
Generations QP1326	General Line	2002	$10	$10
Gentle Angel QP1426	Memories Of Christmas Collection	2002	$15	$15
George Brett QXI5296	General Line	2002	$15	$10
Germany QP1704	Gold Crown Exclusives	2004	$13	$13
Get Your Kicks! QXG6386	General Line	2006	$10	$10
Getting Ready For Christmas QXD4212	General Line	2005	$32	$32
Giddy-Up, Christmas! QP1437	General Line	2003	$13	$13
Gift Bearers 2nd Ed. QX6651	Gift Bearers	2000	$13	$12
Gift Bearers 3rd Ed. QX8115	Gift Bearers	2001	$13	$12
Gift Bearers 4th Ed. QX8883	Gift Bearers	2002	$13	$10
Gift Bearers 5th Ed. QX8239	Gift Bearers	2003	$13	$13
Gift Bearers 6th Ed. QX8401	Gift Bearers	2004	$13	$9

Lionel Hiawatha Observation Car, 2004, **$13.**

1939 Hiawatha Steam Locomotive, 2004, 9th in the Lionel Trains series, **$19.**

The Winning Bounce, 2004, Winnie the Pooh, **$10.**

Lionel Hiawatha Tender, 2004, **$13.**

Winter Garden, 2004, **$8.**

Winter Fun With Snoopy, 2004, 7th in the Winter Fun With Snoopy series, **$7.**

Santa Wanna-Be, 2004, 1st in the Forever Friends series, **$6.**

Ornament Title	Series	Year	Issue Price	Current Value
Gift Bearers 7th Ed. QX2222	Gift Bearers	2005	$13	$13
Gift Exchange QXD4105	General Line	2005	$15	$15
Gift For A Friend With Miniature Teddy Bear QXC4545C	Collector's Club	2001	N/A	$75
Gift For Gardening QXM4463	Miniature Ornaments	2002	$5	$5
Gift For Jesus, A, Book & Ornament Set QKK3053	Gold Crown Exclusives	2006	$25	$25
Gift For Raggedy Ann, A QXI8417	General Line	2003	$13	$12
Gift Of Children, The QEP2029	Heart Of Motherhood Collection	2004	$17	$17
Gift Of Children, The QP2029	Heart Of Motherhood Collection	2003	$17	$17
Gift Of Friendship QXG5611	General Line	2004	$13	$9
Gift Of Love, The QX2142	Holiday Angels	2006	$17	$17
Gifts For Everyone QP1409	General Line	2003	$17	$17
Gifts For The Grinch QXI5344	Dr. Seuss' How The Grinch Stole Christmas	2000	$13	$35
Gifts Of The Season QXM4576	Miniature Ornaments	2002	$28	$28
Gilda QP1815	Joyful Tidings	2005	$13	$13
Gingerbread Church QX8244	General Line	2000	$10	$9
Gingerbread Cottage QLX7683	Magic Ornaments	2002	$20	$20
Gingerbread Home QXI5294	General Line	2004	$13	$13
Girl Token QEP2099	Heart Of Motherhood Collection	2004	$6	$6
Girl Token QEP2099	Heart Of Motherhood Collection	2003	$6	$6
Glass Slipper QXD4182	Disney Collection	2001	$8	$8
Glimpse Of Santa, A QXC6007	Collector's Club	2006	$28	$28
Glinda The Good Witch Arrives! QXI6103	Wizard Of Oz Collection	2006	$15	$15
Glistening Icicles QP1742	Gold Crown Exclusives	2001	$13	$22
Glory Shining Down QXG8667	General Line	2003	$11	$9
Go Teams! QXG5401	General Line	2004	$10	$7
God With Us QX8893	General Line	2002	$7	$7
Godchild QX8161	General Line	2000	$8	$8
Godchild QX8452	General Line	2001	$8	$8
Godchild QX8953	General Line	2002	$13	$13
Godchild QXG3213	General Line	2006	$10	$10
Godchild QXG4735	General Line	2005	$10	$10
Godchild QXG5644	General Line	2004	$13	$9
Godchild QXG8939	General Line	2003	$13	$13
Gold-Star Teacher QX6951	General Line	2000	$8	$5
Golfer Supreme QX6991	General Line	2000	$11	$11
Good Book, The QX8254	Collector's Choice	2000	$14	$18
Good Morning Doves QEO8314	Nature's Sketchbook-Bastin	2004	N/A	$13
Goodcuppa Coffee QXG2276	General Line	2006	$13	$13
Goofy Clockworks QXD4923	Disney Collection	2002	$15	$15
Goofy Helps Out QXD5037	Disney Collection	2003	$13	$13

Scarlett O'Hara, 2005, from the Gone With the Wind series, **$16.**

Lionelville, 2004, **$65.**

Scarlett O'Hara and Rhett Butler, 2004, from the Gone With the Wind series, **$19.**

Scarlett O'Hara and Rhett Butler, 2005, from the Gone With the Wind series, **$19.**

Ornament Title	Series	Year	Issue Price	Current Value
Goofy Toots The Tuba 6th & Final Ed. QXD4903	Mickey's Holiday Parade	2002	$14	$14
Gopher Par QXG8587	General Line	2003	$10	$10
Gouda Reading QX2855	General Line	2001	$10	$10
Graceful Angel Bell QX8182	General Line	2001	$10	$7
Graceful Angel Tree Topper QXM5385	Tree Topper	2001	$13	$13
Graceful Glory QX8304	General Line	2000	$19	$29
Graceful Reindeer QX8912	General Line	2001	$16	$16
Grand Theater, The 20th Ed. QX8149	Nostalgic Houses & Shops	2003	$15	$19
Grandchild's First Christmas QX8485	General Line	2001	$9	$10
Grandchild's First Christmas QXG2437	General Line	2003	$10	$10
Grandchild's First Christmas QXG4612	General Line	2005	$10	$10
Grandchild's First Christmas QXG5741	Child's Age Collection	2004	$10	$7
Granddaughter QX8091	General Line	2000	$9	$10
Granddaughter QX8435	General Line	2001	$9	$10
Granddaughter QX8663	General Line	2002	$10	$10
Granddaughter QXG2936	General Line	2006	$10	$10
Granddaughter QXG4692	General Line	2005	$10	$10
Granddaughter QXG5571	General Line	2004	$10	$10
Granddaughter QXG8907	General Line	2003	$10	$10
Grandma QX8676	General Line	2002	$7	$7
Grandma Tillie & Willie QFO6302	Hauntington U.S.A. Collection	2005	$13	$10
Grandmother QX8445	General Line	2001	$8	$9
Grandmother's House & Covered Bridge 4th Ed. QX8156	Town & Country	2002	$17	$13
Grandmother's Treasure, A QEP2014	Heart Of Motherhood Collection	2004	$17	$17
Grandson QX8094	General Line	2000	$9	$10
Grandson QX8442	General Line	2001	$9	$10
Grandson QX8666	General Line	2002	$10	$10
Grandson QXG2993	General Line	2006	$10	$10
Grandson QXG4685	General Line	2005	$10	$10
Grandson QXG5564	General Line	2004	$10	$7
Grandson QXG8909	General Line	2003	$10	$10
Great Oz, The QLX7361	Wizard Of Oz Collection	2000	$32	$50
Great Ski Challenge, The QXD4926	Disney Collection	2002	$13	$13
Green Bay Packers QSR5114	NFL Collection	2000	$10	$9
Green Bay Packers QSR5625	NFL Collection	2001	$10	$9
Green Eggs & Ham 4th Ed. QX8083	Dr. Seuss Books	2002	$15	$15
Green Eggs & Ham QXM6034	Dr. Seuss Books	2000	$20	$19
Grinch & Cindy-Lou Who, The QXI8377	Dr. Seuss' How The Grinch Stole Christmas	2003	$15	$16
Grinch & Max, The QXI8534	Dr. Seuss' How The Grinch Stole Christmas	2004	$15	$15
Grinchy Claus QXI6183	Dr. Seuss' How The Grinch Stole Christmas!	2006	$15	$15

Ruby Slippers, 2005, from the Keepsake Ornament Collector's Club, **$20.**

See No Humbug!, 2005, **$13.**

Frosty Friends, 2005, 26th in the Frosty Friends series, **$13.**

Rocking Horse special repainted edition, 2005, from the Rocking Horse series, **$20.**

Snow Bear Buddies, 2005, **$10.**

Victorian Home, 2005, 22nd in the Nostalgic Houses and Shops series, **$15.**

Ornament Title	Series	Year	Issue Price	Current Value
Guiding Star QX8962	General Line	2001	$10	$8
Gungan Submarine QXI7351	General Line	2000	$24	$21
Hagrid & Norbert The Dragon QXE4412	Harry Potter	2001	$16	$16
Happiness Isö QXI6163	Peanuts Collection	2006	$13	$13
Happy Birthday, Jesus! QXG5334	General Line	2004	$10	$10
Happy Diploma Day QEO8431	World Of Wishes	2000	$11	$11
Happy Haulers QLX7613	Magic Ornaments	2006	$32	$32
Happy Hopper QEO8505	Easter Ornaments	2001	N/A	$8
Happy Hues QXI6225	General Line	2005	$13	$13
Happy Life Together, A, Ornament Set QXM2206	Miniature Ornaments	2006	$24	$24
Happy Snowman, A 995PR3570	General Line	2005	N/A	$11
Happy Snowman QX8942	General Line	2001	$9	$9
Hard At Work QXI6326	Bob The Builder	2006	$10	$10
Harley-Davidson Barbie Ornament QXI8554	Barbie	2000	$15	$14
Harley-Davidson Barbie Ornament QXI8885	Barbie	2001	$16	$20
Harry Potter & Hedwig QXI4044	Harry Potter & The Sorcerer's Stone	2004	$15	$13
Harry Potter QXE4402	Harry Potter	2001	$13	$13
Hatched Before Your Eyes QEO8571	Easter Ornaments	2004	N/A	$9
Heads-Up Play QXI4061	Scooby-Doo	2004	$13	$13
Heart Of The Season, The QXG4645	General Line	2005	$7	$7
Heartful Of Grateful, A QP1523	General Line	2002	$10	$10
Heavenly Carols QXI7713	Mary's Angels	2002	$17	$17
Heavenly Peace QLZ4314	Laser Gallery	2000	$7	$7
Hello, Dumbo! QXD4162	Disney Collection	2001	$13	$13
Hello, Ricky? QXI6366	I Love Lucy	2006	$17	$17
Here Comes Santa QXM4929	Miniature Ornaments	2003	$15	$22
Here Comes The Band QEO8235	Easter Ornaments	2005	N/A	$16
Hermione Granger's Trunk Set Of 6 QXE4422	Harry Potter	2001	$15	$15
Hidden Wishes 1QXC4001	Collector's Club	2004	N/A	$20
Hide & Seek QEO8324	Nature's Sketchbook-Bastin	2004	N/A	$13
Hockey Thrills 2nd Ed. QX2152	Nick & Christopher	2005	$13	$13
Hogwarts School Crests QXE4452	Harry Potter	2001	$13	$13
Holiday Adventure QXI8289	Scooby-Doo	2003	$15	$12
Holiday Advice Booth QXI4257	Peanuts Collection	2003	$15	$15
Holiday Bouquet QXM5244, Set Of 5	Miniature Ornaments	2004	$20	$20
Holiday Confections QP1776	Merry Bakers	2006	$12	$12
Holiday Flurries 2nd Ed. QXM5311	Holiday Flurries	2000	$7	$7
Holiday Flurries 3rd & Final Ed. QXM5272	Holiday Flurries	2001	$7	$7
Holiday For Two, A QXG3016	General Line	2006	$15	$15
Holiday Gathering, A QX8561	Thomas Kinkade General Line	2000	$11	$19
Holiday Headliner QXM8942	Disney Collection	2005	$10	$10
Holiday Hug QXI5284	General Line	2004	$15	$15
Holiday Mail QXG2753	Winter Garden	2006	$13	$13
Holiday Serenade QXG4422	General Line	2005	$24	$17

Snow Day Magic, 2005, **$20.**

Bounce Practice-Tigger, 2005, Winnie the Pooh, **$13.**

Crack the Whip!, 2005, from the Peanuts Collection, **$20.**

Christmas Window 3, 2005, 3rd in the Christmas Windows series, **$20.**

Ornament Title	Series	Year	Issue Price	Current Value
Holiday Shoe QXM5365	Miniature Ornaments	2001	$5	$5
Holiday Sledding QXI6282	Raggedy Ann & Andy	2005	$15	$13
Holiday Snowflake Skater 8th Ed. QX8137	Madame Alexander	2003	$15	$18
Holiday Spa Tweety QX6945	Looney Tunes	2001	$10	$10
Holiday Treat Taz QX8263	Looney Tunes	2002	$10	$10
Holly Berry Bell QX8291	General Line	2000	$15	$25
Holy Family QX6523	Blessed Nativity Collection	2000	$25	$25
Home Bright Home Mickey & Pluto QXD2509	Disney Collection	2003	$15	$15
Home For The Holidays QXG8837	Thomas Kinkade General Line	2003	$17	$17
Home Improvement Pro QXG2303	General Line	2006	$13	$13
Home Sweet Home Book & Ornament Set QKK3056	Gold Crown Exclusives	2006	$25	$25
Home, Family, Memories QP1323	General Line	2002	$10	$10
Hometown Church 6th & Final Ed. QX8201	Town & Country	2004	$17	$12
Hooray For The USA QX8281	General Line	2000	$10	$17
Hop On Pop 5th Ed. QXI8179	Dr. Seuss Books	2003	$15	$12
Hopalong Cassidy QX6714	General Line	2000	$15	$12
Hopalong Cassidy Velocipede 4th Ed. QEO8411	Sidewalk Cruisers	2000	$13	$30
Hope Cross QX8886	General Line	2002	$10	$10
Hope QP1206	Perfect Harmony Collection	2002	$10	$10
Hope, Joy, & Love QX8433	General Line	2002	$16	$16
Horse Car & Milk Car 2nd Ed. QXM5971	Lionel Norfolk & Western	2000	$13	$12
Horse Of A Different Color QXL7673	Wizard Of Oz Collection	2002	$36	$24
Horton Hatches The Egg 3rd Ed. QX6282	Dr. Seuss Books	2001	$15	$19
Hot Wheels 1968 Deora QXI6891	General Line	2000	$15	$13
Hot Wheels Lunchbox Set QXI8427	Hot Wheels	2003	$15	$13
Hugh QP1756	Merry Bakers	2006	$13	$13
Hugo The Handyman QFO6044	Halloween	2004	$13	$13
I Don'T Do Jolly! Maxine QX2806	Magic Ornaments	2002	$20	$20
I Heard The Bells On Chrismtas Day QP1136	Yuletide Harmony Collection	2006	$15	$15
I Love Grandma QXG3193	General Line	2006	$13	$13
I Love Grandpa QXG3196	General Line	2006	$13	$13
I Love My Dog Photoholder QX8802	General Line	2001	$8	$8
I.C. Pete's Frozen Treats QLX7595	Magic Ornaments	2005	$20	$20
Ice Block Buddies 1st Ed. QXM6011	Ice Block Buddies	2000	$6	$6
Ice Block Buddies 2nd Ed. QXM5295	Ice Block Buddies	2001	$5	$5
Ice Block Buddies 3rd Ed. QXM4356	Ice Block Buddies	2002	$5	$5
Ice Block Buddies 4th Ed. QXM4899	Ice Block Buddies	2003	$5	$5
Ice Block Buddies 5th Ed. QXM5141	Ice Block Buddies	2004	$5	$5
Ice Block Buddies 6th Ed. QXM8972	Ice Block Buddies	2005	$5	$5
Ice-Skaters' Delight 4th Ed. QX2182	Winter Wonderland	2005	$13	$13
I'll Always Be Pooh QXE4565	Premiere Exclusive	2006	$15	$15
I'll Be Home For Christmas QLX7519	Magic Ornaments	2003	$20	$20
I'll Get You, My Pretty! QFM4476	Wizard Of Oz Collection	2006	$65	$65
I'm Melting! I'M Melting! QXI4024	Wizard Of Oz Collection	2004	$36	$36

Santa's Woody Special Edition, 2005, from the Here Comes Santa series, no established value.

1926 Murray Steelcraft Speedster, 2005, 12th in the Kiddie Car Classics series, **$14.**

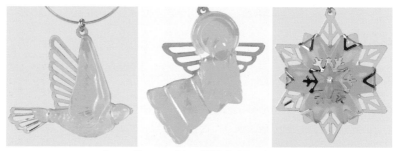

Peace, Hope, and Joy, 2005, **$13 for the set.**

Snow Buddies, 2005, 8th in the Snow Buddies series, **$9.**

1968 Pontiac Firebird, 2005, 15th in the Classic American Cars series, **$15.**

1961 Chevrolet Impala, 2006, 16th in the Classic American Cars series, **$15.**

Ornament Title	Series	Year	Issue Price	Current Value
I'm Snow Angel! QP1109	Snowman's Land	2003	$10	$10
Imperial At-At & Rebel Snowspeeder QXI6193	General Line	2006	$28	$28
Imperial Stormtrooper QXI6711	General Line	2000	$15	$15
In Excelsis Deo QXG2427	General Line	2003	$15	$15
Invisibility Cloak, The QXI8663	Harry Potter	2002	$13	$28
Ireland QP1714	Gold Crown Exclusives	2004	$13	$13
It Came Upon A Midnight Clear QP1113	Yuletide Harmony Collection	2006	$15	$15
It Had To Be You QX2815	General Line	2001	$10	$10
Italy QP1724	Gold Crown Exclusives	2004	$13	$13
It's Christmas Eve! QXC5007	Collector's Club Exclusive	2005	$28	$28
It's Snowtime! 6th Ed. QX2593	Snowball & Tuxedo	2006	$9	$9
It's The Easter Beagle-Peanuts QEO8361	Easter Ornaments	2004	N/A	$19
Ivana Hacketoff QFO6305	Hauntington, U.S.A.	2005	$8	$8
Jack In The Box QLZ4321	Laser Gallery	2000	$9	$5
Jack Skellington QXI8644	Nightmare Before Christmas, The	2004	$17	$17
Jango Fett QXI4386	General Line	2002	$15	$15
Jarjar Binks QX6882	General Line	2001	$15	$15
Jaromir Jagr 5th Ed. QXI6852	Hockey Greats	2001	$16	$16
Jason Giambi QX2449	At The Ballpark	2003	$15	$11
Jason Kidd 10th Ed. QXI8531	Hoop Stars	2004	$15	$10
Jeannie I Dream Of Jeannie QXI8564	General Line	2000	$15	$18
Jedi Council Members: Saesee Tiin, Yoda & Ki-Adi-Mundi QXI6744	General Line	2000	$20	$18
Jedi Master Yoda QXI8337	General Line	2003	$15	$15
Jeremy Fisher 5th & Final Ed. QEO8441	Beatrix Potter	2000	$9	$10
Jerry Rice 9th Ed. QX2457	Football Legends	2003	$15	$15
Jerry Rice QXI4267	General Line	2003	$15	$15
Jesus & Friends QX2843	General Line	2002	$15	$15
Jetsons, The, Lunchbox Set Of 2 QX6312	General Line	2001	$15	$13
Jewelry Box Ballet 1st Ed. QX8183	Treasures & Dreams	2002	$20	$20
Jewelry Box Carol 4th Ed. QX2172	Treasures & Dreams	2005	$20	$20
Jewelry Box Carousel 2nd Ed. QX8197	Treasures & Dreams	2003	$20	$18
Jewelry Box Castle 5th Ed. QX2546	Treasures & Dreams	2006	$20	$20
Jewelry Box Gazebo 3rd Ed. QX8121	Treasures & Dreams	2004	$20	$12
Jiminy Cricket QXD4185	Disney Collection	2001	$8	$8
Jimmie Johnson QXI8389	NASCAR	2003	$15	$15
Jingle All The Way QXI8267	Looney Tunes	2003	$15	$15
Jingle Ball, The QXG2616	General Line	2006	$10	$10
Jingle Bell Express 9th Ed. QXM4867	Miniature Kiddie Car Classics	2003	$7	$12
Jingle Bell Kringle QXC4481	Collector's Club	2000	N/A	$20
Jingle Bell Memories-The Polar Express QXI6462	Polar Express	2005	$15	$15
Jingle Belle QXM4483	Miniature Ornaments	2002	$6	$6
Jingle Bells QP1133	Yuletide Harmony Collection	2006	$15	$15

A Happy Snowman, 2005, $11.

Frosty Friends, 2006, 27th in the Frosty Friends series, **$13.**

Holiday Headliner, 2005, Disney, **$10.**

Frosty Friends, 2006 (a recolored remake of the 1980 1st edition titled A Cool Yule, from the Frosty Friends series), **$15.**

Christmas Window 2006, 4th in the Christmas Windows series, **$20.**

Ornament Title	Series	Year	Issue Price	Current Value
Jingle Bells QXG8777	General Line	2003	$7	$7
Job Switching QXI5316	I Love Lucy	2002	$17	$17
Joe Cool 6th Ed. QX8099	Spotlight On Snoopy	2003	$10	$12
Joe Coolest QXI3203	Peanuts Collection	2006	$10	$10
John Elway 6th Ed. QXI6811	Football Legends	2000	$15	$20
Join The Caravan! Corvette 50th Anniversary QXM4977	Miniature Ornaments	2003	$30	$30
Jolly Li'l Santa QXM4433	Miniature Ornaments	2003	$5	$6
Jolly Ol' St. Nicholas Storybook Set QKK3011	Keepsake Kids	2004	$25	$25
Jolly Old Kris Jingle QXG5501	General Line	2004	$13	$9
Jolly Santa Bells Set Of 3 QX8915	General Line	2001	$20	$20
Jolly Snowmen QXM3176	Miniature Ornaments	2006	$20	$20
Jolly Visitor QX2235	General Line	2001	$7	$7
Jonah & The Great Fish 2nd Ed. QX6701	Favorite Bible Stories	2000	$14	$20
Josefina With Memory Box QAC6434	American Girls Collection	2004	$15	$15
Josephine "Jo" March 2nd Ed. QX8125	Madame Alexander Little Women	2002	$16	$16
Journey Of The Kings, The QXG4382	Magic Ornaments	2005	$19	$19
Journey Of The Train QSR5804	Polar Express	2004	$17	$17
Journey To Bethlehem Bell QX8386	General Line	2001	$15	$15
Joy Of Music, The QXG4322	General Line	2005	$10	$10
Joy Of Nursing, The QXG4305	General Line	2005	$10	$10
Joy QP1233	Perfect Harmony Collection	2002	$10	$10
Joy To The Birds! QXM4967	Peanuts Collection	2003	$6	$8
Joyful Bells QXG1125	General Line	2005	$7	$7
Joyful Garden-Peanuts QEO8252	Easter Ornaments	2005	N/A	$19
Joyful Jumping Jacks QXG4462	General Line	2005	$17	$13
Joyful Noise, A QX2816	Magic Ornaments	2002	$15	$15
Joyful Noise, A QXG5374	General Line	2004	$13	$13
Joyful Santa 2nd Ed. QX6784	Joyful Santa	2000	$15	$22
Joyful Santa 3rd & Final QX8152	Joyful Santa	2001	$15	$15
Joyful Trio QXG5481	General Line	2004	$13	$13
Joyous Angel QP1433	Memories Of Christmas Collection	2002	$15	$15
Juice Machine & Revvin' Heaven QX8236	Hot Wheels Sizzlers	2002	$15	$15
Jumping For Joy QXM2116	Disney Collection	2006	$13	$13
Just What They Wanted! QXD4142	General Line	2001	$13	$13
Kaleidoscope Fairy QXG5461	General Line	2004	$10	$10
Kansas City Chiefs QSR5131	NFL Collection	2000	$10	$9
Kansas City Chiefs QSR5542	NFL Collection	2001	$10	$8
Karl Malone 6th Ed. QXI6901	Hoop Stars	2000	$15	$14
Kaya With Moccasins QAC6461	American Girls Collection	2004	$15	$15
Keeping It "Reel" QXG2636	General Line	2006	$13	$13
Kevin Garnett 8th Ed. QXI8146	Hoop Stars	2002	$15	$15
Khan QXI6202	Star Trek	2005	$15	$17

Lucy and the Wardrobe, 2006, Narnia, **$15.**

I'll Always Be Pooh, 2006, Winnie the Pooh Collection, **$15.**

Monocoupe 110 Special, 2006, 10th in the Sky's the Limit series, **$15.**

1948 Ford F-1, 2006, 12th in the All-American Trucks series, **$15.**

Union Pacific Veranda Turbine Locomotive, 2006, 11th in the Lionel Trains series, **$19.**

Lionel Santa Fe F3A Diesel Locomotive, 2006 (a recolored remake of the 1997 ornament titled 1950 Lionel Santa Fe F3A Diesel Locomotive, from the Lionel Trains series), **$19.**

Ornament Title	Series	Year	Issue Price	Current Value
Kind World, A QP1203	Perfect Harmony Collection	2002	$10	$10
Kindly Lions QXM5314	Miniature Ornaments	2000	$6	$6
Kindred Spirits QP1546	General Line	2002	$10	$10
Kindred Spirits QXG5781	General Line	2004	$13	$13
King Of The Ring QX6864	General Line	2000	$11	$8
Kirsten With Swedish Tine QAC6424	American Girls Collection	2004	$15	$10
Kiss The Cook QX2852	General Line	2001	$10	$10
Kiss, The QXG4412	General Line	2005	$13	$13
Kit With Notebook QAC6441	American Girls Collection	2004	$15	$15
Kitchen Angels QXM5029	Miniature Ornaments	2003	$10	$15
Kitchen Angels Spoon Tree QXM5027	Miniature Ornaments	2003	$20	$25
Kitty Catch QXM4997	Miniature Ornaments	2003	$5	$8
Kitty For Christmas, A QXG2793	General Line	2006	$15	$15
Kobe Bryant 9th Ed. QX8237	Hoop Stars	2003	$15	$15
Kris & The Kringles 1st Ed. QX8112	Kris & The Kringles	2001	$24	$20
Kris & The Kringles 2nd Ed. QX8173	Kris & The Kringles	2002	$24	$24
Kris & The Kringles 3rd Ed. QX7439	Kris & The Kringles	2003	$24	$24
Kris & The Kringles 4th Ed. QX8114	Kris & The Kringles	2004	$24	$24
Kris & The Kringles 5th Ed. QX2185	Kris & The Kringles	2005	$24	$9
Kris Cross Country Kringle QX6954	General Line	2000	$13	$21
Kristi Yamaguchi QXI6854	Sports Collection	2000	$14	$20
Kurt Warner 8th Ed. QXI8143	Football Legends	2002	$15	$15
L.A. At Last! QXI6252	I Love Lucy	2005	$17	$13
Land Of Christmastime QX8282	General Line	2001	$13	$13
Laptop Santa QX8972	General Line	2001	$8	$8
Larry, Moe & Curly QX6861	Three Stooges	2000	$30	$40
Lawn Patrol QXM4979	Miniature Ornaments	2003	$6	$8
Lazy Afternoon QX8335	General Line	2001	$10	$8
Leap Of Love QXG4395	General Line	2005	$10	$10
Legal Beagle, The 9th Ed. QX2316	Spotlight On Snoopy	2006	$10	$10
Leonardo QXI6435	Teenage Mutant Ninja Turtles	2005	$13	$13
Let It Snow, Man! QXM5234	Miniature Ornaments	2004	$7	$7
Letters To Santa QLX7606	Gold Crown Exclusives	2006	$32	$32
Lieutenant Commander Worf QBG4064	Star Trek Voyager	2000	$30	$20
Life's Greatest Blessing QEP1383	Family Tree	2004	$10	$10
Lifesavers QXG3183	General Line	2006	$10	$10
Light Of Liberty QXG4332	General Line	2005	$13	$13
Light Within, The QX2846	General Line	2002	$13	$13
Lighted Display Tree QXM4536	Miniature Ornaments	2002	$15	$15
Lighted Display Tree QXM4536	Miniature Ornaments	2003	$15	$15
Lighthouse Greetings 10th Ed. QX2396	Lighthouse Greetings	2006	$24	$24
Lighthouse Greetings 4th Ed. QLX7344	Lighthouse Greetings	2000	$24	$24
Lighthouse Greetings 5th Ed. QLX7572	Lighthouse Greetings	2001	$24	$24
Lighthouse Greetings 6th Ed. QLX7646	Lighthouse Greetings	2002	$24	$24
Lighthouse Greetings 7th Ed. QX7409	Lighthouse Greetings	2003	$24	$24
Lighthouse Greetings 8th Ed. QX8104	Lighthouse Greetings	2004	$24	$24

Ornament Title	Series	Year	Issue Price	Current Value
Lighthouse Greetings 9th Ed. QX2272	Lighthouse Greetings	2005	$24	$24
Lightning McQueen QXD8386	Cars	2006	$15	$15
Like A Snowflake QP1533	General Line	2002	$10	$10
Li'l Apple QBG4261	Li'l Blown Glass	2000	$8	$8
Li'l Cascade Red QBG4241	Li'l Blown Glass	2000	$8	$8
Li'l Cascade White QBG4244	Li'l Blown Glass	2000	$8	$8
Li'l Christmas Tree QBG4361	Li'l Blown Glass	2000	$8	$8
Li'l Gift Green Bow QBG4344	Li'l Blown Glass	2000	$8	$8
Li'l Gift Red Bow QBG4341	Li'l Blown Glass	2000	$8	$8
Li'l Grapes QBG4141	Li'l Blown Glass	2000	$8	$8
Li'l Jack In The Box QBG4274	Li'l Blown Glass	2000	$8	$8
Li'l Mr. Claus QBG4364	Li'l Blown Glass	2000	$8	$8
Li'l Mrs. Claus QBG4371	Li'l Blown Glass	2000	$8	$8
Li'l Partridge QBG4374	Li'l Blown Glass	2000	$8	$8
Li'l Pear QBG4254	Li'l Blown Glass	2000	$8	$8
Li'l Pineapple QBG4251	Li'l Blown Glass	2000	$8	$8
Li'l Robot QBG4271	Li'l Blown Glass	2000	$8	$8
Li'l Roly Poly Penguin QBG4281	Li'l Blown Glass	2000	$8	$8
Li'l Roly Poly Santa QBG4161	Li'l Blown Glass	2000	$8	$8
Li'l Roly Poly Snowman QBG4284	Li'l Blown Glass	2000	$8	$8
Li'l Santa Traditional QBG4354	Li'l Blown Glass	2000	$8	$8
Li'l Snowman Traditional QBG4351	Li'l Blown Glass	2000	$8	$8
Li'l Stars Metallic Look QBG4221	Li'l Blown Glass	2000	$8	$8
Li'l Stars Patriotic QBG4214	Li'l Blown Glass	2000	$8	$8
Li'l Stars Traditional QBG4224	Li'l Blown Glass	2000	$8	$8
Li'l Swirl Green QBG4234	Li'l Blown Glass	2000	$8	$8
Li'l Swirl Red QBG4231	Li'l Blown Glass	2000	$8	$8
Li'l Teddy Bear QBG4264	Li'l Blown Glass	2000	$8	$8
Link To Yesterday, A QP1313	General Line	2002	$15	$15
Linus & The Pumpkin Patch QFO6076	It's The Great Pumpkin	2006	N/A	$25
Linus QRP4204	A Snoopy Christmas	2000	$5	$5
Lionel 4501 Southern Mikado Steam Locomotive QBG4074	General Line	2000	$35	$29
Lionel Blue Comet 400E Steam Locomotive 7th Ed. QX8166	Lionel Trains	2002	$19	$19
Lionel Blue Comet 400T Oil Tender QX8243	General Line	2002	$19	$19
Lionel Blue Comet Passenger Car QX8833	General Line	2002	$13	$13
Lionel Blue Comet Steam Locomotive & Tender QXM4887	Miniature Ornaments	2003	$13	$13
Lionel Chessie Steam Special Locomotive 6th Ed. QX6092	Lionel Trains	2001	$19	$19
Lionel Daylight Observation Car QXI8327	General Line	2003	$13	$15
Lionel Daylight Oil Tender QXI8249	General Line	2003	$13	$15
Lionel General Steam Locomotive 5th Ed. QX6684	Lionel Trains	2000	$19	$25
Lionel Hiawatha Observation Car QXI4104	General Line	2004	$13	$13

Ornament Title	Series	Year	Issue Price	Current Value
Lionel Hiawatha Tender QXI4101	General Line	2004	$13	$13
Lionel I-400E Blue Comet Locomotive QBG4355	General Line	2001	$35	$35
Lionel No. 714 Boxcar QXI6125	General Line	2005	$13	$13
Lionel No. 717 Caboose QX2122	General Line	2005	$13	$13
Lionel Pennsylvania B6 Tender QXI6122	General Line	2005	$13	$13
Lionel Plays With Words QXI6902	Between The Lions	2001	$15	$11
Lionel Santa Fe F3A Diesel Locomotive QXE3233 (Recolored Version Of 1997 Ornament)	Premiere Exclusive	2006	$19	$19
Lionel Steam Locomotive & Tender QXM2075	Miniature Ornaments	2005	$13	$13
Lionel Union Pacific Veranda Stockcar QXI6176	General Line	2006	$13	$13
Lionel Union Pacific Veranda Tender QXI6173	General Line	2006	$13	$13
Lionelville QXI4111	Magic Ornaments	2004	$44	$65
Lisette Barbie QXI8541	Barbie Fashion Model Collection	2004	$25	$25
List, The QXG8829	General Line	2003	$13	$13
Literary Ace 5th Ed. QX8043	Spotlight On Snoopy	2002	$10	$10
Little Bunny Hug-Peanuts QEO8381	Easter Ornaments	2004	N/A	$15
Little Christmas Helper QXG8747	General Line	2003	$13	$13
Little Helpers-Baking Cookies QXG4445	General Line	2005	$13	$13
Little Helpers-Hanging The Wreath QXG4442	General Line	2005	$13	$13
Little Helpers Mailing A Letter To Santa QXG4435	General Line	2005	$13	$13
Little Nap, A 1st Ed. QX0072	Snowball & Tuxedo	2001	$8	$16
Little Nurse, Big Heart QXG5424	General Line	2004	$10	$7
Little Rain Cloud 6th Ed.QXD5117	Winnie The Pooh Collection	2003	$14	$14
Little Shepherd QXG4345	General Line	2005	$10	$10
Locomotive Monopoly 3rd & Final Ed. QXM4353	Monopoly Game: Advance To Go!	2002	$9	$19
Loggin' On To Santa QX8224	General Line	2000	$9	$9
Lone Ranger QX6941	General Line	2000	$16	$15
Look Out Below! Sylvester & Tweety QX8273	Looney Tunes	2002	$10	$10
Look Who's Here QEO8509	Tweedle Dee Deet	2003	N/A	$10
Looking For Santa QXG2783	General Line	2006	$13	$13
Lotus Of Borg QXI6205	Star Trek: First Contact	2005	$28	$28
Love Lives On QP1333	General Line	2002	$13	$13
Love QP1226	Perfect Harmony Collection	2002	$10	$10
Love Remains QEP1384	Family Tree	2004	$10	$10
Love To Dance! QXI4114	Peanuts Collection	2004	$24	$24
Love To Shop! 2nd Ed. QXM8935	Forever Friends	2005	$6	$6
Love Ya, Grandma! QXG8917	General Line	2003	$10	$10
Love Ya, Grandpa! QXG8919	General Line	2003	$10	$10
Love You A Latte QXI6143	Looney Tunes	2006	$13	$13

Ornament Title	Series	Year	Issue Price	Current Value
Lovely Dove QLZ4294	Laser Gallery	2000	$8	$8
Lovey Lamb QEO8512	Easter Ornaments	2001	N/A	$8
Loving Angel QX8366	General Line	2002	$10	$10
Loving Grandmother, A QEP2007	Heart Of Motherhood Collection	2004	$17	$17
Loving Grandmother, A QP2007	Heart Of Motherhood Collection	2003	$17	$17
Loyal Elephant QXM6041	Miniature Ornaments	2000	$7	$9
Lucky Sisters-Lucky Us QP1516	General Line	2002	$10	$10
Lucky Slot Machine QXM8135	Miniature Ornaments	2005	$8	$8
Lucy & The Wardrobe QXD8393	Disney Collection	2006	$15	$15
Lucy Does A TV Commercial QX6862	I Love Lucy	2001	$16	$16
Lucy Is Enciente QX6884	I Love Lucy	2000	$16	$19
Lucy QFO6073	It's The Great Pumpkin	2006	$9	$9
Lucy QRP4174	A Snoopy Christmas	2000	$5	$5
Lucy's Italian Movie QXI8387	I Love Lucy	2003	$17	$17
Luke Skywalker & Yoda 10th Ed.QX2366	Star Wars	2006	$15	$15
Luke Skywalker QX8206	General Line	2002	$15	$15
Lullabye League QX6604	Wizard Of Oz Collection	2000	$20	$18
Lunch Wagon For Porky Pig QXI4051, Set Of 2	Looney Tunes	2004	$15	$10
Madeline & Genevieve QXI5286	General Line	2002	$13	$13
Madeline QXI8409	General Line	2003	$13	$13
Magic Bell, The QSR5801	Polar Express	2004	$24	$24
Magic Of Glinda, The QXM2043	Wizard Of Oz Collection	2006	$15	$15
Magical Dress For Briar Rose QXD4202	Disney Collection	2001	$15	$9
Mailbox Melodies QLX7632	Magic Ornaments	2005	$32	$32
Majestic Lion 1st Ed. QX8464	Carousel Ride	2004	$13	$11
Make A Wish QP1526	General Line	2002	$10	$10
Make Way! QXI8772	Looney Tunes	2005	$13	$13
Malibu Barbie 10th Ed. QX8107	Barbie	2003	$16	$16
Man Of Steel, The QXI6323	Superman	2006	$15	$15
Margaret "Meg" March 1st Ed. QX6315	Madame Alexander Little Women	2001	$16	$16
Marguerite 13th Ed. QX6571	Mary's Angels	2000	$8	$10
Mark McGwire QXI5361	At The Ballpark	2000	$15	$11
Marlin & Nemo QXD5147	Finding Nemo	2003	$13	$13
Mary & Joseph QX8195	General Line	2001	$19	$19
Mary Hamilton Angel Chorus QX2232	General Line	2001	$7	$7
Mary's Angels QLX7561	General Line	2000	$19	$18
Master, The QFO6031	Halloween	2004	$13	$13
Matilda The Cook QFO6041	Halloween	2004	$13	$13
Matt Kenseth QXI6272	NASCAR	2005	$15	$15
Max QX8584	Snowmen Of Mitford	2000	$8	$8
Maxine's Crabby Mall-idays QLX7641	Magic Ornaments	2004	$20	$20
Medal For America QX2936	General Line	2002	$10	$10

Ornament Title	Series	Year	Issue Price	Current Value
Megarocketron 3000 QXL7583	Magic Ornaments	2006	$17	$17
Melchior-The Magi QX6819	Blessed Nativity Collection	2000	$13	$18
Melody Of Praise QXG4365	General Line	2005	$13	$13
Memories & Joy QEP1311	General Line	2005	$17	$17
Memories Of Christmas QX8264	General Line	2000	$13	$21
Memories Of Love QEP1329	Family Tree	2003	$13	$13
Memory Keeper QEP2017	Heart Of Motherhood Collection	2004	$6	$6
Memory Keeper QP2017	Heart Of Motherhood Collection	2003	$6	$6
Merrier By The Dozen QXM5049	Miniature Ornaments	2003	$15	$15
Merry & Bright QXM2183	Miniature Ornaments	2006	$20	$20
Merry Bakers Ornament Display Stand QP1773	Merry Bakers	2006	$30	$30
Merry Ballooning QX8384	General Line	2000	$17	$28
Merry Carolers QXD7585	Disney Collection	2001	$24	$24
Merry Christmas, Snoopy! QXI4081	Peanuts Collection	2004	$15	$15
Merry Christmas, World! QLX7449	Magic Ornaments	2003	$20	$20
Merry Glitzmas! QLX7537	Magic Ornaments	2003	$15	$12
Merry Kitchen Magic QXG2623	General Line	2006	$13	$13
Merry Music Makers QX8523	Magic Ornaments	2002	$24	$24
Mesmerelda QFO6039	Halloween	2003	$7	$10
Mexico QP1721	Gold Crown Exclusives	2004	$13	$13
Miami Dolphins QSR5144	NFL Collection	2000	$10	$9
Miami Dolphins QSR5555	NFL Collection	2001	$10	$9
Michael Vick 11th Ed. QX2292	Football Legends	2005	$15	$13
Michigan Wolverines QSR2142	Collegiate Collection	2001	$10	$3
Michigan Wolverines QSR2271	Collegiate Collection	2000	$10	$3
Mickey & Minnie Mouse QXD4041	Mickey & Co.	2000	$13	$21
Mickey Mantle-New York Yankees QXI6804	Sports Collection	2001	$15	$26
Mickey's Bedtime Reading QXD4077	Mickey & Co.	2000	$11	$15
Mickey's Skating Party QXD4913	Disney Collection	2002	$10	$10
Mickey's Sky Rider QXD4159	Mickey & Co.	2000	$19	$18
Mickey's Sweetheart-Minnie Mouse QXD4192	Disney Collection	2001	$10	$10
Midnight Serenade QFO6047	Halloween	2003	$7	$7
Mighty Simba QXD4222	Lion King	2005	$15	$15
Millennium Express QLX7364	General Line	2000	$42	$100
Millennium Time Capsule QX8044	General Line	2000	$15	$15
Minnesota Vikings QSR5164	NFL Collection	2000	$10	$9
Minnesota Vikings QSR5575	NFL Collection	2001	$10	$8
Mirror Of Erised QXI8645	Harry Potter	2001	$16	$19
Mischievous Kittens 2nd Ed. QX6641	Mischievous Kittens	2000	$10	$9
Mischievous Kittens 3rd Ed. QX8025	Mischievous Kittens	2001	$10	$13
Mischievous Kittens 4th Ed. QX8046	Mischievous Kittens	2002	$10	$10
Mischievous Kittens 5th Ed. QX8109	Mischievous Kittens	2003	$10	$12

Ornament Title	Series	Year	Issue Price	Current Value
Mischievous Kittens 6th Ed. QX8194	Mischievous Kittens	2004	$10	$10
Mischievous Kittens 7th Ed. QX2225	Mischievous Kittens	2005	$10	$10
Mischievous Kittens 8th Ed. QX2483	Mischievous Kittens	2006	$10	$10
Mistletoad QXM4563	Miniature Ornaments	2002	$5	$5
Mistletoe Miss 1st Ed. QX8092	Mistletoe Miss	2001	$15	$12
Mistletoe Miss 2nd Ed. QX8113	Mistletoe Miss	2002	$15	$15
Mistletoe Miss 3rd Ed. QX8219	Mistletoe Miss	2003	$19	$19
Mistletoe Time Mickey & Minnie QXD5057	Disney Collection	2003	$15	$15
Mitford Snowman Jubilee Set Of 4 QX2825	General Line	2001	$20	$20
Model 4010 Tractor QXI5291	John Deere	2004	$15	$15
Model 8420 Tractor QXI4259	John Deere	2003	$15	$18
Model B Tractor QXI6245	John Deere	2005	$15	$11
Molly With Envelope QAC6444	American Girls Collection	2004	$15	$15
Mom & Dad QX8061	General Line	2000	$10	$10
Mom & Dad QX8462	General Line	2001	$10	$10
Mom & Daughter QXG2983	General Line	2006	$13	$13
Mom QP1543	General Line	2002	$10	$10
Mom QX8064	General Line	2000	$9	$9
Mom QX8415	General Line	2001	$9	$20
Mom QX8933	General Line	2002	$10	$10
Mom QXG2913	General Line	2006	$10	$10
Mom QXG4665	General Line	2005	$10	$10
Mom QXG5544	General Line	2004	$10	$7
Mom QXG8887	General Line	2003	$10	$10
Monkey See QXI8654	General Line	2004	$10	$10
Monocoupe 110 Special 10th Ed. QX2363	Sky's The Limit	2006	$15	$15
Monsters Inc. QXI6145	Disney Collection	2001	$15	$24
Month Tags QEP2037-QEP2089	Heart Of Motherhood Collection	2004	$6	$6
Moose On The Loose QXG8579	General Line	2003	$10	$10
Moose's Merry Christmas QX8835	General Line	2001	$13	$13
Mooster Fix-It QXG4272	General Line	2005	$13	$13
Mosaic Of Faith QXG4352	General Line	2005	$13	$13
Mother & Daughter Ornaments QX2926	General Line	2002	$15	$15
Mother & Daughter QX6962	General Line	2001	$10	$10
Mother & Daughter QX8154	General Line	2000	$10	$12
Mother & Daughter QXG4745	General Line	2005	$13	$13
Mother & Daughter QXG5651	General Line	2004	$13	$13
Mother & Daughter QXG8949	General Line	2003	$13	$13
Mother-Daughter Photoholder QX8683	General Line	2002	$13	$13
Mother's Arms, A QEP2013	Heart Of Motherhood Collection	2004	$17	$17
Mother's Touch, A QEP2009	Heart Of Motherhood Collection	2004	$17	$17
Mother's Touch, A QP2009	Heart Of Motherhood Collection	2003	$17	$17

Ornament Title	Series	Year	Issue Price	Current Value
Mountain Man 3rd & Final Ed. QX6594	Old West	2000	$16	$20
Mouse-Warming Gift QXM4999	Miniature Ornaments	2003	$7	$9
MP3 Player QXG2476	General Line	2006	$17	$17
Mr. Incredible QXD5081	Disney Collection	2004	$13	$13
Mr. Monopoly QX8101	Monopoly Game 65th Anniversary Edition	2000	$11	$12
Mr. Potato Head QXI4277	General Line	2003	$13	$13
Mr. Potato Head QXM6014	Miniature Ornaments	2000	$6	$6
Mr. Tap Happy QFO6017	Halloween	2003	$7	$7
Mrs. Claus's Chair QX6955	General Line	2001	$10	$10
Mrs. Claus's Holiday QX8011	General Line	2000	$10	$8
Mrs. Claus's Polarola QXG2466	General Line	2006	$17	$17
Mrs. Potts & Chip QXD4165	Disney Collection	2001	$13	$16
Mufasa & Simba QXD5087	Lion King	2003	$13	$13
Mumble Moves! QXI3086	Happy Feet	2006	$13	$13
Muscle Cars QXC5009	Collector's Club Exclusive	2005	$34	$34
Music QXG3356	Kid Speak	2006	$13	$13
Music QXG4792	General Line	2005	$10	$10
My Angel Token Set QEP2004	Heart Of Motherhood Collection	2004	$13	$13
My Christmas Slippers QLX7554	Magic Ornaments	2004	$15	$15
My Fifth Christmas-Boy QXG2876	Child's Age Collection	2006	$10	$10
My Fifth Christmas-Boy QXG4562	Child's Age Collection	2005	$10	$7
My Fifth Christmas-Boy QXG5701	Child's Age Collection	2004	$10	$7
My Fifth Christmas-Girl QXG2903	Child's Age Collection	2006	$10	$10
My Fifth Christmas-Girl QXG4585	Child's Age Collection	2005	$10	$7
My Fifth Christmas-Girl QXG5704	Child's Age Collection	2004	$10	$7
My First Christmas Memory Book QX8613	General Line	2002	$13	$13
My First Christmas-Boy QXG2856	Child's Age Collection	2006	$10	$10
My First Christmas-Boy QXG4542	Child's Age Collection	2005	$10	$7
My First Christmas-Boy QXG5661	Child's Age Collection	2004	$10	$7
My First Christmas-Boy QXG8697	Child's Age Collection	2003	$10	$7
My First Christmas-Girl QXG2487	Child's Age Collection	2003	$10	$7
My First Christmas-Girl QXG2883	Child's Age Collection	2006	$10	$10
My First Christmas-Girl QXG4565	Child's Age Collection	2005	$10	$7
My First Christmas-Girl QXG5671	Child's Age Collection	2004	$10	$7
My First Snow QX8403	General Line	2002	$13	$10
My First Snowman QX4442	Nature's Sketchbook	2001	$10	$14
My Fourth Christmas-Boy QXG2873	Child's Age Collection	2006	$10	$10
My Fourth Christmas-Boy QXG4555	Child's Age Collection	2005	$10	$7
My Fourth Christmas-Boy QXG5684	Child's Age Collection	2004	$10	$7
My Fourth Christmas-Girl QXG2896	Child's Age Collection	2006	$10	$10
My Fourth Christmas-Girl QXG4582	Child's Age Collection	2005	$10	$7
My Fourth Christmas-Girl QXG5694	Child's Age Collection	2004	$10	$7
My Second Chrismtas-Girl QXG2886	Child's Age Collection	2006	$10	$10
My Second Christmas-Boy QXG2863	Child's Age Collection	2006	$10	$10

Ornament Title	Series	Year	Issue Price	Current Value
My Second Christmas-Boy QXG4545	Child's Age Collection	2005	$10	$7
My Second Christmas-Boy QXG5664	Child's Age Collection	2004	$10	$7
My Second Christmas-Girl QXG4572	Child's Age Collection	2005	$10	$7
My Second Christmas-Girl QXG5674	Child's Age Collection	2004	$10	$7
My Third Christmas-Boy QXG2866	Child's Age Collection	2006	$10	$10
My Third Christmas-Boy QXG4552	Child's Age Collection	2005	$10	$7
My Third Christmas-Boy QXG5681	Child's Age Collection	2004	$10	$7
My Third Christmas-Girl QXG2893	Child's Age Collection	2006	$10	$10
My Third Christmas-Girl QXG4575	Child's Age Collection	2005	$10	$7
My Third Christmas-Girl QXG5691	Child's Age Collection	2004	$10	$7
My Very Own Christmas Tree QKK3004	Keepsake Kids	2004	$15	$15
Mystery Machine: Scooby-Doo QX6295	Scooby-Doo	2001	$14	$14
Naboo Royal Starship QX8475	General Line	2001	$19	$15
Nacio El Amor WXG4362	General Line	2005	$13	$13
Nativity QLZ4301	Laser Gallery	2000	$9	$17
Nativity, The 3rd Ed. QXM5961	Nativity	2000	$10	$7
Nativity, The 4th & Final Ed. QXM5255	Nativity	2001	$10	$10
Nature's Secret Artist QEO8272	Nature's Sketchbook-Bastin	2005	N/A	$15
Nature's Sketchbook 1st Ed. QX8679	Nature's Sketchbook	2003	$10	$10
Nature's Sketchbook 2nd Ed. QX8554	Nature's Sketchbook	2004	$10	$10
Nature's Sketchbook 3rd Ed. QX2115	Nature's Sketchbook	2005	$10	$10
Nature's Sketchbook 4th Ed. QX2382	Nature's Sketchbook	2006	$10	$10
Naughty Or Nice? Elf QX2823	Magic Ornaments	2002	$10	$10
Nebraska Cornhuskers QSR2135	Collegiate Collection	2001	$10	$3
Nebraska Cornhuskers QSR2321	Collegiate Collection	2000	$10	$3
New Address QEO8275	Nature's Sketchbook-Bastin	2005	N/A	$13
New Breed Of Super Heroes, A QXM2233	Miniature Ornaments	2006	$24	$24
New Friend-Peanuts QEO8364	Easter Ornaments	2004	N/A	$15
New Home QX8171	General Line	2000	$9	$9
New Home QX8636	General Line	2002	$13	$13
New Home QXG3003	General Line	2006	$13	$13
New Home QXG4635	General Line	2005	$13	$13
New Home QXG5621	General Line	2004	$13	$9
New Home QXG8957	General Line	2003	$13	$13
New Hope, A QP1213	Perfect Harmony Collection	2002	$10	$10
New Joys QEO8265	Nature's Sketchbook-Bastin	2005	N/A	$15
New Millennium Baby QX8581	General Line	2000	$11	$11
Newborn Prince QXD4194	Disney Collection	2000	$14	$14
No. 1 Teacher QX2865	General Line	2001	$10	$8
Noah's Ark QXG2676	General Line	2006	$18	$18
Noah's Ark QXG4355	Magic Ornaments	2005	$15	$15
Noah's Ark QXG5371	General Line	2004	$17	$17
Noah's Ark QXG8997	General Line	2003	$17	$17
Noche De Paz QX8192	General Line	2001	$13	$10
North Carolina Tar Heels QSR2155	Collegiate Collection	2001	$10	$3
North Carolina Tar Heels QSR2304	Collegiate Collection	2000	$10	$3

Ornament Title	Series	Year	Issue Price	Current Value
North Pole Band Teddy QXG3026	General Line	2006	$15	$15
North Pole Network QX6994	General Line	2000	$11	$9
North Pole Patriot QXG5451	General Line	2004	$13	$13
North Pole Towing Service 24th Ed. QX8106	Here Comes Santa	2002	$15	$15
Northern Art Bear QX8294	General Line	2000	$9	$15
Northern Cardinal QX2135	Beauty Of Birds	2005	$15	$15
Norway QP1711	Gold Crown Exclusives	2004	$13	$13
Nose So Bright! QXG2756	Rudolph The Red-Nosed Reindeer	2006	$15	$15
Notre Dame Fighting Irish QSR2284	Collegiate Collection	2000	$10	$3
Nuestra Familia QXG2537	General Line	2003	$13	$10
Nuestra Familia QXG4732	General Line	2005	$13	$13
Nuestra Familia QXG5744	General Line	2004	$13	$13
Nurse With A Magic Touch QXG8567	General Line	2003	$10	$10
Nutcracker Guild 7th & Final Ed. QXM5991	Nutcracker Guild	2000	$7	$6
Nutcracker King 1QXC4006	Collector's Club Exclusive	2004	$17	$17
Nutcracker, The QLZ4284	Laser Gallery	2000	$6	$6
O Christmas Tree QP1126	Yuletide Harmony Collection	2006	$15	$15
O Come, All Ye Faithful QP1123	Yuletide Harmony Collection	2006	$15	$15
O Kitchen Rack QXG4282	General Line	2005	$10	$10
Obi-Wan Kenobi 4th Ed. QXI6704	Star Wars	2000	$15	$15
Obi-Wan Kenobi QXI8216	General Line	2002	$15	$15
Oddball, Domino, & Little Dipper QXD4936	Disney Collection	2002	$13	$13
Oddball, Little Dipper, & Domino QXD5074	Disney Collection	2004	$15	$15
Off To Neverland! QXD4004	Peter Pan	2000	$13	$13
Off To See The Wizard! QXI8925	Wizard Of Oz Collection	2005	$20	$20
Officer Rob Graver QFO6315	Hauntington U.S.A. Collection	2005	$8	$10
Oh, So Sweet! QXG2273	General Line	2006	$10	$10
Oh, The Places You'll Go! 7th Ed. QX2112	Dr. Seuss Books	2005	$15	$15
Oh, What A Grill! QXG2443	General Line	2006	$13	$13
Oh, What Fun! QP1427	General Line	2003	$13	$13
Old Ned The Musician QFO6034	Halloween	2004	$13	$13
Old Stone Church 9th Ed. QX2313	Candlelight Services	2006	$20	$20
Old-World Santa QX8975	General Line	2001	$10	$10
On Frozen Pond QXI4289	General Line	2003	$15	$12
On The Slopes-Miniature QXD4553	General Line	2002	$7	$7
On Track: Deora II & Sweet Sixteen II QXI8429	Hot Wheels	2003	$17	$17
On, Tweety! On, Daffy! QXI4011	Looney Tunes	2004	$20	$20
Once Upon A Starry Night QXG4385	General Line	2005	$13	$13
One Cool Snowboarder QX2876	General Line	2002	$10	$10
One Cute Cookie QXG4632	General Line	2005	$10	$10
One Fish Two Fish Red Fish Blue Fish 2nd. Ed. QX6781	Dr. Seuss Books	2000	$15	$14
One Little Angel QX8935	General Line	2001	$9	$9

Ornament Title	Series	Year	Issue Price	Current Value
Opening Game, The QXC5002	Collector's Club	2005	$20	$20
Order Up! QRP4082	Debut Event Ornament	2005	$19	$19
Ornament For Grandmother QEP2036	General Line	2005	$15	$15
Ornament For Mother QEP2028	General Line	2005	$15	$15
Our Best Buddy QXD5129	Toy Story 2	2003	$15	$12
Our Christmas QXG4405	General Line	2005	$13	$13
Our Christmas QXG5341	General Line	2004	$13	$9
Our Christmas QXG5344	General Line	2004	$15	$12
Our Christmas Together QX8054	General Line	2000	$10	$7
Our Christmas Together QX8623	General Line	2002	$10	$10
Our Christmas Together QX8926	General Line	2002	$15	$15
Our Christmas Together QXG2726	General Line	2006	$13	$13
Our Christmas Together Set Of 4 QX8412	General Line	2001	$8	$8
Our Family Photoholder QX8995	General Line	2001	$9	$9
Our Family QX8211	General Line	2000	$8	$10
Our Family QXG2943	General Line	2006	$15	$15
Our Family QXG4725	General Line	2005	$13	$13
Our Family QXG5601	General Line	2004	$13	$13
Our Family QXG8947	General Line	2003	$13	$13
Our First Christmas QX8816	General Line	2002	$19	$19
Our First Christmas QXG4415	General Line	2005	$19	$19
Our First Christmas QXG5351	General Line	2004	$19	$12
Our First Christmas QXG8877	General Line	2003	$19	$19
Our First Christmas Together Photoholder QX6012	General Line	2001	$9	$15
Our First Christmas Together Photoholder QX8051	General Line	2000	$9	$12
Our First Christmas Together QX3104	General Line	2000	$11	$15
Our First Christmas Together QX3233	General Line	2002	$8	$8
Our First Christmas Together QX8405	General Line	2001	$10	$10
Our First Christmas Together QX8626	General Line	2002	$10	$10
Our First Christmas Together QX8701	Commemoratives	2000	$11	$12
Our First Christmas Together QXG5324	General Line	2004	$9	$6
Our Friendship QXD5067	General Line	2003	$13	$13
Our Lady Of Guadalupe QX8231	Feliz Navidad	2000	$13	$9
Our Love Story QXG8859	General Line	2003	$13	$13
Outdoor Dining QEO8007	Nature's Sketchbook-Bastin	2003	N/A	$19
Over Par Snowman QXG5421	General Line	2004	$10	$10
Over The Rainbow QXI8932	Wizard Of Oz Collection	2005	$28	$28
Packed With Love QXG4642	General Line	2005	$10	$10
Padme Amidala QXI8339	General Line	2003	$15	$15
Pals At The Pole QXG8827	General Line	2003	$15	$15
Pansy Fairy 2nd. Ed. QX2563	Fairy Messengers	2006	$10	$10
Parents-To-Be QXG2469	General Line	2003	$13	$13
Parents-To-Be QXG2853	General Line	2006	$13	$13
Parents-To-Be QXG4605	General Line	2005	$13	$13

Ornament Title	Series	Year	Issue Price	Current Value
Parents-To-Be QXG5734	Child's Age Collection	2004	$13	$13
Part Of Our Legacy QP1343	General Line	2002	$13	$13
Part Of Your World QXD8366	Disney Collection	2006	$15	$15
Partridge In A Pear Tree QX8215	General Line	2001	$13	$13
Pat The Bunny QX8582	General Line	2001	$10	$10
Peace & Goodwill QP1223	Perfect Harmony Collection	2002	$10	$10
Peace On Earth Harmony Bell QX8393	General Line	2002	$10	$10
Peace QP1216	Perfect Harmony Collection	2002	$10	$10
Peace, Hope & Joy QXM8172	Gifts Of Christmas	2005	$13	$13
Peanuts Christmas Pageant QXC5011	Collector's Club Exclusive	2005	$26	$26
Peanuts Christmas Pageant QXM3146	Miniature Ornaments	2006	$20	$20
Peanuts Game, The QXI8691	Peanuts Collection	2004	$19	$15
Peanuts Pageant QX2832	Peanuts Collection	2001	$15	$15
Peanuts QEO8444	Easter Ornaments	2000	$15	$15
Pedal Power QXI5304	General Line	2004	$15	$15
Peek-A-Boo Present QX8302	General Line	2001	$10	$10
Peek-A-Boo! QXI8755	Looney Tunes	2005	$15	$15
Peep A Boo Chicks QEO8037	Peekaboo	2003	N/A	$16
Peggy Fleming QXI6845	Sports Collection	2001	$15	$10
Penguin Races QXM8155	Miniature Ornaments	2005	$13	$13
Penguins At Play QX8982	General Line	2001	$10	$10
Penn State Nittany Lions QSR2122	Collegiate Collection	2001	$10	$3
Penn State Nittany Lions QSR2311	Collegiate Collection	2000	$10	$3
Pennsylvania B6 Steam Locomotive 10th Ed. QX2052	Lionel Trains	2005	$19	$19
Peppermint Candy Cane Barbie QXI0544	Barbie	2004	$15	$15
Peppermint Pals QXE3263	Premiere Exclusive	2006	N/A	$24
Perfect Blend, A QX8985	General Line	2001	$10	$10
Perfect Christmas, A QXI6895	Arthur 25th Anniversary	2001	$13	$13
Perfect Evening Out, The QFM4483	Barbie	2006	$35	$35
Peter Rabbit QEO8545	Easter Ornaments	2001	N/A	$12
Peyton Manning 10th Ed. QX8521	Football Legends	2004	$15	$15
Piglet's First Ride QXD4963	General Line	2002	$13	$13
Piglet's Jack-In-The-Box QXD4187	Classic Pooh Collection	2000	$15	$14
Pinball Action QXI8775	Looney Tunes	2005	$24	$24
Pinocchio Marionette QXM5121	Miniature Ornaments	2004	$8	$8
Pirates Of The Caribbean QXD6376	Disney Collection	2006	$17	$17
Pittsburgh Steelers QSR5124	NFL Collection	2000	$10	$9
Pittsburgh Steelers QSR5565	NFL Collection	2001	$10	$8
Place In The Sun QEO8007	Nature's Sketchbook-Bastin	2003	N/A	$24
Platform 9-3/4 QXI4279	Harry Potter & The Chamber Of Secrets	2003	$13	$13
Play It Again, Santa! QLX7469	Magic Ornaments	2003	$24	$24
Playful Minnie QXD4906	Disney Collection	2002	$10	$9
Playful Pup, A QX2263	General Line	2006	$10	$10
Plotting The Course 1QXC4002	Collector's Club	2004	N/A	$20

Ornament Title	Series	Year	Issue Price	Current Value
Pluto Plays Triangle 5th Ed. QXD4112	Mickey's Holiday Parade	2001	$14	$25
Pocket Watch Ornament QXD5001	Mickey Mouse	2004	$24	$24
Poinsettia Fairy 1st Ed. QX2145	Fairy Messengers	2005	$10	$10
Polar Coaster QLX7459	Magic Ornaments	2003	$42	$40
Pony For Christmas, A 3rd Ed. QX6624	Pony For Christmas	2000	$13	$12
Pony For Christmas, A 4th Ed. QX6995	Pony For Christmas	2001	$13	$14
Pony For Christmas, A 5th Ed. QX8056	Pony For Christmas	2002	$13	$13
Pony For Christmas, A 6th Ed. QX8229	Pony For Christmas	2003	$13	$13
Pony For Christmas, A 7th Ed. QX8221	Pony For Christmas	2004	$13	$13
Pony For Christmas, A 8th Ed. QX2265	Pony For Christmas	2005	$13	$13
Pony For Christmas, A 9th Ed. QX2496	Pony For Christmas	2006	$13	$13
Pooh Bells QFM4486	General Line	2006	$60	$60
Pooh Chooses The Tree QXD4157	General Line	2000	$13	$12
Pooh's Christmas List QXD8323	General Line	2006	$10	$10
Pop! Goes The Reindeer 3rd Ed. QX2125	Jack-In-The-Box Memories	2005	$15	$15
Pop! Goes The Santa 2nd Ed. QX8411	Jack-In-The-Box Memories	2004	$15	$10
Pop! Goes The Snowman 1st Ed. QX8457	Jack-In-The-Box Memories	2003	$15	$15
Pop! Goes The Teddy Bear 4th Ed. QX2493	Jack-In-The-Box Memories	2006	$15	$15
Poppy Field QLX7565	Wizard Of Oz Collection	2001	$24	$34
Portrait Of Scarlett QX2885	Gone With The Wind	2001	$16	$29
Potions Master QXI8652	Harry Potter	2001	$15	$15
Prancing Reindeer 3rd Ed. QX2486	Carousel Ride	2006	$13	$13
Precious Penguin QXM6104	Precious Edition	2000	$10	$9
Precocious Tink QXD2126	Peter Pan	2006	$7	$7
Pretty As A Princess QXD5079	Disney Collection	2003	$13	$13
Priceless Memories QEP1319	Family Tree	2003	$13	$13
Priceless Treasure QEP2014	General Line	2005	$17	$17
Primera Navidad De Bebe QXG2517	General Line	2003	$13	$10
Primera Navidad De Bebe QXG4595	General Line	2005	$13	$13
Primera Navidad De Bebe QXG5751	General Line	2004	$13	$9
Prince Charming QXM5224	Miniature Ornaments	2004	$6	$6
Princess Aurora & Prince Phillip QXD8383	Sleeping Beauty	2006	$24	$24
Princess Leia 9th Ed. QX2015	Star Wars	2005	$15	$13
Princess Tower, The QXD8373	Disney Collection	2006	$19	$19
Proud & The Brave, The QXG2646	General Line	2006	$10	$10
Proud Giraffe 2nd Ed. QX2012	Carousel Ride	2005	$13	$13
Puppies On The Doorstep QXM4989	Miniature Ornaments	2003	$7	$10
Puppy For Christmas, A QXG2806	General Line	2006	$15	$15
Puppy Love 10 Ed. QX6554	Puppy Love	2000	$8	$12
Puppy Love 11th Ed. QX6982	Puppy Love	2001	$8	$17
Puppy Love 12th Ed. QX8006	Puppy Love	2002	$8	$12
Puppy Love 13th Ed. QX8127	Puppy Love	2003	$8	$13
Puppy Love 14th Ed. QX8441	Puppy Love	2004	$9	$25
Puppy Love 15th Ed. QX2312	Puppy Love	2005	$9	$12
Puppy Love 16th Ed. QX2533	Puppy Love	2006	$10	$10
Purr-Fectly Contented QXM5241, Set Of 3	Miniature Ornaments	2004	$10	$10

Ornament Title	Series	Year	Issue Price	Current Value
Purring Friend, A QX2266	General Line	2006	$10	$10
Putter For Santa, A QXG4312	General Line	2005	$10	$10
Putting On The Glitz QXM5111	Miniature Ornaments	2004	$10	$10
Queen Aurora Tree Topper QP1662	Frostlight Faeries Collection	2001	$35	$35
Queen Of Cuisine QP1831	Queen Of Collection	2004	$13	$13
Queen Of Cuisine QP1841	Queen Of Collection	2004	$13	$13
Queen Of Cuisine QP1844	Queen Of Collection	2004	$13	$13
Queen Of Do-It-Yourself QP1821	Queen Of Collection	2004	$13	$13
Queen Of Fitness QP1811	Queen Of Collection	2004	$13	$13
Queen Of Multi-Tasking QP1814	Queen Of Collection	2004	$13	$13
Queen Of Shoes QP1801	Queen Of Collection	2004	$13	$13
Queen Of Shopping QP1824	Queen Of Collection	2004	$13	$13
Queen Of The Garden QP1804	Queen Of Collection	2004	$13	$13
Quidditch Match QXI8915	Harry Potter	2005	$15	$15
Quidditch Season QXI8656	Harry Potter	2002	$24	$28
Qui-Gon Jinn QXI6741	General Line	2000	$15	$15
Quilt Of Memories QEP1307	Family Tree	2003	$13	$13
R2-D2 5th Ed. QX6875	Star Wars	2001	$15	$39
Rabbit 2nd Ed. QEO8461	Easter Egg Surprise	2000	$15	$15
Race Car 2nd Ed. QXM5292	Monopoly Game: Advance To Go!	2001	$9	$9
Race Down Main Street QXI5244	Snowmen of Mitford	2000	N/A	$16
Raggedy Andy QX8574	General Line	2001	$11	$12
Raggedy Ann & Raggedy Andy QXM4496	Miniature Ornaments	2002	$10	$10
Raggedy Ann QX8571	General Line	2001	$11	$19
Rainbow Brito & Starlite QXI8681	General Line	2004	$13	$13
Rainbow Snowman QX8283	General Line	2002	$10	$10
Rainy Day Rescue 8th Ed. QXD4102	Winnie The Pooh Collection	2005	$15	$15
Raspberry 3rd & Final Ed. QEO8565	Fairy Berry Bears	2001	$10	$9
Reaching For Christmas QXG5474	General Line	2004	$15	$15
Reader To The Core, A QX6974	General Line	2000	$10	$9
Ready For A Ride QXM5302	Miniature Ornaments	2001	$7	$7
Ready For Delivery QXC4552A	Collector's Club Exclusive	2001	N/A	$18
Ready For Flight QP1745	Santa's Midnight Ride	2005	$15	$15
Ready For Sledding QXG2766	General Line	2006	$13	$13
Ready Reindeer QX8295	General Line	2001	$14	$14
Ready Teddy QX8842	General Line	2001	$10	$10
Ready, Set, Grow QXG3006	Winter Garden	2006	$13	$13
Red Power Ranger QXD2439	Power Rangers: Ninja Storm	2003	$13	$13
Red Power Ranger QXI8604	Power Rangers: Dinothunder	2004	$15	$15
Reflections Of Love QXG3216	General Line	2006	$10	$10
Relaxing Robins QEO8321	Nature's Sketchbook-Bastin	2004	N/A	$13
Remembering The Past QEP1327	Family Tree	2003	$13	$13
Rhett Butler QX6674	Gone With The Wind	2000	$13	$23
Riding On The Breeze-Winnie The Pooh QEO8612	Easter Ornaments	2001	N/A	$17

Ornament Title	Series	Year	Issue Price	Current Value
Ring-A-Ling Pals QXM5077	General Line	2003	$13	$13
Ringing In Christmas QXD8303	Disney Collection	2006	$10	$10
Ringing Reindeer QXC4484	Collector's Club	2000	N/A	$15
Rippling Dream QEO8007	Nature's Sketchbook-Bastin	2003	N/A	$13
Road Trip Barbie Ornament Set QXM8982	Barbie	2005	$15	$15
Robot Parade 1st Ed. QX6771	Robot Parade	2000	$15	$15
Robot Parade 2nd Ed. QX8162	Robot Parade	2001	$15	$17
Robot Parade 3rd & Final Ed. QX8133	Robot Parade	2002	$15	$20
Rock Candy Railroad QLX7616	Magic Ornaments	2006	$42	$42
Rock 'N' Roll Stitch QXD2447	Lilo & Stitch	2003	$10	$10
Rockin' & Rollin'! QLX7457	Magic Ornaments	2003	$32	$32
Rockin' With Santa QLX7622	Magic Ornaments	2005	$28	$28
Rocking Horse Repainted Edition QXE2352	Rocking Horse	2005	$20	$20
Rocking Reindeer QX8261	General Line	2001	$13	$13
Ron Weasley & Scabbers QXE4405	Harry Potter	2001	$13	$28
Rosette Dreams Bride & Groom QXM2082	Miniature Ornaments	2005	$13	$13
Royal Princesses, The QXM8952	Disney Collection	2005	$20	$20
Ruby Slippers QXC5004	Collector's Club	2005	$20	$20
Rudolph & Bumble The Abominable Snowmonster QXG4475	Rudolph The Red-Nosed Reindeer	2005	$15	$15
Rudolph & Santa QXG5654	General Line	2004	$13	$13
Rudolph The Red-Nosed Reindeer QXM8995	Miniature Ornaments	2005	$8	$8
Ruff & Tuff Hero QXG8557	General Line	2003	$10	$10
Russia QP1701	Gold Crown Exclusives	2004	$13	$13
Sack Of Money 1st Ed. QXM5341	Monopoly Game: Advance To Go!	2000	$9	$8
Safe & Snug 1st Ed. QX8342	Safe & Snug	2001	$13	$19
Safe & Snug 2nd Ed. QX8036	Safe & Snug	2002	$13	$13
Safe & Snug 3rd & Final Ed. QX8217	Safe & Snug	2003	$13	$13
Safe In Noah's Ark QX8514	General Line	2000	$11	$18
Sailor 6th & Final Ed. QXM5334	Miniature Clothespin Soldier	2000	$5	$20
Sally QFO6056	It's The Great Pumpkin	2006	$9	$9
Samantha "Sam" Stephens QXI6892	Bewitched	2001	$15	$15
Samantha With Sampler QAC6451	American Girls Collection	2004	$15	$15
Sammy Sosa QXI6375	At The Ballpark	2001	$15	$15
San Francisco 49ers QSR5134	NFL Collection	2000	$10	$9
San Francisco 49ers QSR5562	NFL Collection	2001	$10	$8
Santa Beagle & Friends QXI6485	Peanuts Collection	2005	$15	$15
Santa Claus QRP4495	General Line	2001	N/A	$4
Santa Claus With Miniature Panda Bear QXI5395	Collector's Club	2001	$19	$14
Santa From England QXG4822	Santas From Around The World	2005	$13	$13
Santa Jumping Jack QXM4473	Miniature Ornaments	2002	$6	$6
Santa Knows QLX7612	Magic Ornaments	2005	$24	$24

Ornament Title	Series	Year	Issue Price	Current Value
Santa Nutcracker QXC5005	Collector's Club Exclusive	2005	$17	$17
Santa Paws QXI4054	Scooby-Doo	2004	$13	$8
Santa QX3326	Yuletide Treasures	2006	$17	$17
Santa Sneaks A Sweet QX8862	Cooking For Christmas	2001	$16	$17
Santa To The Rescue QXG5431	General Line	2004	$10	$10
Santa Wanna-Be 1st Ed. QXM5151	Forever Friends	2004	$6	$6
Santa, Look At Me! QXG5484, Set Of 2	General Line	2004	$15	$10
Santa-In-The-Box QXM5355	Miniature Ornaments	2001	$7	$7
Santa's Balloon Tree QXM5221	Miniature Ornaments	2004	$6	$6
Santa's Big Rig 25th Ed. QX8167	Here Comes Santa	2003	$15	$18
Santa's Chair QX8314	General Line	2000	$10	$12
Santa's Day Off QX2872	General Line	2001	$10	$10
Santa's Desk-2001 Studio Limited Ed. QXC4562A	Collector's Club	2001	N/A	$150
Santas From Around The World QXM3143	Miniature Ornaments	2006	$20	$20
Santa's Helpers QXD4012	Disney Collection	2005	$15	$15
Santa's Hula-Day QLX7631	Magic Ornaments	2004	$28	$28
Santa's Journey Begins QXM6004	Miniature Ornaments	2000	$10	$10
Santa's Little Shopper QXG4302	General Line	2005	$10	$10
Santa's Magic Sack QXG4465	General Line	2005	$13	$13
Santa's Magic Sack QXG4472	General Line	2005	$13	$13
Santa's Mailbox QX6943	General Line	2002	$13	$13
Santa's On His Way QXG8809	General Line	2003	$15	$22
Santa's Racin' Sleigh QXI5306	NASCAR	2002	$15	$16
Santa's Sleigh With Sack & Miniature Ornament QX8872	Collector's Club	2001	$19	$15
Santa's Snowplow 23rd Ed. QX8065	Here Comes Santa	2001	$15	$15
Santa's Sweet Surprise QX8275	General Line	2001	$15	$15
Santa's Toy Box With 3 Miniature Ornaments QXI5392	Collector's Club	2001	$13	$10
Santa's Wittle Helper QXI3163	Tweety-Looney Tunes	2006	$7	$7
Santa's Woody Special Ed. QXE2355	Here Comes Santa	2005	N/A	N/A
Santa's Workshop Countdown Calendar Set Of 25 QKK3066	Gold Crown Exclusives	2006	$40	$40
Santa's Workshop Lunchbox QXC4586	Collector's Club	2002	$19	$19
Santa's Workshop QX2812	General Line	2001	$10	$10
Saturday Morning Cartoons QXI6136	Looney Tunes	2006	$24	$24
Scarecrow QXM5091	Miniature Ornaments	2004	$7	$7
Scarlett O'Hara 4th & Final Ed. QX6671	Scarlett O'Hara	2000	$15	$25
Scarlett O'Hara & Rhett Butler QXI4034	Gone With The Wind	2004	$19	$19
Scarlett O'Hara & Rhett Butler QXI4287	Gone With The Wind	2003	$19	$19
Scarlett O'Hara & Rhett Butler QXI6015	Gone With The Wind	2005	$19	$19
Scarlett O'Hara & Rhett Butler QXI6116	Gone With The Wind	2006	$19	$19
Scarlett O'Hara QX6671	Gone With The Wind	2000	$15	$16
Scarlett O'Hara QX8253	Gone With The Wind	2002	$16	$16
Scarlett O'Hara QXI4031	Gone With The Wind	2004	$16	$16

Ornament Title	Series	Year	Issue Price	Current Value
Scarlett O'Hara QXI6002	Gone With The Wind	2005	$16	$16
Scarlett O'Hara QXI8307	Gone With The Wind	2003	$16	$16
School Days 5th Ed. QXD4983	Winnie The Pooh Collection	2002	$14	$14
School Days QXG5624	General Line	2004	$10	$10
School Photoholder QXG8929	General Line	2003	$10	$10
School QXG3333	Kid Speak	2006	$13	$13
Schoolhouse 17th Ed. QX6591	Nostalgic Houses & Shops	2000	$15	$26
Schoolhouse & Flagpole 5th Ed. QX8247	Town & Country	2003	$17	$12
Scooby-Doo & Shaggy QXI5283	Scooby-Doo	2002	$17	$17
Scooby-Doo QXI8394	General Line	2000	$13	$19
Scooby-Doo QXM5322	Scooby-Doo	2001	$7	$9
Scooby-Doo Takes Aim QXI8287	Scooby-Doo	2003	$10	$7
Scoops McGore QFO6312	Hauntington, U.S.A.	2005	$8	$8
Scorpion, The QXI7509	Star Trek: Nemesis	2003	$32	$35
Scuffy The Tugboat QX6871	General Line	2000	$12	$15
Seaside Scenes 2nd Ed. QXM5974	Seaside Scenes	2000	$8	$7
Seaside Scenes 3rd & Final Ed. QXM5275	Seaside Scenes	2001	$8	$9
Season To Sing, A QXI6242	Kermit The Frog	2005	$13	$13
See No Humbug! QXM8152	Miniature Ornaments	2005	$13	$13
Self-Portrait QX6644	General Line	2000	$11	$14
Serial Number One & 2003 Harley-Davidson Ultra Classic Electra Glide QXI8317	General Line	2003	$28	$25
Service Station 18th Ed. QX8045	Nostalgic Houses & Shops	2001	$15	$22
Seven Of Nine Star Trek: Voyager QX6844	Star Trek Voyager	2000	$15	$14
Sew Merry, Sew Bright! QXG5434	General Line	2004	$10	$10
Sew Sweet Angel QX2862	General Line	2001	$10	$10
Shake It, Santa! WD3533	Collector's Club	2005	$7	$7
Sharing Santa's Snacks QX8212	General Line	2001	$9	$9
Sharing The Stars 1QXC4004	Collector's Club	2004	N/A	$25
Shepherds, The QX8361	Blessed Nativity Collection	2000	$25	$46
Shimmering Carrot Trimmers QEO8563	Easter Ornaments	2002	N/A	$6
Shimmering Carrot Trimmers QEO8563	Easter Ornaments	2003	N/A	$6
Shimmering Easter Eggs QEO8553	Easter Ornaments	2002	N/A	$15
Shimmering Easter Eggs, Pink QEO8047	Easter Ornaments	2003	N/A	$12
Shimmering Easter Eggs, Purple QEO8049	Easter Ornaments	2003	N/A	$12
Shining Promise QXG5364	General Line	2004	$13	$13
Shiver-Me Tim Brrr QLX7582	Magic Ornaments	2005	$17	$17
Shopping For Shoes Barbie QXM4949	Miniature Ornaments	2003	$15	$15
Shrek & Donkey QXI8759	Shrek	2003	$15	$15
Shrek & Princess Fiona QXI6492	Shrek 2	2005	$15	$15
Shrek, Donkey & Puss In Boots QXI6226	Shrek	2006	$15	$15
Silent Night QLX7591	Magic Ornaments	2004	$25	$25
Silent Night QP1116	Yuletide Harmony Collection	2006	$15	$15
Silent Night QXG4482	Thomas Kinkade General Line	2005	$15	$15
Silken Flame Barbie QXM6031	Barbie	2000	$13	$20
Sing-Along Pals QXD8316	Disney Collection	2006	$32	$32

Ornament Title	Series	Year	Issue Price	Current Value
Sister To Sister QX8144	General Line	2000	$13	$11
Sister To Sister QXG8969	General Line	2003	$17	$17
Sisters Photoholder QX8455	General Line	2001	$9	$9
Sisters QX8686	General Line	2002	$13	$13
Sisters QXG2963	General Line	2006	$13	$13
Sisters QXG4715	General Line	2005	$13	$13
Sisters QXG4722	General Line	2005	$13	$13
Sisters QXG5761	General Line	2004	$13	$9
Sittin' On Santa's Lap QLX7594	Magic Ornaments	2004	$25	$16
Skating In Circles QXD7526	General Line	2002	$24	$24
Skating Lesson QXD4242	Disney Collection	2005	$17	$17
Skating Sugar Bear Bell QX6005	General Line	2001	$10	$8
Skylar A. Woolscarf 1st Ed. QX2405	Snowtop Lodge	2005	$19	$13
Slave I Starship QXI8223	General Line	2002	$19	$19
Sleeping Beauty's Maleficent 3rd Ed. QXD4001	Unforgettable Villains	2000	$15	$15
Sleeping Village, The QXC6002	Collector's Club	2006	$20	$20
Sleepy-Time Mouse QXM8145	Miniature Ornaments	2005	$7	$7
Sleigh Ride 2nd Ed. QX8207	Winter Wonderland	2003	$13	$13
Sleigh Ride QXD8313	Disney Collection	2006	$19	$19
Sleigh X-2000 22nd Ed. QX6824	Here Comes Santa	2000	$15	$20
Small World QXD5021	Magic Ornaments	2004	$32	$32
Smasheroo Barbie 11th Ed. QXI8544	Barbie	2004	$16	$16
S'Mittens QXG8857	General Line	2003	$13	$13
Snackercize! QLX7581	Magic Ornaments	2003	$20	$18
Sneakaboo QFO6009	Halloween	2003	$7	$7
Sneaking A Treat QRP4294	Mickey Mouse	2004	N/A	$18
Snicker & Doodle QP1743	Merry Bakers	2006	$15	$15
Snoopy QFO6063	It's The Great Pumpkin	2006	$14	$14
Snoopy QRP4184	A Snoopy Christmas	2000	$5	$5
Snoopy The Magnificent 8th Ed. QX2132	Spotlight On Snoopy	2005	$10	$10
Snoozing Santa QX8165	General Line	2001	$19	$19
Snow Angel QXG8749	General Line	2003	$10	$10
Snow Bear Buddies QXG4432	General Line	2005	$10	$10
Snow Belles QX8446	General Line	2002	$16	$16
Snow Blossom QX8494	General Line	2001	$10	$10
Snow Buddies 3rd Ed. QX6654	Snow Buddies	2000	$8	$15
Snow Buddies 4th Ed. QX6972	Snow Buddies	2001	$8	$10
Snow Buddies 5th Ed. QX8003	Snow Buddies	2002	$8	$8
Snow Buddies 6th Ed. QX8097	Snow Buddies	2003	$8	$8
Snow Buddies 7th Ed. QX8131	Snow Buddies	2004	$9	$9
Snow Buddies 8th Ed. QX2245	Snow Buddies	2005	$9	$9
Snow Buddies 9th Ed. QX2473	Snow Buddies	2006	$10	$10
Snow Cozy 1st Ed. QXM4546	Snow Cozy	2002	$5	$5
Snow Cozy 2nd Ed. QXM4917	Snow Cozy	2003	$5	$5
Snow Cozy 3rd Ed. QXM5144	Snow Cozy	2004	$5	$5

Ornament Title	Series	Year	Issue Price	Current Value
Snow Cozy 4th Ed. QXM8965	Snow Cozy	2005	$5	$5
Snow Day Magic QXC5001	Collector's Club	2005	$20	$20
Snow Fort Fun QX2803	General Line	2006	$15	$15
Snow Girl QX8274	General Line	2000	$10	$8
Snow Ho Ho! QP1107	Snowman's Land	2003	$10	$10
Snow News Is Good News! QP1117	Snowman's Land	2003	$10	$10
Snow Place Like Home! QP1129	Snowman's Land	2003	$10	$10
Snow Sculpture QXD5014	Mickey Mouse	2004	$10	$10
Snow Time Like The Present! QP1137	Snowman's Land	2003	$10	$10
Snow What Fun! QP1127	Snowman's Land	2003	$10	$10
Snowbody Does It Better! QP1119	Snowman's Land	2003	$10	$10
Snowflake Fun QXG5524, Set Of 3	General Line	2004	$16	$10
Snowflake Garland QP1745	Gold Crown Exclusives	2001	$13	$12
Snowflakes QP1436	Memories Of Christmas Collection	2002	$13	$13
Snowie Rolie QXD2477	Rolie Polie Olie	2003	$13	$13
Snowman Surprise QXG8807	General Line	2003	$13	$10
Snowmen Of Mitford, The QXM4959	Miniature Ornaments	2003	$13	$13
Snowshoe Taxi 3rd Ed. QX8227	Snowball & Tuxedo	2003	$8	$10
Snowy Day QXG5454	General Line	2004	$7	$7
Snowy Friend QP1406	General Line	2002	$10	$10
Snowy Garden QX8284	Nature's Sketchbook	2000	$14	$18
Snowy Push 'N' Pull QLX8259	Magic Ornaments	2003	$20	$20
Snug Hug, A QEO8424	Easter Ornaments	2000	$10	$14
Snuggle Time QXD4916	Disney Collection	2002	$15	$15
Snuggly Sugar Bear Bell QX8922	General Line	2001	$10	$10
So Much To Do! 995PR3035	General Line	2004	$13	$13
So Much To Remember QEP1356	Family Tree	2003	$13	$13
So Much To Remember QP1356	General Line	2002	$13	$13
Soccer QXG4755	General Line	2005	$10	$10
Soccer Tigger-Style QXD5119	General Line	2003	$10	$10
Soda Shop Sweethearts QRP4072	Magic Ornaments	2005	$17	$17
Solo In The Spotlight Case & Barbie Ornament QXM5312	Barbie	2001	$13	$11
Son QX8084	General Line	2000	$9	$7
Son QX8432	General Line	2001	$9	$15
Son QX8943	General Line	2002	$10	$10
Son QXG2923	General Line	2006	$10	$10
Son QXG4675	General Line	2005	$10	$10
Son QXG5554	General Line	2004	$10	$10
Son QXG8897	General Line	2003	$10	$10
Song For The Lamb Of God, A QX8376	General Line	2002	$15	$15
Sooo Fast Custom Car Set QX8876	Hot Wheels	2002	$17	$17
Sooper Loop QXI6243	Hot Wheels	2006	$13	$13
Sorcerer's Apprentice, The QXD4082	Disney Collection	2005	$32	$32
Sorcerer's Apprentice, The QXD5011	Walt Disney's Fantasia	2004	$15	$10

Ornament Title	Series	Year	Issue Price	Current Value
Space Alien Alert! QXI6505	Power Rangers S.P.D.	2005	$15	$15
Space Station Deep Space 9 QX6065	Star Trek: Deep Space Nine	2001	$32	$39
Spaghetti Supper QXD5099	Lady & The Tramp	2003	$15	$15
Spartan Model 7-W Executive 8th Ed. QX8391	Sky's The Limit	2004	$15	$17
Speak! QXI8905	Scooby-Doo	2005	$17	$17
Special Cat Photoholder QXG8609	General Line	2003	$10	$10
Special Cat QX2863	General Line	2002	$10	$10
Special Cat QXG2973	General Line	2006	$10	$10
Special Cat QXG5591	General Line	2004	$10	$10
Special Dog Photoholder QXG8607	General Line	2003	$10	$10
Special Dog QX8716	General Line	2002	$10	$10
Special Dog QXG2966	General Line	2006	$10	$10
Special Dog QXG5584	General Line	2004	$10	$10
Special Event Photoholder QXG8959	General Line	2003	$13	$13
Special Event QXG5614	General Line	2004	$13	$9
Special Friend QXG8927	General Line	2003	$10	$10
Speedy Delivery 3rd Ed. QX2586	Nick & Christopher	2006	$13	$13
Speedy Style Christmas QXI3093	Looney Tunes	2006	$13	$13
Spider-Man QXI6236	Spider-Man	2006	$15	$15
Spider-Man QXI6265	Spider-Man	2005	$15	$15
Spider-Man QXI8611	Spider-Man	2004	$15	$15
Spirit Of St. Louis 4th Ed. QX6634	Sky's The Limit	2000	$15	$55
Spirit Of St. Louis 4th Ed. QXM5181	Sky's The Limit Miniature Series	2004	$7	$7
Spirit Of St. Nick Colorway QXE3226	Gold Crown Exclusive	2006	N/A	$32
Spirit Of St. Nick QLX7645	Magic Ornaments	2005	$20	$20
Sports QXG3343	Kid Speak	2006	$13	$13
Spring Daydreams QEO8273	Nature's Sketchbook-Bastin	2006	N/A	$10
Spring Peepers QEO8543	Peekaboo	2002	N/A	$8
Springing Santa QX8085	General Line	2001	$8	$8
Spring's Peaceful Promise QEO8262	Nature's Sketchbook-Bastin	2005	N/A	$13
Springtime Inspirations-Peanuts QEO8255	Easter Ornaments	2005	N/A	$17
Sprinkle QP1766	Merry Bakers	2006	$15	$15
Sprinkle Sunshine	Nature's Sketchbook-Bastin	2006	N/A	$11
Sprucing Up Sylvester QXI6126	Tweety-Looney Tunes	2006	$15	$15
Stack-O'-Lanterns QFO6049	Halloween	2003	$7	$7
Staggerwing 6th Ed. QX8093	Sky's The Limit	2002	$15	$57
Stanley & Dennis QXD8674	Disney Collection	2004	$13	$11
Star Destroyer & Blockade Runner QXI4064	General Line	2004	$28	$28
Star Fairy QXM6101	Miniature Ornaments	2000	$5	$10
Star Trek Insignias QXM5211, Set Of 3	Miniature Ornaments	2004	$13	$9
Star Trek: The Next Generation Crown Reflections QBG4345	Star Trek	2001	$24	$24
Starfleet Legends Set Of 3 QXM5325	Star Trek	2001	$15	$15
Stargazer Shepherd QX2836	General Line	2002	$10	$10

Ornament Title	Series	Year	Issue Price	Current Value
Stars & Stripes For Santa QXE3266	Premiere Exclusive	2006	N/A	$22
Stars & Stripes Forever QHB2892	General Line	2001	N/A	$15
Star-Spangled Banner QXM5204	Miniature Ornaments	2004	$9	$9
Starter Kit Photoholders QP1346	General Line	2002	$17	$17
Starter Kit QEP1308	General Line	2005	$17	$17
Starter Kit QEP1376, Set Of 5	Family Tree	2004	$17	$17
Starter Kit QEP1388, Set Of 3	Family Tree	2004	$17	$17
Starter Kit QEP1389	General Line	2005	$17	$17
Starter Kit QEP1391	General Line	2005	$17	$17
Steam Locomotive & Tender Lionel, The General QXM4366	Miniature Ornaments	2002	$13	$13
Steam Locomotive & Tender QXM2096	Lionel Pennsylvania B6	2006	$13	$13
Steam Locomotive & Tender QXM5131	Miniature Ornaments	2004	$13	$13
Steam Locomotive & Tender-Lionel-Blue Comet QXM4887	Miniature Ornaments	2003	$13	$16
Steve Young-San Francisco 49ers QXI6309	Sports Collection	2001	$15	$15
Sticky Situation, A 7th Ed. QXD5084	Winnie The Pooh Collection	2004	$15	$10
Stocking Stuffers QXD5041	General Line	2004	$15	$15
Stolen Magic Barbie QXC6006	Collector's Club	2006	$25	$25
Story For Pooh 3rd & Final Ed. QXD4135	Winnie The Pooh & Christopher Robin Too	2001	$14	$20
Story Time With Pooh 2nd Ed. QXD4024	Winnie The Pooh & Christopher Robin Too	2000	$14	$18
Stroll Around The Pole QX8164	General Line	2000	$11	$10
Stuck On You QXG8867	General Line	2003	$10	$10
Sub-Commander T'Pol QXI8757	Enterprise	2003	$15	$18
Sugar Plum Fairies QXM4513	Miniature Ornaments	2002	$15	$15
Sugar Plum Tabletop Topiary QXM4506	Miniature Ornaments	2002	$20	$20
Sugarplum Fairy 5th & Final Ed. QXM5984	Nutcracker Ballet	2000	$6	$22
Sulley & Mike QXD4613	Disney Collection	2002	$15	$15
Sunday Evening Sleigh Ride QX2903	Thomas Kinkade General Line	2002	$15	$15
Super Friends QX6724	General Line	2000	$15	$13
Surprise Package QXI8391	Blue's Clues	2000	$11	$10
Sweeeet Friendship QXD4812	Finding Nemo	2005	$15	$15
Sweet Contribution QXM4492	Cooking For Christmas	2001	$5	$10
Sweet For Tweety, A QXM5057	Looney Tunes	2003	$6	$8
Sweet Irish Dancer 10th Ed. QX2055	Madame Alexander	2005	$15	$15
Sweet Little Lad QP1469	General Line	2003	$10	$10
Sweet Memories QXI6283	General Line	2006	$15	$15
Sweet Pea 17th Ed. QX8324	Mary's Angels	2004	$8	$8
Sweet Shop QX2456	Noelville	2006	$17	$17
Sweet Shopper QP1447	General Line	2003	$10	$10
Sweet Slipper Dream QXM5345	Miniature Ornaments	2001	$5	$5
Sweet Smackerel Of Honey WD3931	Premiere Exclusive	2006	N/A	N/A
Sweet Tooth Treats 1st Ed. QX8193	Sweet Tooth Treats	2002	$15	$15

Ornament Title	Series	Year	Issue Price	Current Value
Sweet Tooth Treats 2nd Ed. QX8199	Sweet Tooth Treats	2003	$15	$15
Sweet Tooth Treats 3rd Ed. QX8191	Sweet Tooth Treats	2004	$15	$10
Sweet Tooth Treats 4th Ed. QX2175	Sweet Tooth Treats	2005	$15	$15
Sweet Tooth Treats 5th & Final Ed. QX2526	Sweet Tooth Treats	2006	$15	$15
Sweet William 16th Ed. QX8119	Mary's Angels	2003	$8	$10
Sweeter By The Dozen QXM5274, Set Of 12	Miniature Ornaments	2004	$15	$15
Sweetest Little Angel QLX7574	Magic Ornaments	2003	$17	$17
Sweetest Little Shepherd QLX7634	Magic Ornaments	2004	$17	$17
Swing With Friends, A QEO8414	Easter Ornaments	2000	$15	$15
Swinging On A Star 1QXC4005	Collector's Club Exclusive	2004	$17	$17
Swooshing Through The Snow QXD8346	Winnie The Pooh Collection	2006	$28	$28
Sylvester's Bang-Up Gift Wx6912	Looney Tunes	2001	$13	$13
Taz As The Nutcracker QXI8269	Looney Tunes	2003	$10	$10
Taz Paint Egg QEO8572	Easter Ornaments	2001	N/A	$10
Taz The Snowman Wizard QXI6133	Looney Tunes	2006	$15	$15
Teacher QX8973	General Line	2002	$10	$10
Teacher QXG5631	General Line	2004	$10	$10
Teachers Rule QXG8629	General Line	2003	$10	$10
Ted Williams QXI8397	General Line	2003	$15	$15
Teddy Bear Band QLX7603	Magic Ornaments	2006	$28	$28
Teddy-Bear Style 4th & Final Ed. QXM5954	Teddy-Bear Style	2000	$6	$5
Tee's The Season QX8726	General Line	2002	$13	$13
Teetering Toddler WX8916	General Line	2002	$15	$15
Tender-Lionel Chessie Steam Special QX6285	General Line	2001	$14	$14
Tender-Lionel General Steam Locomotive QX6834	General Line	2000	$14	$18
Tending Her Topiary QX8004	General Line	2000	$10	$7
Tennessee Volunteers QSR2125	Collegiate Collection	2001	$10	$3
Tennessee Volunteers QSR2334	Collegiate Collection	2000	$10	$3
Thank You Ball QX8986	General Line	2003	N/A	$10
Thank You Ball QX8986	General Line	2002	$7	$7
Thank You Hug QX2893	General Line	2002	$10	$10
Thanks, Coach! QX8976	General Line	2002	$10	$8
Thanks, Mom! QX8963	General Line	2002	$10	$10
That Holy Night QXG5391, Set Of 3	General Line	2004	$17	$17
That's What Christmas Is About, Charlie Brown QFM3316	Peanuts Collection	2006	$34	$34
Thimble Soldier QBG4061	General Line	2000	$22	$33
Thing One & Thing Two! QXM5315	Miniature Ornaments	2001	$15	$15
Thirsty Cardinal QEO8301	Nature's Sketchbook-Bastin	2004	N/A	$13
This Is The Life QXG8597	General Line	2003	$10	$10
Thomas O'Malley & Duchess QXD4175	Disney Collection	2001	$15	$14
Thomas The Tank Engine QXI6235	Thomas The Tank Engine	2005	$13	$13
Those Who Serve QXG5444	General Line	2004	$13	$9
Threadbear QX2916	General Line	2002	$10	$10

Ornament Title	Series	Year	Issue Price	Current Value
Three Beautiful Princesses QXD5054	Disney Collection	2004	$17	$17
Three Kings From Afar Book & Ornament Set QKK3002	Gold Crown Exclusives	2006	$25	$25
Three Kings From Afar Storybook Set QKK3002	Keepsake Kids	2005	$25	$25
Three Kings Lantern QX8853	General Line	2002	$13	$13
Thrill Drivers Corkscrew Race QXI8634	Hot Wheels	2004	$15	$15
Tickle, Tickle Santa QX2826	Magic Ornaments	2002	$20	$20
Ticktock Workshop QLX7614	Magic Ornaments	2004	$28	$28
TIE Advanced X1 & Millennium Falcon QXM2085	General Line	2005	$15	$15
TIE Fighter QXI7507	General Line	2003	$24	$26
Tigger-Ific Tidings To Pooh QXD4014	General Line	2000	$9	$8
Tigger's Springy Tree QXD4966	General Line	2002	$10	$10
Tim Duncan 7th Ed. QXI5235	Hoop Stars	2001	$15	$27
Time For A Party! QXG2613	General Line	2006	$13	$13
Time For Joy QX6904	General Line	2000	$24	$30
Time In A Barden QEO8511	Easter Ornaments	2000	$11	$11
Time To Believe, A QX8506	General Line	2002	$19	$19
Tin Man QXM4556	Wizard Of Oz Collection	2002	$7	$7
Tin Man's Heart 2nd Ed. QXM5981	Wonders Of Oz	2000	$6	$5
Tinker Bell QXD4232	Disney Collection	2004	$17	$17
Tinker Bell QXD4265	Peter Pan	2005	$15	$15
Tinker Bell QXD4943	Peter Pan	2002	$15	$15
Tinker Bell QXD6373	Peter Pan	2006	$15	$15
Tinker Bell QXM5097	Peter Pan	2003	$7	$12
Tiny Ballerina QXM8142	Miniature Ornaments	2005	$6	$6
'Tis The Season QXM5047	Miniature Ornaments	2003	$15	$15
To My Gouda Friend QXG4662	General Line	2005	$10	$10
Toast To Wine, A QXG2296	General Line	2006	$13	$13
Toddler Photoholder QX2856	General Line	2002	$13	$13
Toddler Photoholder QXG8739	General Line	2003	$10	$10
Together We Serve QX8021	General Line	2000	$10	$8
Tonka 1955 Steam Shovel QX6292	Tonka	2001	$14	$22
Tonka 1961 Cement Truck QX8233	Tonka	2002	$15	$36
Tonka Dump Truck QX6681	General Line	2000	$14	$14
Tonka Giant Bulldozer QXI5281	Tonka	2004	$15	$15
Tonka Mighty Crane QXI8367	Tonka	2003	$15	$18
Tonka Mighty Wrecker QXI6255	Tonka	2005	$15	$15
Tony Stewart QXI8651	NASCAR	2004	$15	$15
Tootle The Train QX6052	General Line	2001	$12	$19
Topping The Tree QX6953	General Line	2002	$15	$15
Toto 3rd& Final Ed. QXM5285	Wonders Of Oz	2001	$6	$14
Touchdown, Snoopy QXI6285	Peanuts Collection	2005	$15	$15
Town Hall & Mayor's Christmas Tree QX2467	Nostalgic Houses & Shops	2003	$20	$29
Toy Shop Serenade QX8301	General Line	2000	$17	$19

Ornament Title	Series	Year	Issue Price	Current Value
Toyland Treasures QLX7625	Magic Ornaments	2005	$32	$32
Toymaker Santa 1st Ed. QX6751	Toymaker Santa	2000	$15	$15
Toymaker Santa 2nd Ed. QX8032	Toymaker Santa	2001	$15	$23
Toymaker Santa 3rd Ed. QX8096	Toymaker Santa	2002	$13	$13
Toymaker Santa 4th Ed. QX8159	Toymaker Santa	2003	$13	$13
Toymaker Santa 5th Ed. QX8124	Toymaker Santa	2004	$13	$13
Toymaker Santa 6th Ed. QX2205	Toymaker Santa	2005	$13	$13
Toymaker Santa QX2573	Gold Crown Exclusives	2006	$13	$13
Toymaker Santa QXG3206	General Line	2006	$13	$13
Tracking The Jagular 4th Ed. QXD4132	Winnie The Pooh Collection	2001	$14	$19
Train Set-The Polar Express QXM6475	Polar Express	2005	$24	$24
Transport Chamber, The QXI6296	Star Trek	2006	$28	$28
Treasured Memories QEP2002	Heart Of Motherhood Collection	2004	$17	$17
Tree Guy QX6961	General Line	2000	$9	$9
Tree-Napper At Work QXI6162	Dr. Seuss' How The Grinch Stole Christmas	2005	$13	$13
Treetop Duet QEO8507	Tweedle Dee Deet	2003	N/A	$10
Trick Or Treat! QFO6051	Halloween	2004	$10	$10
Trim A Tiny Tree QXG4295	General Line	2005	$10	$10
Trimming The Tree 5th Ed. QX2553	Winter Wonderland	2006	$13	$13
Triple Dippin'! WD3532	Collector's Club	2005	$7	$7
Triple-Decker Treat QXG5491	General Line	2004	$10	$10
True Friends QXG4652	General Line	2005	$13	$10
True Love Is Our Love QX8923	General Line	2002	$15	$15
True Patriot QXD4005	Disney Collection	2005	$10	$10
Tucked In Tenderly QX2886	General Line	2002	$10	$8
Tweety Plays An Angel QXI8762	Looney Tunes	2005	$15	$15
Tweety QXM5305	Looney Tunes	2001	$7	$7
Twilight Angel 3rd & Final Ed. QX6614	Madame Alexander Holiday Angels	2000	$15	$35
Twinkle, Twinkle QXD8767	General Line	2003	$13	$13
Two For The Skies QP1755	Santa's Midnight Ride	2005	$15	$15
Two Sweet! 5th Ed. QX2192	Snowball & Tuxedo	2005	$8	$8
Two Tiny Penguins QXM4413	Miniature Ornaments	2002	$10	$10
Twuthful Tweety QXI6123	Looney Tunes	2006	$15	$15
U.S.S. Enterprise NCC-1701 40th Anniv. Ed. QXI6293	Star Trek	2006	$32	$32
U.S.S. Enterprise NCC-1701-A	Star Trek	2005	$28	$28
U.S.S. Enterprise QXI2943	Star Trek	2002	$24	$34
Uncle Sam Nutcracker QXG2489	General Line	2003	$10	$10
Union Pacific Veranda Turbine Locomotive 11th Ed. QX2323	Lionel Trains	2006	$19	$19
United States Of America QP1731	Gold Crown Exclusives	2004	$13	$13
United States Of America QP1734	Gold Crown Exclusives	2004	$13	$13
University Of Kentucky Wildcats QSR2152	Collegiate Collection	2001	$10	$3

Ornament Title	Series	Year	Issue Price	Current Value
University Of Kentucky Wildcats QSR2291	Collegiate Collection	2000	$8	$3
Unlikely Friends QXD4215	General Line	2005	$13	$13
Up For Adventure QXM8945	General Line	2005	$13	$13
Up On The Housetop QLX7575	Collector's Choice	2001	$42	$19
Up To The Tweetop! Tweety QXM4396	Looney Tunes	2002	$6	$6
Up, Up, & Away QX8466	General Line	2002	$10	$10
Van Ghoul QFO6007	Halloween	2003	$7	$7
Veggie Tales QXI5293	Veggie Tales	2002	$13	$13
Veggie Tales QXK4337	Veggie Tales	2003	$13	$13
Veronica 19th Ed. QX2556	Mary's Angels	2006	$9	$9
Very Carrot Christmas, A, Bugs Bunny QX8276	Looney Tunes	2002	$10	$10
Very Friendly Christmas Tree, A QXD8343	General Line	2006	$17	$17
Very Good Girl, A QP1477	General Line	2003	$13	$13
Very Important Bunny QEO8242	Easter Ornaments	2005	N/A	$15
Very Merry Snowman, A QP1417	General Line	2003	$15	$15
Victorian Angel Tree Topper QXM4293	Tree Topper	2000	$13	$21
Victorian Barbie With Cedric Bear Ornament QXI6952	Barbie	2001	$16	$16
Victorian Christmas 6th Ed. QX6855	Madame Alexander	2001	$15	$15
Victorian Christmas Memories Set Of 3 QX8292	Thomas Kinkade General Line	2001	$15	$12
Victorian Christmas QXG5521	Thomas Kinkade General Line	2004	$17	$11
Victorian Home 22nd Ed. QX2322	Nostalgic Houses & Shops	2005	$15	$15
Victorian Inn 19th Ed. QX8103	Nostalgic Houses & Shops	2002	$15	$42
Victorian Sleigh QX8855	General Line	2001	$13	$13
Video Games QXG3346	Kid Speak	2006	$13	$13
Village Toy Shop QLX7676	Magic Ornaments	2002	$24	$20
Visit From Santa QLZ4281	Laser Gallery	2000	$9	$9
Visit From St. Nicholas, A QX8344	General Line	2000	$11	$18
Volleyball QXG4765	General Line	2005	$10	$10
Vulcan Command Ship QXI4084	Star Trek	2004	$28	$30
Waddles QX8952	General Line	2001	$9	$9
Waggles QX8945	General Line	2001	$9	$9
Waiting For Santa Larry The Cucumber & Bob The Tomato Veggie Tales QXI6932	Veggie Tales	2001	$13	$15
Walt Disney's Mickey Mouse Steamboat Willie QXD5047	Disney Collection	2003	$24	$24
Walt Disney's Snow White & The Seven Dwarfs QXD5064	Magic Ornaments	2004	$36	$36
Wandering Bluejay QEO8304	Nature's Sketchbook-Bastin	2004	N/A	$13
Warm Kindness QX8014	General Line	2000	$9	$22
Warmed By Candleglow QX2471	General Line	2000	$7	$6
Washington Redskins QSR5151	NFL Collection	2000	$10	$9
Washington Redskins QSR5552	NFL Collection	2001	$10	$9
We Call Him Santa QX2883	General Line	2002	$13	$13

Ornament Title	Series	Year	Issue Price	Current Value
Weatherbird QEO8519	Tweedle Dee Deet	2003	N/A	$10
Wedding Day Dance QXD4245	Cinderella	2005	$24	$24
Welcome Sound QXD5231	Miniature Ornaments	2004	$6	$6
Welcoming Angel QXM5321	Miniature Ornaments	2000	$6	$6
Welcoming The Savior QX8356	General Line	2002	$13	$13
What A Grinchy Trick! QXI6405	Dr. Seuss' How The Grinch Stole Christmas	2001	$15	$15
What Child Is This QXG8989	General Line	2003	$13	$13
Wheely Wonderful Easter QEO8029	Peekaboo	2003	N/A	$14
Where Life Begins QEP1363	Family Tree	2003	$13	$13
Where Life Begins QP1363	Family Tree	2002	$13	$13
Where's Pickles? Storybook Set QKK3015	Keepsake Kids	2005	$25	$25
Whirlwind Decorating QXI4014	Looney Tunes	2004	$15	$10
Whisk QP1753	Merry Bakers	2006	$13	$13
White Poinsettia QX2953	General Line	2002	$7	$7
Who Goes There! QXM5094	Miniature Ornaments	2004	$6	$6
Wiggles QX8955	General Line	2001	$9	$9
Wild Thornberrys, The QXI5263	General Line	2002	$13	$13
Willie Mays QXI5314	Sports Collection	2004	$15	$15
Willow 15th Ed. QX8013	Mary's Angels	2002	$8	$8
Wings For Eeyore QXD5031	General Line	2004	$15	$15
Winning Bounce, The QXD8561	General Line	2004	$10	$10
Winning Ticket, The 7th Ed. QX8371	Spotlight On Snoopy	2004	$10	$8
Winter Angel QP1423	Memories Of Christmas Collection	2002	$10	$10
Winter Friends QX2242	General Line	2001	$7	$7
Winter Friends QXM8165	Miniature Ornaments	2005	$28	$28
Winter Fun With Barbie & Kelly QXI6561	Barbie	2000	$16	$15
Winter Fun With Snoopy 3rd Ed. QXM5324	Winter Fun With Snoopy	2000	$7	$8
Winter Fun With Snoopy 4th Ed. QXM5262	Winter Fun With Snoopy	2001	$7	$8
Winter Fun With Snoopy 5th Ed. QXM4343	Winter Fun With Snoopy	2002	$7	$8
Winter Fun With Snoopy 6th Ed. QXM4869	Winter Fun With Snoopy	2003	$7	$8
Winter Fun With Snoopy 7th Ed. QXM5184	Winter Fun With Snoopy	2004	$7	$7
Winter Fun With Snoopy 8th Ed. QXM2092	Winter Fun With Snoopy	2005	$7	$7
Winter Fun With Snoopy 9th Ed. QXM2066	Winter Fun With Snoopy	2006	$7	$7
Winter Garden QXG5534	General Line	2004	$13	$8
Winter In Paris QXI5321	General Line	2004	$13	$13
Winter Perch, A QXG2786	Winter Garden	2006	$13	$13
Winter Trimmers QP1497	General Line	2003	$10	$10
Winter Wonderland 7th Ed. QX8086	Madame Alexander	2002	$15	$15
Winterberry Santa QXI4331	General Line	2000	$15	$14
Winterfest QX8474	Frosty Friends Special Anniversary Edition	2004	$17	$17
Winter's Here! QXM4423	Miniature Ornaments	2002	$7	$7
Winter's Ride, A QP1416	Memories Of Christmas Collection	2002	$13	$11

Ornament Title	Series	Year	Issue Price	Current Value
Wish 3rd Ed. QXM5174	Paintbox Pixies	2004	$7	$7
Wish For Peace, A QXC4013A	Collector's Club Exclusive	2004	$24	$24
Wishing Star, The 2nd Ed. QX8033	Snowball & Tuxedo	2002	$8	$8
With Help From Pup QXC4565	Collector's Club Exclusive	2001	N/A	$50
Woodland Friends QX8536	General Line	2002	$15	$15
Woodland Frolic QX8543	General Line	2002	$15	$15
Woodstock On Doghouse Display Piece QRP4211	A Snoopy Christmas	2000	$5	$5
Woody & Bullseye QXD4933	Toy Story 2	2002	$15	$15
Words Of Love QXG8869	General Line	2003	$15	$15
Workout Warrior QXG2293	General Line	2006	$10	$10
Workshop Clock, The QXC6006	Collector's Club	2006	$35	$35
World-Class Shoppers QXD5004	Mickey & Minne	2004	$19	$19
World-Famous Christmas Decorator QXC3004	Peanuts Collection	2003	N/A	$50
Worldwide Celebration QX2833	General Line	2002	$13	$13
Woven Out Of Love QEP1309	Family Tree	2003	$13	$13
Wreath Of Evergreens QX8832	General Line	2001	$9	$9
Wreath Of Peace QXG8687	General Line	2003	$10	$10
Write-On Tag QP2109	Heart Of Motherhood Collection	2003	$6	$6
Write-On Token QEP2109	Heart Of Motherhood Collection	2004	$6	$6
Yankee Doodle & Celebrating America QXM2103	Miniature Ornaments	2006	$13	$13
Yankee Doodle Santa QXG4335	General Line	2005	$13	$13
Year To Remember, A-2002 QX2813	Magic Ornaments	2002	$24	$24
Year-Dated Tag QP2119	Heart Of Motherhood Collection	2003	$6	$6
Yellow Submarine QXI6841	Beatles	2000	$14	$10
Yertle The Turtle 6th Ed. QXI8421	Dr. Seuss Books	2004	$15	$15
You Inspire Me QP1513	General Line	2002	$10	$10
You're A Star QX8966	General Line	2002	$10	$10
You've Been Caught! QXG4292	General Line	2005	$10	$10
You've Got Games QXG8627	General Line	2003	$10	$10
Yule Express QLX7644	Magic Ornaments	2004	$20	$20
Yule Tide Runner QX6981	General Line	2000	$10	$16
Yuletide Harmony Tree QP1143	Yuletide Harmony Collection	2006	$20	$20
Yuletide Santa QP1403	General Line	2002	$10	$10
Zephyr QFO6019	Halloween	2003	$7	$7

More Expert Collecting References

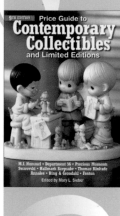